THE

THIRD AFGHAN WAR

1919

OFFICIAL ACCOUNT

Compiled in the General Staff Branch, Army Headquarters India

---

CALCUTTA: GOVERNMENT OF INDIA
CENTRAL PUBLICATION BRANCH
1926

G. S. A. 157.

Government of India Publications are obtainable from the Government of India Central Publication Branch, 8, Hastings Street, Calcutta, and from the following Agents :—

EUROPE.

OFFICE OF THE HIGH COMMISSIONER FOR INDIA,
42, GROSVENOR GARDENS, LONDON, S.W. 1.

And at all Booksellers.

INDIA AND CEYLON.

Provincial Book Depôts:

MADRAS :—Office of the Superintendent, Government Press, Mount Road, Madras.
BOMBAY :—Superintendent, Government Book Depôt, Town Hall Bombay.
SIND :—Library attached to the Office of the Commissioner in Sind, Karachi.
BENGAL :—Office of the Bengal Secretariat Book Depôt, Writers' Buildings, Room No. 1, Ground Floor, Calcutta.
UNITED PROVINCES OF AGRA AND OUDH :—Office of the Superintendent of Government Press, United Provinces of Agra and Oudh, Allahabad.
PUNJAB :—Office of the Superintendent, Government Printing, Punjab, Lahore.
BURMA :—Office of the Curator, Government Book Depôt, Burma, Rangoon.
CENTRAL PROVINCES AND BERAR :—Office of the Superintendent, Government Printing, Central Provinces, Nagpur.
ASSAM :—Officer in charge, Secretariat, Book Depôt, Shillong.
BIHAR AND ORISSA :—Office of the Superintendent, Government Printing, Bihar and Orissa, P. O. Gulzarbagh, Patna.
COORG :—Office of the Chief Commissioner of Coorg, Bangalore.
NORTH-WEST FRONTIER PROVINCE :—Office of the Manager, Government Printing and Stationery, Peshawar.

Thacker, Spink & Co., Calcutta and Simla
W. Newman & Co., Ltd., Calcutta.
R. Cambray & Co., Calcutta.
S. K. Lahiri & Co., Calcutta.
The Indian School Supply Depôt, 309, Bow Bazar Street, Calcutta, and 226, Nawabpur, Dacca.
Butterworth & Co. (India), Ltd., Calcutta.
Rai M. C. Sarcar Bahadur & Sons, 90-2A, Harrison Road, Calcutta.
The Weldon Library, 17, Park Street, Calcutta.
Standard Literature Company, Limited, Calcutta.
Association Press, Calcutta.
Chukervertty, Chatterjee & Co., Ltd., 13, College Square, Calcutta.
The Book Company, Calcutta.
James Murray & Co., 1, Government Place, Calcutta (For Meteorological Publications only).
Higginbotham & Co., Madras.
V. Kalyanarama Iyer & Co., Madras.
P. R. Rama Iyer & Co., Madras.
Rochouse and Sons, Madras.
G. A. Nateson & Co., Publishers, George Town, Madras.
The Modern Stores, Salem, Madras.
Bright & Co., Trivandrum.
The Booklover's Resort, Taikad, Trivandrum, South India.
V. S. Swaminathan, Bookseller, West Tower Street, Madura.
Thacker & Co., Ltd., Bombay.
D. B. Taraporevala, Sons & Co., Bombay.
Sunder Pandurang, Bombay.
Ram Chandra Govind & Sons, Kalbadevi, Bombay.
N. M. Tripathi & Co., Booksellers, Princess Street, Kalbadevi Road, Bombay.
R. B. Umadikar & Co., The Bharat Book Depôt, Dharwar.
Proprietor, New Kitabkhana, Poona.
The Manager, Oriental Book Supplying Agency, 15, Shukrawar, Poona City.
R. S. Gondhalekar's Book Depôt, Publisher and Bookseller, Budhwar Chawk, Poona City.
Managing Director, Co-operative Bookstall, Booksellers and Publishers, Poona City.
The Standard Bookstall, Karachi, Delhi, Quetta, Murree and Rawalpindi.
J. Ray & Sons, 43 K. & L., Edwardes Road, Rawalpindi and Murree.
The Standard Book Depôt, Lahore, Lucknow, Nainital, Mussoorie, Dalhousie and Ambala Cantonment.
The Standard Bookstall, Quetta.
Raghunath Prosad & Sons, Patna City.
Karsandas Narandas & Sons, Surat.
Mangaldas & Sons, Booksellers and Publishers, Bhaga Talao, Surat.
Mrs. Radhabai Atmaram Sagoon, Kalbadevi Road, Bombay.
A. H. Wheeler & Co., Allahabad, Calcutta and Bombay.
N. B. Mathur, Supdt., Nazir Kanun Hind Press, Allahabad.
The North India Christian Tract and Book Society, 18, Clive Road, Allahabad.
Ram Dayal Agarwala, 184, Katra, Allahabad.
Manager, Newal Kishore Press, Lucknow.
The Upper India Publishing House, Ltd., 41, Aminabad Park, Lucknow.
Munshi Seeta Ram, Managing Proprietor, Indian Army Book Depôt, Juhi, Cawnpore.
Rai Sahib M. Gulab Singh & Sons, Mufid-i-Am Press, Lahore and Allahabad.
Rama Krishna & Sons, Booksellers, Anarkali, Lahore.
Puri Brothers, Booksellers and Publishers, Katcheri Road, Lahore.
The Tilak School Book-shop, Lahore.
The Standard Bookstall, Lahore.
Manager of the Imperial Book Depôt, 63, Chandni Chawk Street, Delhi.
Oxford Book and Stationery Company, Delhi.
Supdt., American Baptist Mission Press, Rangoon.
Proprietor, Rangoon Times Press, Rangoon.
The Modern Publishing House, Ltd., 30, Phayre Street, Rangoon.
The International Buddhist Book Depôt, Post Box No. 971, Rangoon.
Burma Book Club, Ltd., Rangoon.
Manager, the "Hitavada," Nagpur.
S. C. Talukdar, Proprietor, Students & Co., Cooch Behar.
Times of Ceylon Co., Ltd.
The Manager, Ceylon Observer, Colombo.
The Manager, The Indian Book Shop, Benares City.
B. C. Basak, Esq., Proprietor, Albert Library, Dacca.
The Srivilliputtur Co-operative Trading Union, Ltd., Srivilliputtur (Satur S. I. R.)
Banwari Lal, Esq., Pakariya Street, Pilibhit, United Provinces.
Manager, Educational Book Depôt, Jubbulpore.

CONTENTS.

APPENDICES

LIST OF MAPS AND PLANS.

The coloured maps in this reprint are placed after this page.

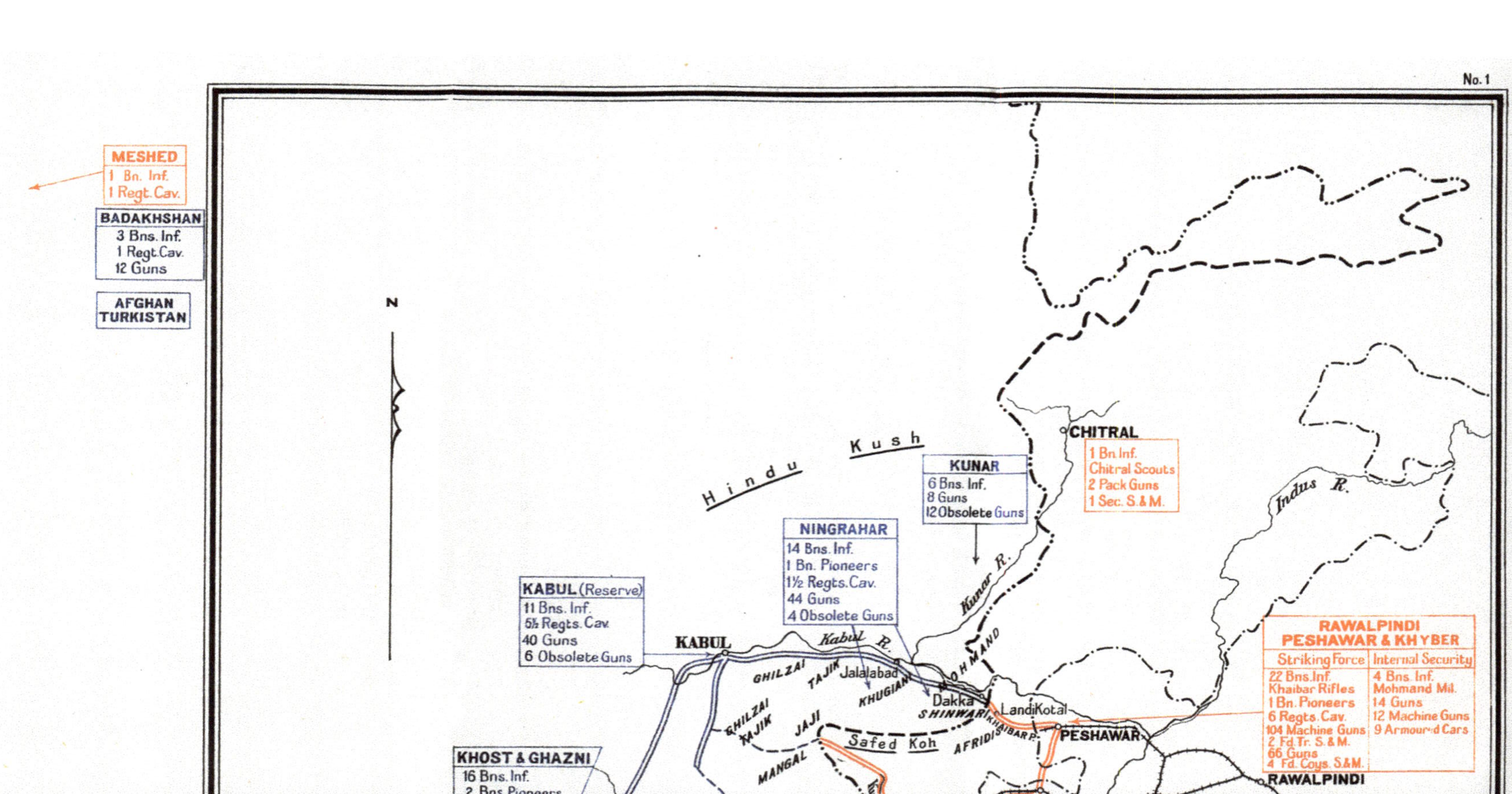
No. 1
MESHED
1 Bn. Inf.
1 Regt. Cav.
BADAKHSHAN
3 Bns. Inf.
1 Regt. Cav.
12 Guns
AFGHAN TURKISTAN
N
Hindu Kush
KUNAR
6 Bns. Inf.
8 Guns
12 Obsolete Guns
CHITRAL
1 Bn. Inf.
Chitral Scouts
2 Pack Guns
1 Sec. S. & M.
Indus R.
NINGRAHAR
14 Bns. Inf.
1 Bn. Pioneers
1½ Regts. Cav.
44 Guns
4 Obsolete Guns
Kunar R.
KABUL (Reserve)
11 Bns. Inf.
5½ Regts. Cav.
40 Guns
6 Obsolete Guns
KABUL
Kabul R.
GHILZAI
TAJIK
Jalalabad
KHUGIANI
MOHMAND
Dakka
SHINWARI
KHAIBAR P.
Landi Kotal
PESHAWAR
GHILZAI
TAJIK
JAJI
Safed Koh
AFRIDIS
MANGAL
KHOST & GHAZNI
16 Bns. Inf.
2 Bns. Pioneers
RAWALPINDI PESHAWAR & KHYBER
Striking Force
22 Bns. Inf.
Khaibar Rifles
1 Bn. Pioneers
6 Regts. Cav.
104 Machine Guns
2 Fd. Tr. S. & M.
66 Guns
4 Fd. Coys. S. & M.
Internal Security
4 Bns. Inf.
Mohmand Mil.
14 Guns
12 Machine Guns
9 Armoured Cars
RAWALPINDI

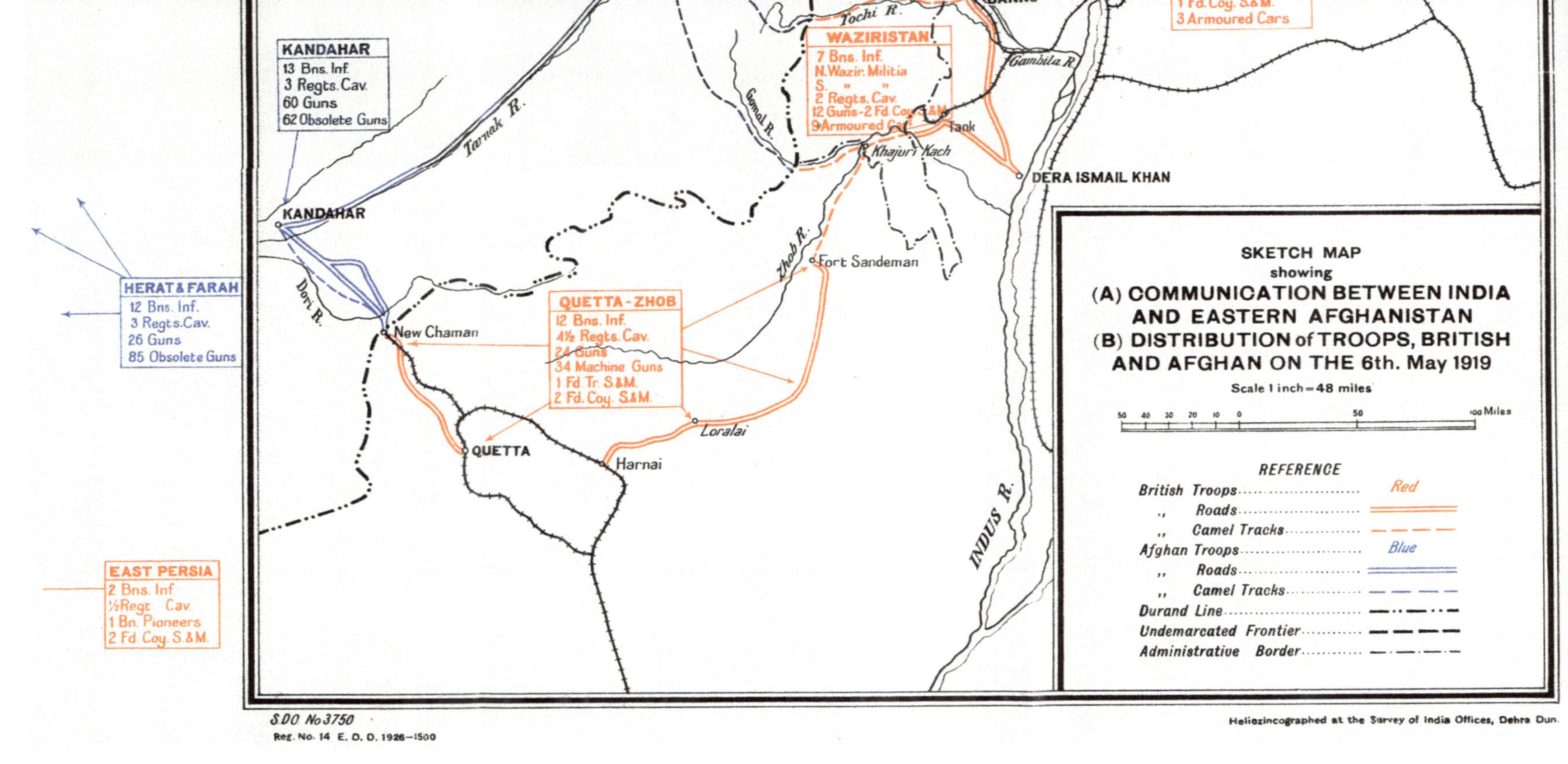
SKETCH MAP
showing
(A) COMMUNICATION BETWEEN INDIA AND EASTERN AFGHANISTAN
(B) DISTRIBUTION of TROOPS, BRITISH AND AFGHAN ON THE 6th. May 1919
Scale 1 inch = 48 miles
50 40 30 20 10 0 50 100 Miles
REFERENCE
British Troops .... Red
,, Roads
,, Camel Tracks
Afghan Troops .... Blue
,, Roads
,, Camel Tracks
Durand Line
Undemarcated Frontier
Administrative Border
KANDAHAR
13 Bns. Inf.
3 Regts. Cav.
60 Guns
62 Obsolete Guns
HERAT & FARAH
12 Bns. Inf.
3 Regts. Cav.
26 Guns
85 Obsolete Guns
EAST PERSIA
2 Bns. Inf.
½ Regt. Cav.
1 Bn. Pioneers
2 Fd. Coy. S.&M.
QUETTA - ZHOB
12 Bns. Inf.
4½ Regts. Cav.
24 Guns
34 Machine Guns
1 Fd. Tr. S.&M.
2 Fd. Coy. S.&M.
WAZIRISTAN
7 Bns. Inf.
N. Wazir. Militia
S. " "
2 Regts. Cav.
12 Guns - 2 Fd. Coy. S.&M.
9 Armoured Cars
1 Fd. Coy. S.&M.
3 Armoured Cars
KANDAHAR
Tarnak R.
Dori R.
New Chaman
QUETTA
Harnai
Loralai
Fort Sandeman
Zhob R.
Gomal R.
Tochi R.
BANNU
Gambila R.
Tank
Khajuri Kach
DERA ISMAIL KHAN
INDUS R.
S.D.O. No 3750
Reg. No. 14 E. D. O. 1926—1500
Heliozincographed at the Survey of India Offices, Dehra Dun.

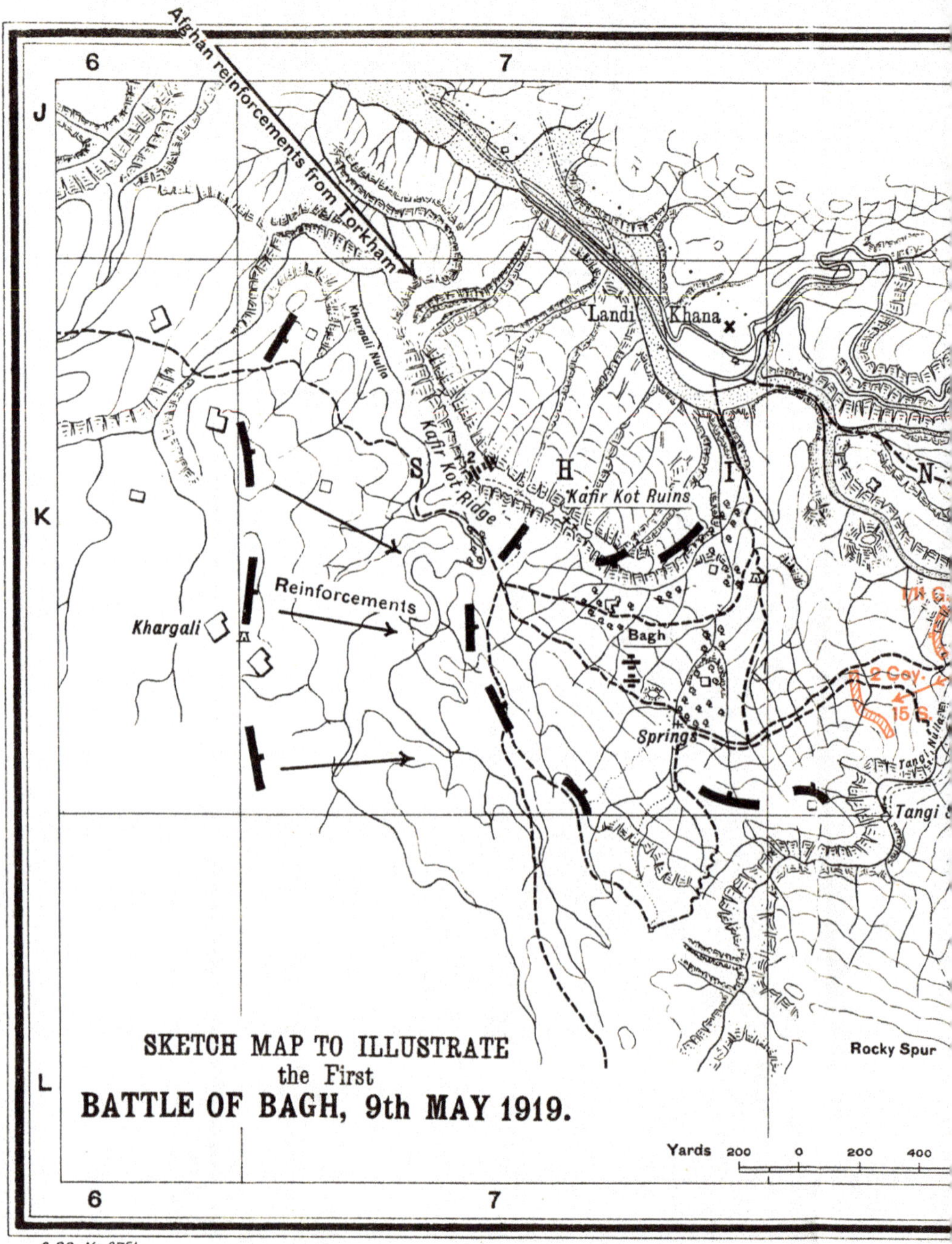

S.D.O. No 3751

Reg. No. 14 E. D. D. 1926-1500

No. 3

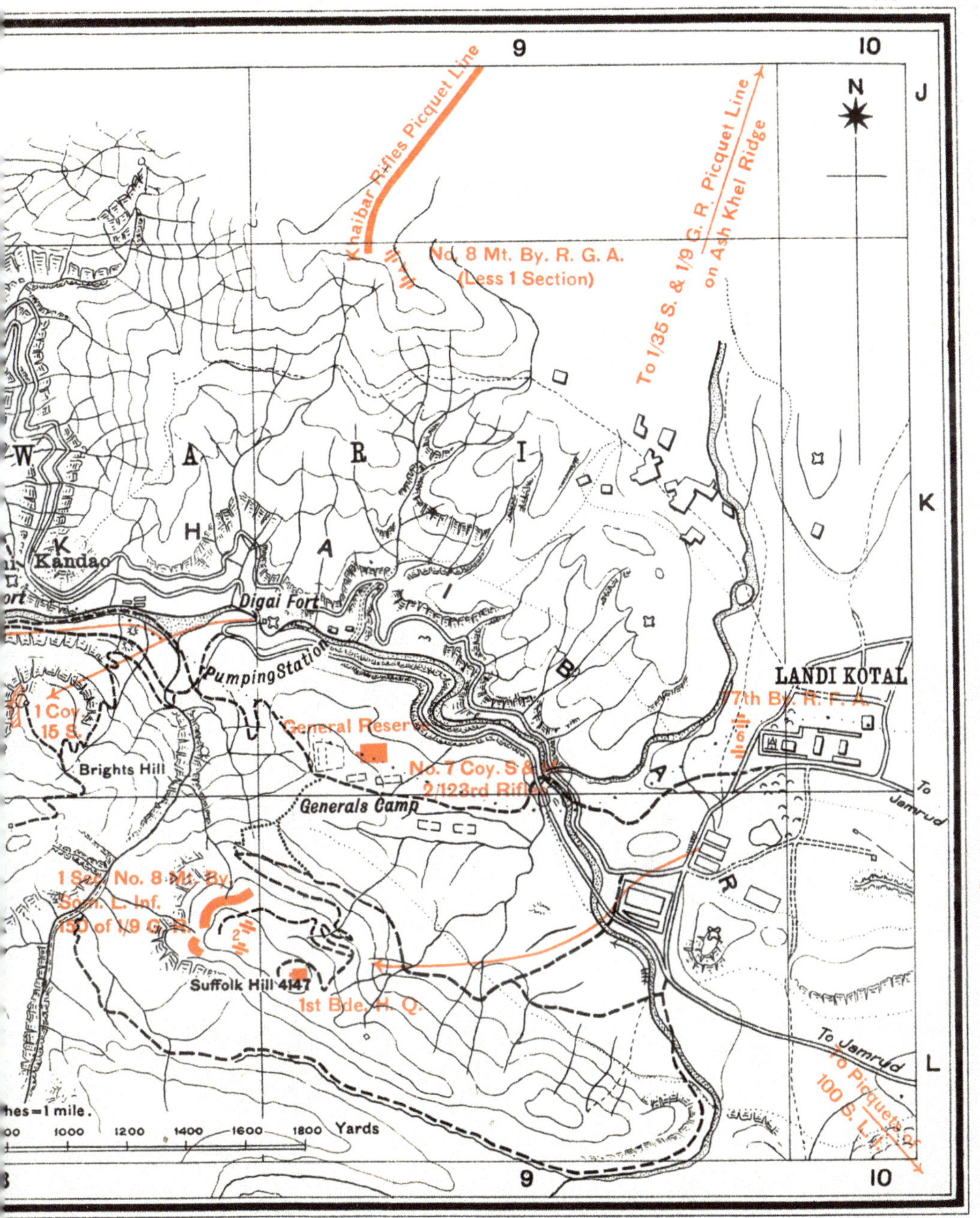

Heliozincographed at the Survey of India Offices, Dehra Dun.

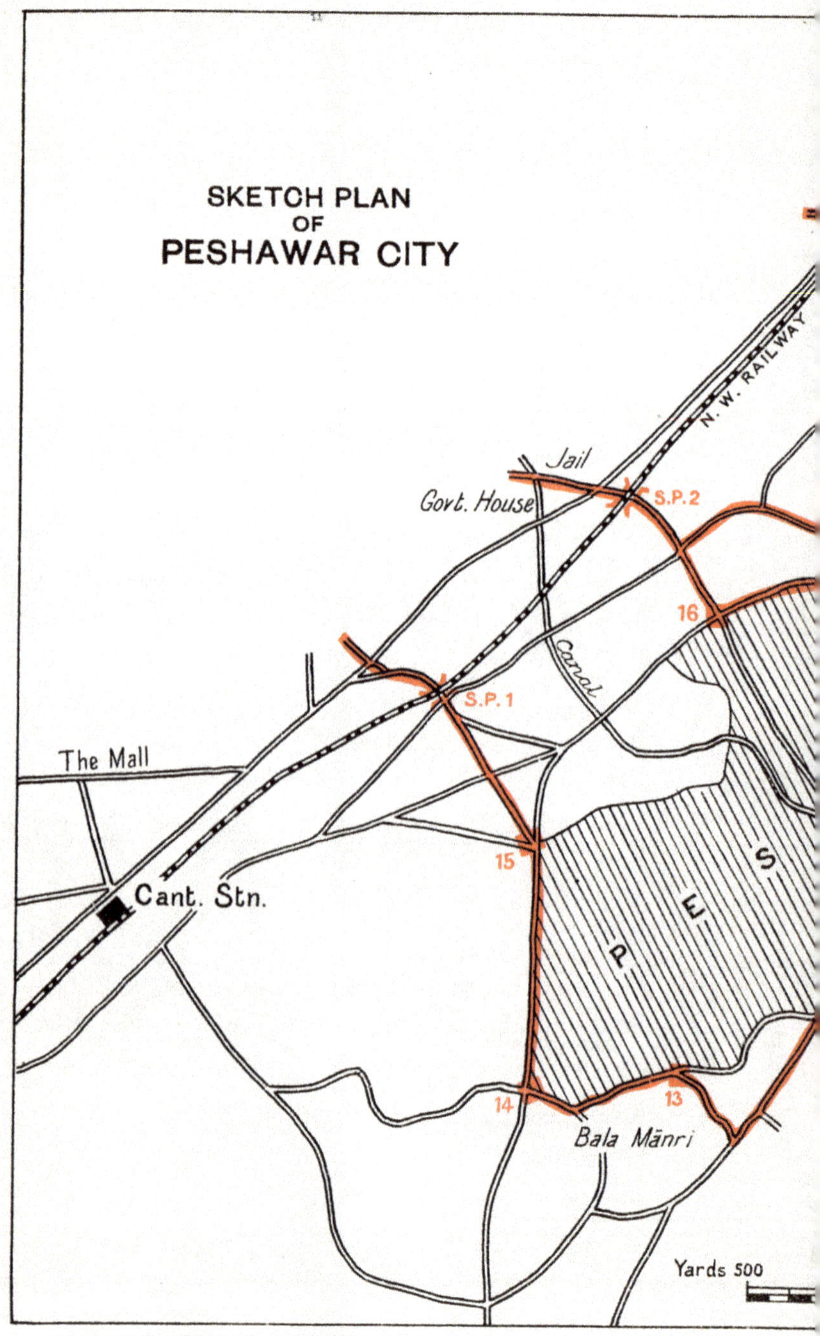

S. D. O. No. 3753, May 1925.

Reg. No. 14 E. D. D. 1926–1500.

No. 4

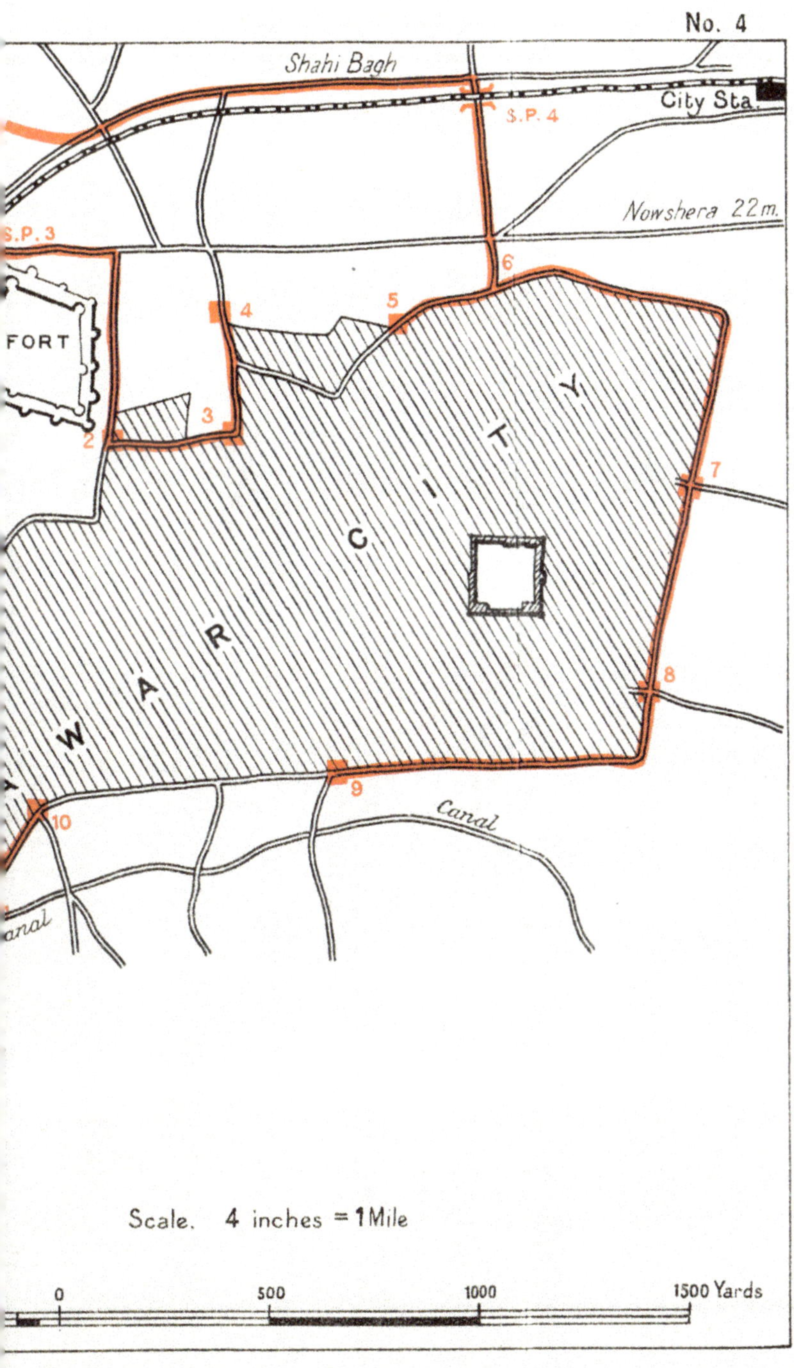

Heliozincographed at the Survey of India Offices, Dehra Dun.

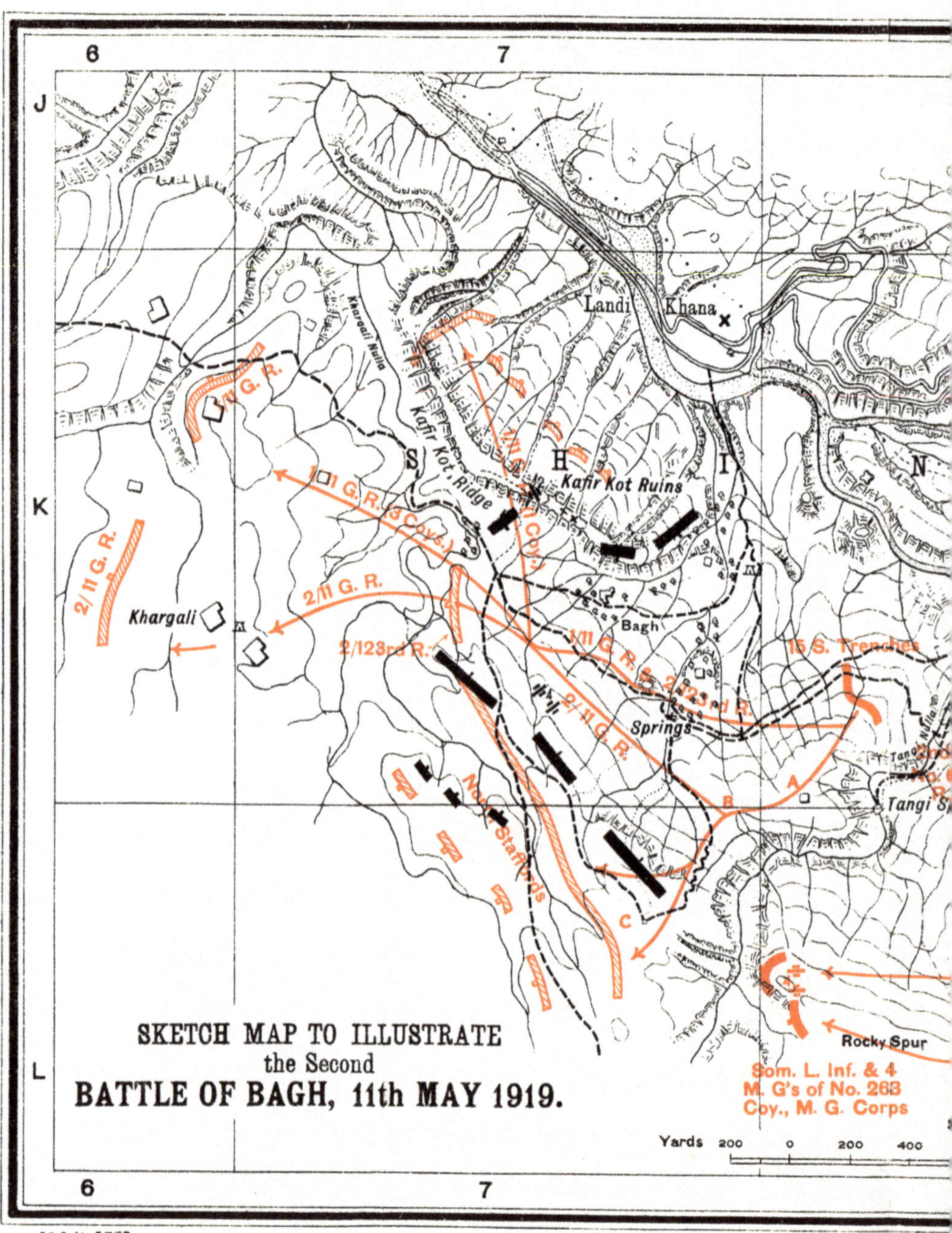

S.D.O. No.3752

Reg. No. 14 E. D. D. 1926–1500

No. 5

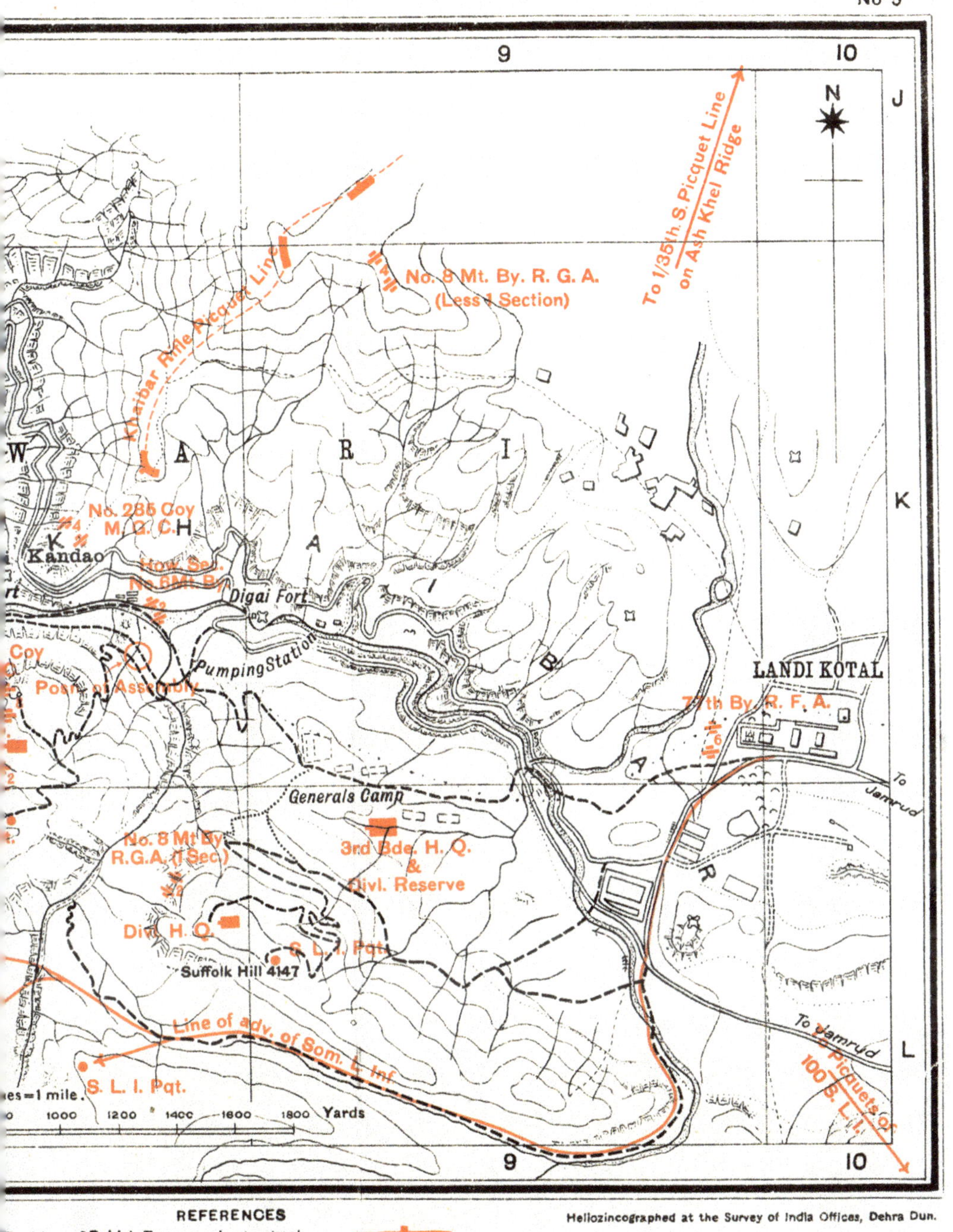

REFERENCES

Position of British Troops prior to attack.........

Final Objective reached..........................

Afghans..

Heliozincographed at the Survey of India Offices, Dehra Dun.

No. 20

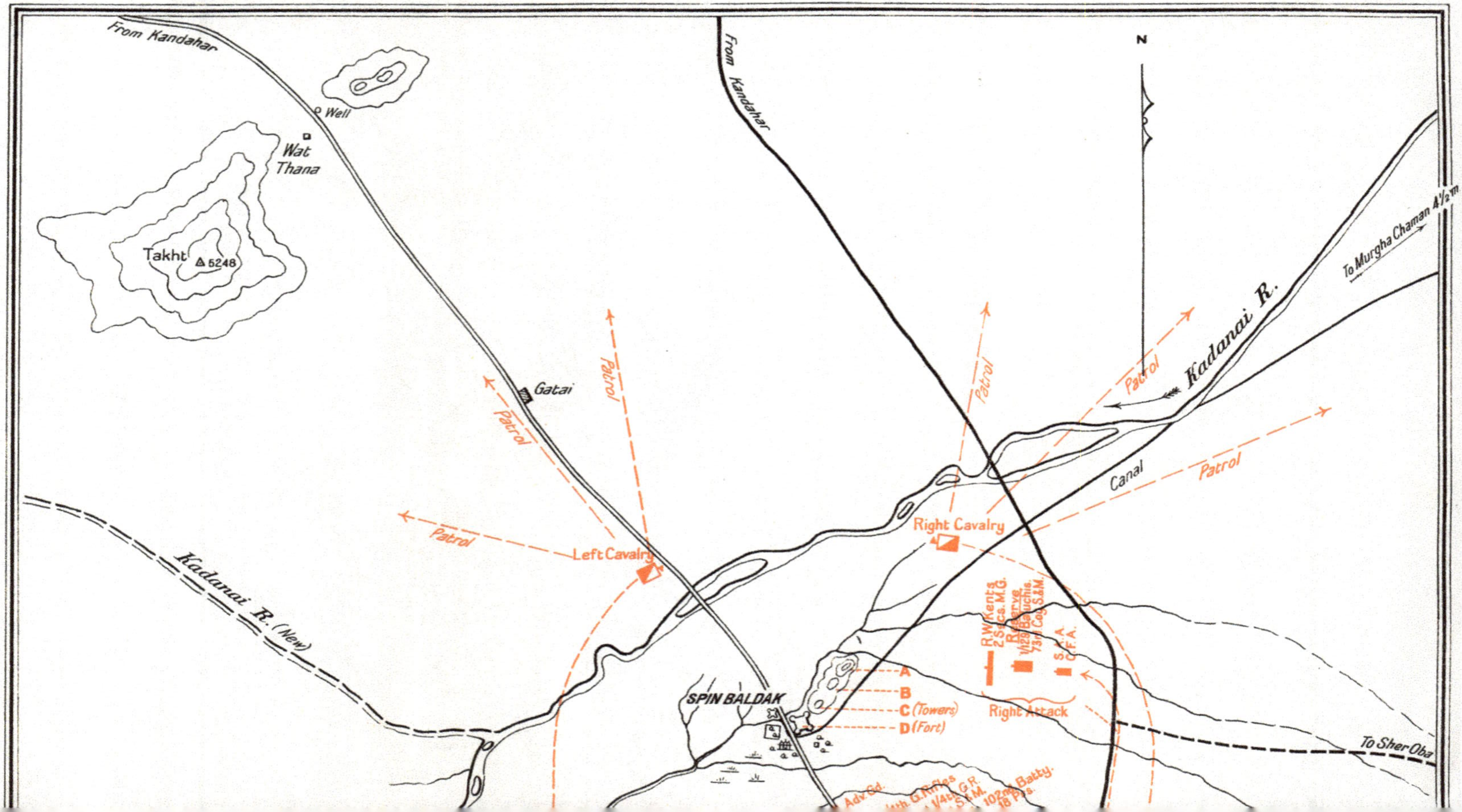

N

From Kandahar

Well

Wat Thana

Takht

5248

Gatai

From Kandahar

To Murgha Chaman 4½m

Kadanai R.

Canal

Patrol

Patrol

Patrol

Patrol

Patrol

Patrol

Left Cavalry

Right Cavalry

R.W.Kents.
2 Secs. M.G.

Reserve.
½128 Baluchis.
73rd Coy. S.&M.

S.A.
C.F.A.

Right Attack

A

B

C (Towers)

D (Fort)

SPIN BALDAK

To Sher Oba

Kadanai R. (New)

Adv. Gd.
4th G. Rifles
½4th G.R.
S.&M.
102nd Batty.
18 Prs.

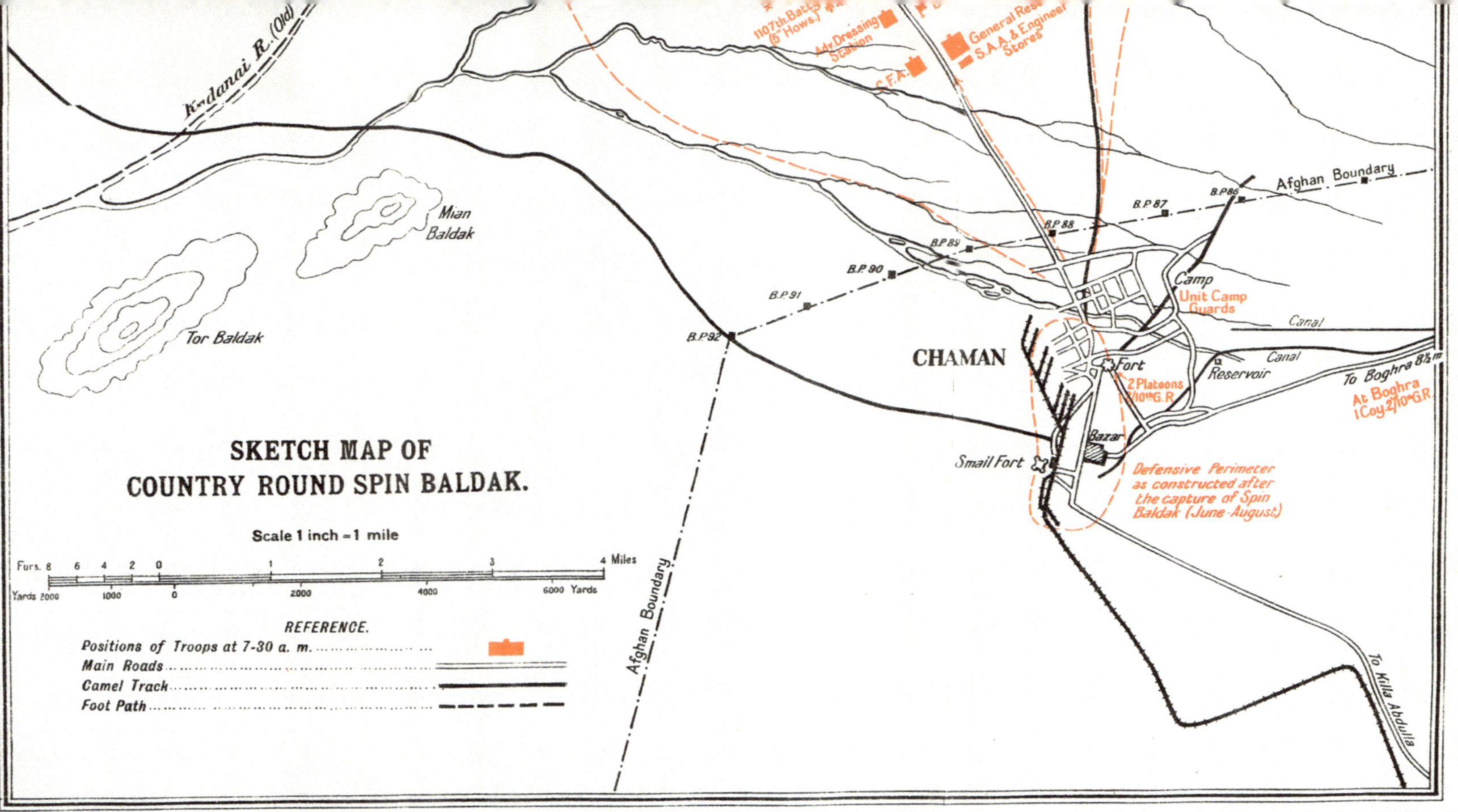

SKETCH MAP OF
COUNTRY ROUND SPIN BALDAK.
Scale 1 inch = 1 mile
Furs. 8 6 4 2 0 1 2 3 4 Miles
Yards 2000 1000 0 2000 4000 6000 Yards
REFERENCE.
Positions of Troops at 7-30 a. m.
Main Roads
Camel Track
Foot Path
K-danai R. (Old)
Mian Baldak
Tor Baldak
Adv. Dressing Station
C.F.A.
S.A.A. & Engineer Stores
Afghan Boundary
B.P. 86
B.P. 87
B.P. 88
B.P. 89
B.P. 90
B.P. 91
B.P. 92
Camp
Unit Camp Guards
Canal
Canal
CHAMAN
Fort
2 Platoons 2/10th G.R.
Reservoir
To Boghra 8½ m
At Boghra 1 Coy 2/10th G.R
Bazar
Smail Fort
Defensive Perimeter as constructed after the capture of Spin Baldak (June-August)
Afghan Boundary
To Killa Abdulla
S.D.O. No 3761
Reg. No. 14 S.D.D. 1926-1500
Heliozincographed at the Survey of India Offices, Dehra Dun.

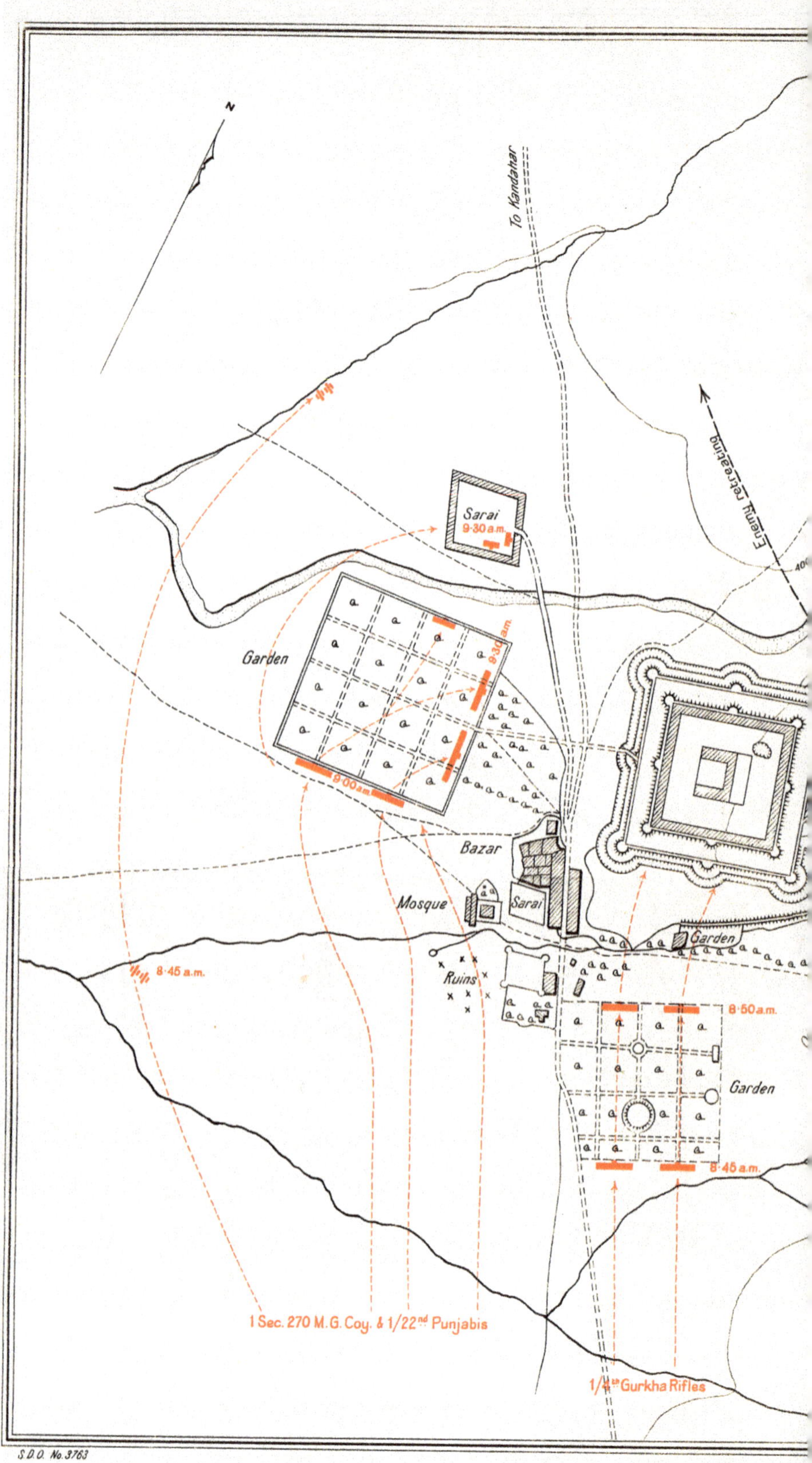

S.D.O. No. 3763
Reg. No. 14 E. D. D. 1926–1500

No. 21

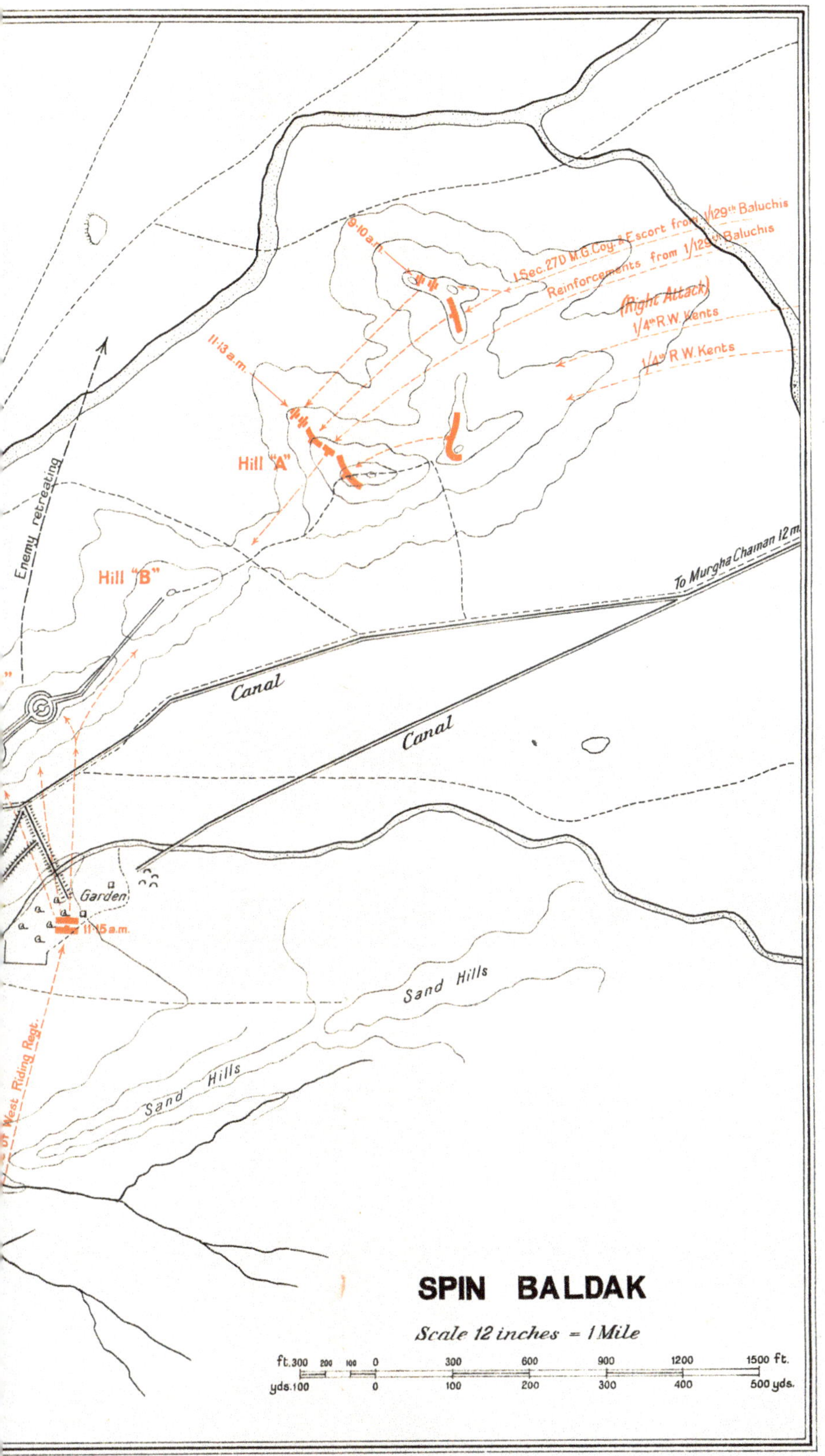

Heliozincographed at the Survey of India Offices, Dehra Dun.

CHAPTER I.

General Description of Afghanistan and the North-West Frontier of India.

Afghanistan may be aptly described as an Asiatic Switzerland. It is a rugged country rising to ranges covered with perpetual snow. It is bounded by four nations each of whose territory exceeds its own, China to the north-east, Russia to the north, Persia to the west and British India to the south and east. Its inhabitants are hardy, warlike, proud and intensely independent. Since the Middle Ages it has provided excellent mercenaries for its more wealthy neighbours. Furthermore it is a land-locked country with no outlet to the Sea.

Boundaries of Afghanistan.

Between Afghanistan and Russian Turkistan the boundary is the Oxus River and the southern edge of the Kum deserts. There is no great natural feature to define the Perso-Afghan frontier, a large portion of which is undemarcated. Between British India and Afghanistan the border is known as the Durand Line after Sir Mortimer Durand, who first signed a Convention at Kabul in 1893 defining the frontier between the two powers. In 1919 boundary pillars existed, with one important exception, along the border line from Chitral in the north to Koh-i-Malik Siah, the extreme south-westerly point of Afghanistan, where the frontiers join those of Persia. This break extended from Nawa Sar, 55 miles N.-W. by N. of Peshawar, through the Mohmand country to the Kabul River, thence west of Landi Kotal across the main Peshawar-Kabul road and along the main ridge of the Safed Koh range to Sikaram Peak. Although this portion had never been demarcated by means of boundary pillars, its position on the map had been defined and agreed to by both parties. Actually on the Peshawar-Kabul road we claimed that a spot known as Torkham was the actual frontier, whilst the Afghans affirmed that their frontier ran as far as Landi Khana.

Debatable portion of Durand Line.

East of the Durand Line, and in British territory, is a tract of country inhabited by Pathans who, although in reality our subjects, are almost independent. A loose form of control is exercised over this area by the Political Officers of the Indian Government, but the inhabitants pay no taxes and manage their own tribal affairs. Between them and the settled districts is a second frontier known as the "Administrative Border". This, with the exception of a narrow belt along the Kurram river, roughly follows the edge of the plain from Amb on the Indus to the Sherani country south of the Gomal, and along the latter river to the Durand Line. We have thus two borders in the North West Frontier Province. The Administrative Border separates the settled districts from independent tribal territory, whilst the Durand Line divides India from Afghanistan. From the Gomal, the southern border of Waziristan, to Koh-i-Malik Siah is British Baluchistan which is administered right up to the Durand Line.

Administrative Border.

Eastern Afghanistan and the tribal country on our North-West Frontier form a tangle of inhospitable hills, often rising to great altitudes. The valleys, with few exceptions are narrow and little cultivated; water is scarce, and, except in favoured localities, the slopes are bare of forest. The products of the soil provide a bare existence for the inhabitants, and the stony hills a scanty pasture for their flocks and herds.

Communications.

In 1919 there were no railways in Afghanistan or in tribal territory, wheeled vehicles were scarce and camels were generally employed for transport. The valleys of the rivers which empty themselves into the Indus are the main highways between India and Afghanistan.

River System.

These are the Kabul, the Kurram, Kaitu and Tochi, whose combined waters form the Gambila; and the Gomal. None of these are navigable, although in 1882 rafts were employed on the Kabul River to transport stores from Jalalabad to Dakka. There are few fords on the Kabul river, but the remainder can be crossed almost any where except during floods. Other routes exist but they are unsuited to the movements of troops owing to the absence of water, difficulties of terrain or other reasons.

South of Ghazni the rivers fall into the Helmund system, eventually emptying their waters into the great lake known as the Hamum-i-Helmund on the borders of Afghanistan and Persia, thus flowing away from India. Between Quetta and Kandahar our frontier at New Chaman is west of the watershed, and the roads from the latter station to Kandahar run roughly parallel to the Dori River. Between this and the Gomal there is no main highway.

Deserts.

South and southwest of Kandahar are extensive deserts reaching into Baluchistan which present a formidable obstacle to the passage of troops.

Particulars of these various routes are given overleaf.

Table showing communications between India and Afghanistan in 1919.

River Routes.	Kabul.	Kurram.	Kaitu.	Tochi.	Gomal.	Dori.
From	Peshawar . .	Kohat	Thal, Bannu . .	Bannu . . .	Dera Ismail Khan.	Quetta.
To	Kabul	Kabul	Matun . . .	Ghazni . . .	Ghazni . .	Kandahar.
Distance from Durand Line.	Peshawar 35 miles, Kabul 154 miles.	Kohat 145 miles, Kabul 103 miles.	Thal 34 miles, Bannu 38 miles, Matun 18 miles.	Bannu 80 miles, Ghazni 87 miles.	Dera Ismail Khan 126 miles, Ghazni 162 miles.	Quetta 78 miles, Kandahar 72 miles.
Roads, British . . .	Double M. T. road.	M. T. road to Parachinar, cart and camel track to Peiwar Kotal.	Camel track . .	M. T. road to Miranshah, cart road to Datta Khel thence camel track.	M. T. road to Murtaza thence camel track.	M. T. road.
Roads, Afghan . . .	Unmetalled to Jalalabad thence metalled. Surface poor and bridges unsafe.	Camel track to Kushi thence unmetalled cart road to Kabul.	Ditto . .	Camel track . .	Camel track . .	Two unmetalled cart roads, one camel track.
Railheads, British . .	Peshawar, later Jamrud.	Broad gauge Kohat, narrow gauge Thal.	Bannu . .	Bannu . .	Broad gauge Darya Khan, narrow gauge Tank.	New Chaman.
Gauge of railways . .	5′ 6″ . .	5′ 6″ . . . 2′ 6″ . . .	2′ 6″ . . .	2′ 6″ . .	5′ 6″ . . . 2′ 6″ . . .	5′ 6″.
Tribal territory traversed, British.	Afridi, Shinwari .	Bangash, Turi .	Wazir . . .	Wazir, Daur . .	Mahsud, Wazir .	Administered territory.
Afghan tribes . . .	Shinwari, Mohmand, Khugiani, Tajik, Ghilzai.	Jajis, Chakmannis, Tajiks, Ghilzais.	Khostwals . .	Ghilzai . . .	Ghilzai . . .	Achakzais, Barcchi, Durani.

Lateral Communications.

Each of these routes is cut off from the others by high mountain chains and there is little lateral communication. Thus troops in any one area cannot be transferred to another without difficulty. The main lateral line in Afghanistan is the historic road from Kabul to Kandahar, 310 miles, a cart road which was metalled and bridged in places, but which was in such disrepair previous to 1919 that Afghan officials transferred from Kabul to Kandahar preferred to travel through India. On our side of the frontier there was a metalled road from Peshawar to Kohat, thence to Bannu and on to Dera Ismail Khan. From Thal a cart track ran to Idak in the Tochi and a camel track down the Kurram to Bannu. Further south a camel track ran up the Zhob from its confluence with the Gomal at Khajuri Kach to Fort Sandeman. From here a metalled road went to Loralai and onwards to Harnai on the loop line to Quetta.

Mountain System.

The mountains of Afghanistan not only impede lateral communication but actually shut off Kabul from some of the outlying provinces during the winter. The giant range of the Hindu Kush is a serious obstacle to traffic between the capital and the northern provinces of Badakhshan and Afghan Turkistan. From December to April the passes are blocked with snow for days at a time. Similarly the route from Kabul to Herat over the Koh-i-Baba is closed at intervals during this period. In winter travellers between the two latter places use the very round-about route by Ghazni, Kandahar and Farah. The snow clad Safed Koh interposes a formidable barrier between the districts of Jalalabad and Khost, whilst the wedge of mountains known as the Hazarajat precludes direct communication between southwest Afghanistan and Herat. The sub-joined table gives the distances between Kabul and the provincial capitals and shows the difficulty of moving troops in Afghanistan even under favourable circumstances.

Table showing distances of the provincial capitals and large military stations from Kabul.

Province.	Capital.	Distance from Kabul.		Type of road.	Obstacles
		Miles.	Stages.		
Badakhshan	Faizabad	335	25	Cart road and camel track	Hindu Kush Range.
Afghan Turkistan	Mazar-i-Sharif	380	30	Ditto	Ditto.
Herat	Herat	490	30	Camel track	Unai Pass, Daulat Yar Pass 7,820.
Kandahar	Kandahar	325	23	Cart road	*Nil.*
Khost District	Matun	147	13	Camel track	Altimur Pass.
Jalalabad	Jalalabad	108	9	Metalled road	*Nil.*

These physical difficulties divide the Indo-Afghan frontier into three main areas both for attack and defence as shown below :—

Area.	Dividing line.	Area.	Dividing line.	Area.
Northern.—Consisting of the basin of the Kabul River.	Safed Koh Range	*Central.*—Consisting of the Kurram, Kaitu, Tochi and Gomal systems.	Watershed between the Indus and Helmund systems.	*Southern.*—Kandahar Plain.

Climate.

The climate of Afghanistan generally is characterised by extremes of temperature, high winds and dryness. The seasons change with startling suddenness: spring comes on rapidly and, within a few weeks of the last signs of snow, the sun's heat becomes tropical; the approach of autumn is equally abrupt after nights of balmy mildness. The extremes of temperature are both seasonal and diurnal; a difference of 80 degrees between night and day temperature having been experienced in August 1880 on the march from Kandahar to Kabul. To take the lowlands between Jalalabad and Dakka and between Kandahar and New Chaman, which were the scenes of operations in 1919, the maximum and minimum temperatures show a great range between winter and summer. In July, the thermometer registers 105 degrees in the shade in Kandahar and 110 in Jalalabad. In 1919 during the same months the temperature at Landi Khana and Dakka in E. P. tents reached 125 degrees on several occasions. That year, however, was exceptional, the average in Peshawar for June and July being 6 degrees above normal. This high temperature is rendered more unbearable by the hot winds and dust storms. In February the temperature drops to 15 degrees both in Jalalabad and Kandahar. The cold is rendered more intense by the strong wind which pierces any clothing less impervious than the skin coat or "poshtin" which is worn by Afghans of all classes during the winter. In the spring and autumn the climate is temperate, and these are the most favourable seasons for military operations. Even during these seasons the range of temperatures is great, and cases of chilblains and sun exhaustion were admitted to hospital at Chaman on the same day in May 1919. The annual rainfall averages 11 inches throughout the country, most of which falls between December and April, during which period the snowfall is general at altitudes over 7,000 feet.

Prevalent diseases.

There are certain diseases which affect troops campaigning in Afghanistan. Cholera takes its toll from every invading force. During the summer, bowel complaints are common, in the autumn malaria is prevalent and in the winter pulmonary diseases such as pneumonia cause heavy casualties.

Inhabitants.

The population of Afghanistan is about six and a half million souls. They are of varied origin, fighting value and loyalty to the Crown. The most warlike of the inhabitants are the Afghan and Pathan tribes of Eastern Afghanistan, and these were opposed to our troops in 1919. The strength of the nation lies in the armed tribesmen rather than in the regular army.

Religion.

The whole of the Afghans and Pathans are bigoted Mohammedans, and are susceptible to a call to a religious war. The Amir of Afghanistan is able, as a temporal ruler of a Mohammedan country, to declare a crusade (jehad) against an infidel, and he resorted to this expedient in 1919.

Government.

The government of Afghanistan was autocratic in the extreme. All power was vested in the Amir whose actions were unchecked by anything except the necessity for complying with Mohammedan common law. Authority was delegated to six provincial governors who were answerable to the Amir alone. These Governors had considerable powers and were the military commanders of their own provinces as well as the heads of the civil administration. The province of Kabul was always directly under the Amir. The army was raised by a form of conscription which took one man in eight for life service. This did not result in the enlistment of the pick of the country, as the more warlike and truculent tribes evaded their obligations, and the remainder provided recruits who could be most easily spared from their communities.

The Semi-Independent tribes and their organisation.

The Pathans living between the Durand Line and the Administrative Border under British jurisdiction are allied by ties of kinship, language and religion to the inhabitants of Eastern Afghanistan. They are first class fighting material, and the best armed and most warlike of them are those tribes which border on Afghanistan. These Pathans number nearly half a million fighting men, a large proportion of whom are armed with rifles. The authorities at Kabul always keep in close touch with our tribesmen, many of whom are in receipt of annual allowances from the Amir. Although they are actually British subjects, they enjoy almost complete independence. North of the Kabul River, the Pathans of the Swat and Panjkora basins have a feudal form of Government under their tribal chiefs. The Bajauris, Mohmands, Shinwaris, Afridis, and Orakzais have their own petty chiefs, but each section and sub-section has a council of elders (jirga) which decides lawsuits, settles policy and keeps the power in their own hands. Among the Mahsuds and Wazirs the headmen have little authority, and every man is a law unto himself. Among all these tribes, religious leaders (*i.e.*, mullahs) arise who sweep aside the authority of the headmen and drag the mass of the people after them by appeals to their fanaticism. The policy of these mullahs is almost invariably anti-British and pro-Afghan and they are thus a constant source of danger to us.

Methods of fighting.

Both Pathans and Afghans are expert in guerilla warfare. They seldom await an assault, but they follow up a retirement relentlessly and with the utmost boldness. They show great skill in cutting off detachments and in laying ambushes for isolated bodies of troops. They are, however, deficient in some important military qualities. They lack steadfastness in adversity and lose heart when subjected to reverses. They have little cohesion and concerted action on their part cannot be expected. Their forces (*lashkars*) are brought to, and kept in, the field by the exertions of their religious leaders, and each man fights as he pleases. Time is lost owing to lengthy discussions which often precede military action or declaration of policy. Mutual jealousies or blood feuds, which are sunk on occasions of fanatical outbursts, are apt to re-appear during prolonged operations.

General Summary.

The factors, then, which affect the situation when hostilities break out with Afghanistan, are the lack of communications, general sterility of the soil in the theatres of war and shortage of water, extremes of climate, epidemic diseases, the natural aptitude of Afghan and Pathan for guerilla warfare, the danger of a general conflagration along the frontier, and the uncertainty as to when and where such fanatical outbursts will take place.

CHAPTER II.

THE HISTORY OF AFGHANISTAN AND ITS CONNECTION WITH INDIA.

Ahmad Shah.

The founder of the kingdom of Afghanistan was Ahmad Khan, an Afghan of the Abdali (now Durani) tribe. He commanded a force of 3,000 horsemen of his tribe who formed the bodyguard of Nadir Shah, the Persian conqueror. When the latter was murdered in 1747, Ahmad seized the treasure and jewels which the deceased monarch had looted from Delhi in 1738, and proclaimed himself Shah of the Afghans at Kandahar under the name of Ahmad Shah. The riches which he had thus acquired enabled him to raise an army by means of which he rapidly wrested the provinces of Kandahar, Kabul and Peshawar from the Governors appointed by Nadir Shah.

Conquests in Persia and India.

Later he conquered Herat and Khorassan (the northeasterly province of Persia), whilst his lieutenants subdued Afghan Turkistan and Kashmir. He over-ran the Punjab, then under Moghul rule, and marched towards Delhi. Further operations in this direction were abandoned as an arrangement was arrived at by which his son and heir, Timur, was married to a niece of the Emperor, Alamgir II, and

Receives Punjab as his son's dowry.

received the Punjab as the dowry of the princess. Timur was installed as Governor of his new province at Lahore, but soon had to fly to Peshawar as the result of a Mahratta invasion. Ahmad Shah returned to India, cleared the Punjab and finally defeated the

Panipat 1761.

Mahrattas with great slaughter at Panipat in 1761. Twelve years later, Ahmad Shah died, leaving Timur a splendid inheritance which included Khorassan, Afghanistan, Kashmir, the Punjab, Sind and Baluchistan.

Timur.

Timur lacked the vigour and military skill of his father, and the power of the kingdom began to decline. On his death, in 1793, a struggle for the throne began between five of his sons, during which the outlying provinces were gradually shorn away.

Shah Zaman.

First, Prince Zaman, the fourth son of Timur and Governor of Kabul, was proclaimed Shah, mainly owing to the assistance he obtained from Painda Khan, the chief of the Muhammadzais, a section of the Barakzai Duranis. During his reign of 8 years the Punjab, which had practically attained independence under Timur, was virtually ceded to the Sikhs by the appointment of Ranjit Singh as Governor. Afghan Turkistan, also fell under the dominion of its local chiefs. Unfortunately for himself, Shah Zaman turned against

Execution of Painda Khan.

the man to whom he owed his throne and caused Painda Khan to be executed in 1801. Painda Khan's son, Fateh Khan, then joined

Shah Mahmud.

forces with Mahmud, another son of Timur. Shah Zaman was defeated, captured and blinded. He eventually escaped to Ludhiana, where he ended his days as a pensioner of the East India Company.

Shah Shuja.

After a reign of two years, Mahmud was deposed by a popular insurrection and was succeeded by another brother, Shah Shuja. During the reign of the latter, Sind declared its independence whilst the Persians reconquered Khorassan. Fateh Khan was retained as

Shah Mahmud again on the throne.

Wazir, but was dismissed in 1809. He and his brother, Dost Mohammed, contrived to release Mahmud from prison and they set him on the throne for a second time, whilst Shah Shuja joined Shah

Zaman as an exile in Ludhiana. This revolution cost the kingdom Multan, which place was taken by the Sikhs in 1810.

Barakzai brothers. Fateh Khan, the eldest of the twenty-one sons of Painda Khan known as the Barakzai brothers, now became the virtual ruler of Afghanistan. In 1817, however, Mahmud and his son Kamran, first blinded Fateh Khan and then put him to death. This roused the Barakzai brothers. They collected their retainers and drove out Mahmud, who took refuge in Herat, where he ruled as an independent prince until his death in 1829.

Death of Fateh Khan.

Mahmud in exile.

Struggle between Barakzai brothers. The expulsion of the descendants of Ahmad Shah left the field open for the sons of Painda Khan. They fought each other for supremacy until 1826, when Dost Mohammed was left in undisputed possession of Kabul. He proclaimed himself ruler with the title of "Amir-ul-Muamin" (lord of the faithful) or more commonly "Amir".

Dost Mohammed proclaimed Amir.

Encroachments of Ranjit Singh. During these internecine wars, Ranjit Singh made use of the opportunity offered him to extend his possessions. Sikh forces crossed the Indus in 1818 and seized the Peshawar and Derajat districts. In 1823, Muhammad Azim, a brother of Dost Mohammed, made a desperate effort to recover the Peshawar plain, but he was defeated with heavy loss at Nowshera. In the same year Ranjit Singh invaded Bannu. The Sikhs, however, did not finally subjugate this district till 1836.

Intrigues of Shah Shuja. Shah Shuja continued to intrigue with his adherents in Afghanistan, and in 1833 he advanced on Kandahar with a force of Hindustani mercenaries with the connivance of the Indian authorities. He reduced the ruler of Kandahar, Kuhan Dil, to great straits, but Dost Mohammed advanced from Kabul and utterly defeated Shah Shuja. The latter again returned to Ludhiana.

Dost Mohammed and the Russians. The loss of his fairest province caused Dost Mohammed to make another attempt to recover Peshawar in 1836 but his effort was unsuccessful. He had tried to secure the aid of the British against Ranjit Singh, but this was refused. The effect of this refusal was to throw the Afghan back on Russia, his powerful neighbour.

Russian policy. Since the Russians had advanced to the Caspian and conquered the Caucasus in 1828, Britain had become intensely suspicious of the activities of this power in Central Asia. Since the days of Peter the Great, a steady policy of aggression had been pursued by the Russians, who were seeking an outlet to the warm waters. This is an economic necessity for Russia with her ice-bound harbours, and must form the keystone of her foreign policy whether under Romanoff or under Bolshevik rule. When Dost Mohammed entered into friendly relations with this power, the Government of India decided to place Shah Shuja on the throne of Afghanistan. An agreement known as the "Tripartite Treaty" was entered into by the Government of India, Ranjit Singh and Shah Shuja to carry this into effect. This began the First Afghan War which is fully described in Frontier and Overseas Expeditions, Volume III. Ranjit Singh died before the expedition started out from India and the Sikhs were then more of a hindrance than a help. Shah Shuja was installed, but proved to be a weak and inefficient ruler and in 1842 Dost Mohammed was permitted to occupy the throne again. Practically nothing had been

First Afghan War.

gained by three and a half years of warfare, nor had our political influence over Afghanistan been materially increased.

Second Sikh War.

In 1849 the Second Sikh War was fought. An Afghan contingent was sent to join the Sikhs against us, but it arrived too late and was swept away in the flight of the Sikh Army after the decisive battle of Gujrat. The kingdom created by Ranjit Singh passed into British hands and our borders then marched with those of Afghanistan. This led to renewed relations with Dost Mohammed, who was apprehensive of an attack by the Persians. Negotiations were opened and in 1855 he signed a treaty of friendship with us, which proved advantageous to both parties. In 1856 a British expedition to Persia frustrated an attack on Afghanistan and led to fresh conversations. These resulted in a further agreement by which in 1857 the British made the Amir a grant of 12 lakhs of rupees and certain arms. During the Indian Mutiny, which broke out soon after this latter arrangement had been come to, persistent efforts were made by the Afghan priesthood to induce Dost Mohammed to declare war on Great Britain. This he steadily refused to do, and this adherence to his treaty engagements enabled troops from the frontier to be moved to Delhi to deal with the centre of revolt there.

Anglo-Afghan treaty.

Indian Mutiny.

British policy in Afghanistan.

Our policy, which was formulated in 1855 and which continues to the present day, is to secure a united Afghanistan under a ruler strong enough to quell internal dissensions and to repel foreign aggression; to attain this object we have in the past supplied successive Amirs with money and arms. This receiving of a subsidy would represent levying blackmail in Europe, but in the East it is regarded as accepting a salary from a superior.

Dost Mohammed was now able to extend his dominions. In 1857 he drove his half brothers out of Kandahar where they had enjoyed independent status. Two years later he extended his borders northwards from the Hindu Kush to the Oxus (1859). In 1863 he reduced Herat. On his death in 1867, he left to his son, Sher Ali, a kingdom roughly corresponding to modern Afghanistan.

Accession of Amir Sher Ali.

At this time the Russians were making steady progress in Central Asia and the conquest of Bokhara in 1868 and of Khiva in 1873 brought their frontiers to the Oxus. Thinking that he had more to gain from Russia than from England, Sher Ali received a Russian Mission in Kabul and refused to admit one from India. This act led up to the Second Afghan War which can be followed in detail in the official account of the campaign, in Colonel Hanna's work, and in the lives of Lord Roberts and Sir Donald Stewart.

Second Afghan War.

Death of Sher Ali.

Yakub succeeds and abdicates.

Murder of Sir Louis Cavagnari.

Abdur Rahman succeeds.

During the opening stages of the war, Sher Ali died. His son and successor, Yakub, feeling his hold on the throne precarious, came to terms with the British. This agreement is known as the Treaty of Gandamak. One of its clauses stipulated that a British Resident should be established permanently at Kabul. Sir Louis Cavagnari was chosen as our representative. Six weeks after his arrival in Kabul, he and his escort were massacred. This led to a resumption of hostilities (1879.) Yakub surrendered and was sent to India to end his days as a pensioner of the British. In 1880 the throne of Afghanistan was offered to, and accepted by, Abdur Rahman, whose father, Mohammed Afzal, was the eldest son of Dost Mohammed. He had been an exile in Russian territory since the accession of Sher

Ali to the throne. He agreed to surrender all claims on the Khyber, the Kurram, Sibi and Peshin.

Durand Treaty.

Three years later (1883), an annual subsidy of twelve lakhs of rupees was granted to Abdur Rahman by the Government of India. In 1893 under the Durand Convention (see page 1) Chagai in Baluchistan, New Chaman and Waziristan (except Birmal) were definitely ceded to Britain, whilst the yearly subsidy was increased to eighteen lakhs. The 21 years of Abdur Rahman's reign were marked by friendliness on his part towards this country. A man of forceful character, he reduced Afghanistan to order, put down rebellions and was generally successful in opposing Russian aggression. In one case he was unsuccessful. In 1885 the Russians seized the Panjdeh, a small tract on the north-west frontier of Afghanistan, where Kushk is now situated. He realized the ideal of British policy, and made his kingdom a strong " Buffer State " between Russia and India.

Amir Habibulla.

On his death in 1901, Abdur Rahman was succeeded by his son Habibulla. The new ruler, though an able man, lacked the forceful nature and decision of character of his father. At first he refused to renew the agreements entered into by the former Amir and commenced intriguing with the Afridis. It was not until 1905 that he fell in with Abdur Rahman's policy. He then received the Dane Mission in Kabul and signed an agreement re-affirming the Durand Convention. He received in turn an annual subsidy of eighteen lakhs of rupees.

From 1905 to 1914 Habibulla maintained, on the whole, a friendly attitude towards the Indian Government. When the Great European War broke out, India's share in the world-wide conflagration was largely dependent on the attitude adopted by Afghanistan. Had the Amir proved hostile, it would not have been possible to denude India of troops for service on other fronts. Habibulla's position was made very difficult when Turkey entered the war. The Sultan of Turkey was the successor of the Prophet (Khalifa) and the head of the Islamic world in the eyes of orthodox or Sunni Mohammadans. The cause of the Khalifa was taken up with enthusiasm by the ignorant and fanatical priesthood, who wield great influence throughout Afghanistan and our North-West Frontier. The British had ample proof of the strength of this movement, as the Afridis in such Indian units as were stationed within easy reach of the Tirah deserted in large numbers during the closing months of 1914. Desertions of trans-frontier Pathans also occurred in theatres of war overseas. Notwithstanding this popular excitement, Habibulla continued to abide by his treaty engagements and Afghanistan remained neutral.

At the same time, he gradually freed Afghan foreign policy from British domination, and the Government of India, preoccupied in more vital matters, tacitly accepted the new situation.

Turco-German Mission to Kabul, 1915.

In October 1915, a Turco-German Mission arrived in Kabul under Captain von Hentig, who had formerly been a member of the German Embassy in Pekin. Other members of the party were Captain Niedermeyer, Kasim Beg, Barkatulla of Bhopal (a well known Indian revolutionary) and Mohendra Partap, a talukdar of Oudh and brother-in-law of the Maharaja of Jind. Von Hentig carried with him a draft treaty between Afghanistan and Germany. Whether this treaty was ever signed by the Amir is open to doubt. There was, at any rate, little intention of ever putting it into effect, and this was so apparent to von Hentig that he left Afghanistan in disgust accompanied by the other Germans. The Indians remained in Kabul, and, under the high-sounding title of "The Provisional Government of India", opened a correspondence with the disaffected elements in India.

Afghan War Party.

Unsuccessful though von Hentig had been in obtaining material assistance for Germany, his intrigues with the Afghan party who were in favour of a war with India had a lasting effect. This faction was influential, and included Nasrulla, the brother of the Amir, the Amir's third son, Amanulla, the Ulya Hazrat, (mother of Amanulla), and the Commander-in-Chief, Nadir Khan. The visit of the German deputation united this party and made them more clamorous for war than ever. The Amir was finally driven to the grave step of calling together the representatives of the people and explaining his policy to them. This assembly passed a resolution expressing confidence in their ruler and approving of his actions. This checkmated the War Party and drove their activities underground.

ROUGH GENEOLOGICAL TABLE OF THE AMIRS OF AFGHANISTAN.

Names of actual rulers with dates in capitals.

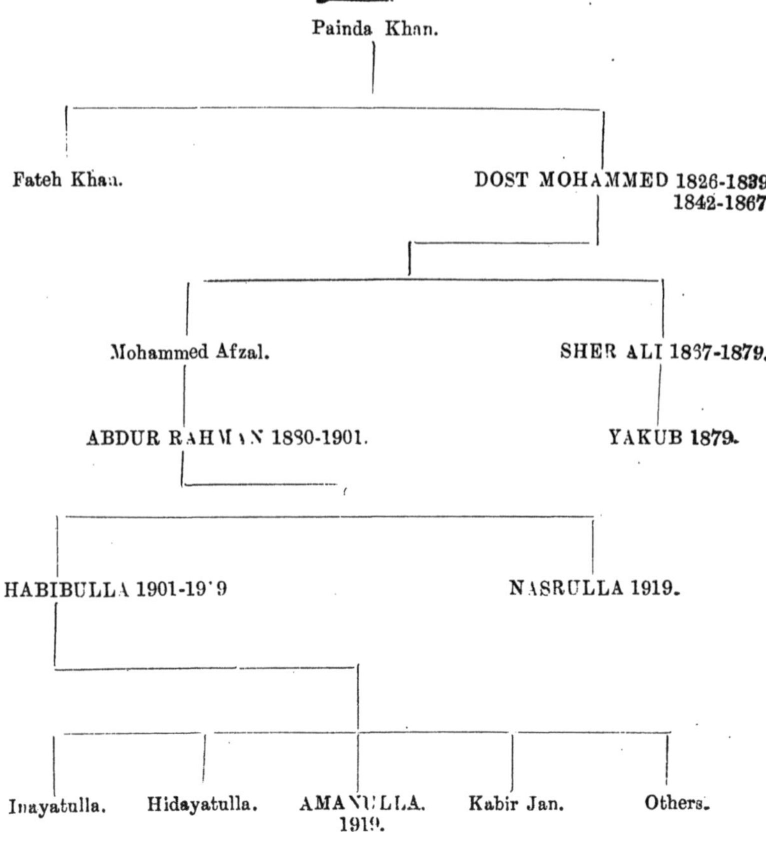

Although public excitement died down, plots against the Amir continued to be hatched, and on the night of the 19th and 20th of February 1919, Habibulla was murdered whilst on a shooting trip in Laghman. **Murder of Habibullah.**

At this time the Court was in Jalalabad. Nasrulla immediately proclaimed himself Amir, and Inayatulla, the heir-apparent, who was a supporter of his father's policy, was compelled to acknowledge his accession. Nasrulla soon found that he had underrated his nephew, Amanulla, who was in Kabul, officiating as Governor during the absence of his father. As soon as Amanulla heard of the murder, he assembled the notables and principal military officers and was proclaimed Amir by them on the 28th of February. Nasrulla felt that he could not rely on the troops in Jalalabad with whom Habibulla had been popular. They were greatly incensed at his murder and had shown their resentment by arresting the Commander-in-Chief, Nadir Khan, who was suspected of complicity in the crime. Therefore, when summoned to Kabul, Nasrulla and Inayatulla felt compelled to obey, and both of them rendered homage to Amanulla. **Succession of Nasrulla. His deposition by Amanulla** **Amanulla succeeds.**

The new Amir then proceeded to placate public opinion. A perfunctory enquiry was held into the murder of Habibulla and one Afghan colonel was executed on rather flimsy evidence. As a concession to the troops, their pay was increased, and their ruffled feelings smoothed by the appointment of Saleh Muhammad as Commander-in-Chief, whilst Nadir Khan was removed to Khost. Still feeling that his hold on the throne was none too secure, Amanulla secretly made preparations for a descent on India in order to divert popular opinion, and to pander to the War Party which had placed him on the throne. **Preparations for war.**

To aid him in his enterprise there were two potential allies. The first was the group of fanatical tribesmen on the British side of the Durand Line. The second was the vociferous section of Indian politicians, who were then busily engaged in engineering an agitation against the Criminal Law Amendment Act (Rowlatt Act). To obtain their assistance, Amanulla summoned the headmen of the Pathan tribes to Kabul, warned them to be ready for war, and sent them back to their homes. He also sent emissaries with money and ammunition across the frontier to prepare the inflammable material in independent territory. Through the "Provisional Government of India" he began to intrigue with the revolutionary party in India. He assured these individuals of his sympathy with their cause, and promised them help.

In addition to the two potential allies referred to above, there were the tempting factors of the war-weariness of the forces in India and the gradual demobilisation of both British and Indian troops.

The Indian revolutionaries were the first to move. Along the main railway line from Bombay to Peshawar, violent outbreaks occurred during the first half of April 1919. Excited mobs, utterly ignorant of what they were fighting for, but guided by extremist leaders, destroyed railway stations, damaged the permanent way and set fire to property. Between Bombay and Delhi there was **Punjab Rebellion, April 1919.**

serious rioting at Ahmadabad. There were disturbances in Delhi itself. On the two main lines from Delhi to Lahore there were more serious outbreaks at Amritsar and Kasur respectively. At Lahore itself the mob came into conflict with the armed police and matters appeared so grave that Martial Law was proclaimed. Further north the railway station and mission church at Gujranwala were burned, and the important railway junction of Wazirabad was attacked by large bands of rioters. Prompt military measures were taken at each place and the rioters were cowed by heavy casualties, especially at Amritsar.

Meanwhile Afghan troops were moving towards the frontier. Towards the end of April, the new Commander-in-Chief, Saleh Muhammad, appeared at Dakka nominally on a frontier tour, with an escort of two guns and two companies of infantry. He made a personal inspection of the springs at Bagh *on our side of the frontier* where later, on the 4th of May, the Afghan troops took up their position. Two thousand troops followed the Commander-in-Chief from Kabul to Dakka, fifteen hundred men were sent to Kandahar, and two thousand to Khost. Finally the Afghan Postmaster in Peshawar was summoned to Kabul. He received copies of a proclamation signed by the Amir calling on all Mohammadans to aid Afghanistan in a war against the Infidels (*i.e.*, British). Returning to Peshawar, the Postmaster had these documents distributed far and wide by Afghan agents. On the 3rd of May the first definite acts of hostility were committed and India, most unwillingly and with the knowledge that she was ill-prepared for it, was forced into war.

Outbreak of war.

On this date (3rd May) the party of Khyber Rifles detailed to escort the caravan, were met by piquets of armed Afghans under one Zar Shah, a notorious raider who lived among the Sangu Khel Shinwaris in Afghanistan, and turned back. Later in the day, Zar Shah, who boasted that he was acting under the orders of the Afghan Commander-in-Chief, killed five harmless labourers who were working on the Landi Kotal water scheme. This outrage was followed by the occupation of Kafir Kot ridge and Bagh village by a party of 150 Afghan regulars. These places were on our side of the border, and the presence of Afghan troops there constituted an act of war. On the 4th of May further reinforcements of Khassadars (see page 24) and Shinwaris reached Bagh, and cut the water supply of Landi Kotal. Afghan Mohmands and Shinwaris poured into Jalalabad, and received rifles with which to carry out a holy war (jehad). On the 5th of May further reinforcements of Afghan regulars arrived at Bagh, whilst a column of two companies of Indian infantry, one section of mountain artillery and one section of sappers and miners reached Landi Kotal, the whole in motor lorries, to assist the Khyber Rifles.

In the Kurram, Jajis and Afghan regulars had commenced to build breastworks on the Peiwar Kotal as early as the 29th of April. The Turi inhabitants, fearing an inroad of their inveterate enemies, were in a state of panic and prepared to evacuate their villages. Regular troops were asked for and a column left Thal on the 5th of

May under Lieutenant-Colonel J. Willans, D.S.O., 57th Wilde's Rifles and arrived at Parachinar on the 7th of May. It consisted of:—

1 squadron, 37th Lancers.

1 section, No. 28 Indian Mountain Battery.

57th Wilde's Rifles F. F.

On the 6th of May, general mobilization was ordered, and war was declared on Afghanistan.

CHAPTER III.

British and Afghan Forces in 1919.

The dispositions of the British and Afghan forces close to the frontiers are shown on the map facing page 1.

British Army in India.

In 1919, the Military Forces in India were organized in two Armies, Northern and Southern. Certain Divisions were directly under Army Headquarters, and were not included in either Army. The composition of these Armies and the formations under Army Headquarters are given below in tabular form:—

Northern Army.	Southern Army.	Under A. H. Q.
1st Cavalry Brigade (Risalpur).	5th Division (Mhow).	12th Mounted Brigade (Baleli near Quetta).
4th Cavalry Brigade (Meerut).	9th Division (Secunderabad).	4th Division (Quetta).
10th Cavalry Brigade (H. Q. and 1 regiment Peshawar).	Independent Brigades—	8th Division (Lucknow).
1 regiment (Mardan).	Karachi.	Burma Division.
1 regiment (Rawalpindi).	Bombay.	
1st Division (Peshawar).	Divisional Area, Poona.	
2nd Division (Rawalpindi).		
16th Division (Lahore).		
Independent Brigades—		
Kohat.		
Bannu.		
Derajat.		
Divisional Area, Meerut.		

Of these the Field Army for service on the North West Frontier of India consisted of the 1st, 2nd, 16th and 4th Divisions, with the 1st, 4th and 10th Cavalry Brigades and the 12th Mounted Brigade.

A Division of the Field Army consisted of three infantry brigades (each consisting of one British and three Indian infantry battalions), one squadron of Indian Cavalry, one field artillery brigade (two 18 pr. batteries and one 4·5 ins. howitzer battery), one mountain (pack) artillery brigade (two batteries of 2·75 ins. guns), two companies of machine guns (16 guns each), two companies of sappers and miners, one pioneer battalion, one divisional signal company, a divisional ammunition column and the usual ancillary units.

The 1st and 4th Cavalry brigades were composed of one horse artillery battery, one British and two Indian cavalry regiments, one squadron of machine guns (12 guns), one field troop sappers and miners, one signal troop and an ammunition column. The 10th Cavalry Brigade and the 12th Mounted Brigade were similarly constituted except that they had no horse artillery battery and three Indian cavalry regiments, but no British cavalry. The 12th Mounted Brigade was composed of newly raised Indian units mounted on undersized country-bred horses.

In addition to the Field Army certain units and formations were detailed for the defence of the North West Frontier and for the maintenance of order within their areas. These were the Kohat, Bannu and Derajat Independent Brigades; the garrisons of the Malakand posts and Chitral; troops for Internal Security at Peshawar and Quetta; and the units stationed in the Zhob valley. Owing to the defensive role assigned to them, they came under the designation of "Internal Security, North West Frontier". The three Independent Brigades were composed of all arms, and had sufficient transport to make them mobile. Each consisted of one regiment of Indian cavalry, one battery of mountain artillery, one armoured car battery of three cars (two in Bannu) and four battalions of Indian infantry (three in the Derajat).

When war broke out, all units, both of the Field Army and Internal Security, were short of their authorized strength. Demobilization of British personnel had begun and large numbers of men had left for England without being replaced. The shortage of skilled artizans and mechanics in the technical branches was specially marked. Eight regular battalions had been left in India for the whole period of the war and numbered many pre-war soldiers in their ranks. They had maintained a high standard of training and efficiency. Of these remnants of the "Old Contemptibles" three battalions were allotted to the 1st Division, three to the 2nd Division and two to the 4th Division. There was a British Territorial battalion in the 57th Brigade of the 4th Division and one in each of the three brigades of the 16th Division. The Indian units throughout were temporarily short of effectives. The rank and file extra to the establishments had been discharged as soon as possible after the Armistice (11th November, 1918), and a full complement of Indian Officers and men had been permitted to proceed on furlough for the first time since August, 1914.

Numbers of men were absent from their peace stations. Every year a proportion of British troops of the Peshawar and Rawalpindi Divisions proceed to the sanitaria in the Murree Hills for the summer months. Many of them had arrived in their hill stations, and more were on their way, when mobilization was ordered. Much of the mechanical transport required for the army in the field was engaged in carrying baggage between Rawalpindi and Murree in connection with these moves. There were many Indian battalions in the hills at the time. Of the 3rd Infantry Brigade of the 1st Division, on whom the early fighting was to devolve, two battalions were at Kakul near Abbottabad, whilst the third should have been on its way there, but was fortunately detained at Nowshera. Of the 2nd Division, three Indian battalions were in the Murree Hills, whilst one British and one

Indian battalion were in the Southern Punjab, whither they had been detached to deal with the risings in the previous month. The 16th Division was incomplete, the Pioneer battalion being at Dhond, one field company at Rurki, one machine gun company at Dalhousie and its transport in the four corners of the Peninsular.

The remainder of the Divisions and Divisional Areas throughout India were able to muster two mobile brigades of all arms for service, but beyond this there were no formations ready to take the field.

In estimating the standard of the troops at this period (and there can be no doubt that this was comparatively low) due weight should be given to the fact that India had risked much in order to contribute to the fullest extent towards the winning of the war. 182 Battalions of Indian Infantry and 131 Squadrons of Indian Cavalry had been sent overseas during the War.* Each of these infantry battalions and cavalry regiments had left behind depots to train the recruits necessary to meet the wastage of modern warfare, and to manage the administrative affairs of the unit. These depots were located in stations distant from the frontier. In few cases had the parent battalions returned from the expeditionary forces, so thus, whilst India was full of soldiers, they were chiefly to be found in the depots. There were, however, a certain number of newly raised battalions which were awaiting despatch to the various fronts on which Indian troops were employed when the Armistice was signed. Some of these were in process of being disbanded when the Afghan war broke out. The mustering out of these battalions was discontinued and they were brought up to strength as quickly as possible to meet the fresh emergency.

In addition to these disadvantages, both British and Indian units were short of senior officers. Although this was not so noticeable in the mass warfare on the Western and Turkish fronts, where the Division or the Brigade was the units of manœuvre, it became more pronounced in the type of fighting in Afghanistan and the North West Frontier of India, which necessitates a high degree of training in all leaders, and particularly in the case of company and platoon commanders.

In one respect India was fortunate. A large number of personnel, *en route* from Mesopotamia to England for demobilization, were detained in India owing to the shortage of shipping. These officers and men were utilized to meet the crisis. The infantry were formed into "Special Service Battalions", which were given emergency numbers. Those numbered from 1 to 4 were made into a Brigade at Rawalpindi, but in June they were split up to provide reinforcements for existing British battalions. Nos. 6, 12, 15, 16 and 18 were employed as Internal Security troops in India, whilst No. 17 was used in the Baluchistan area. Artizan and mechanics were drafted to technical corps and rendered invaluable services during the operations.

In accordance with the principles laid down by Lord Curzon in 1899, regular troops constituting the Field Army and Internal Security troops North West Frontier were mainly concentrated in cantonments

*At the outbreak of the Afghan War no less than 124 Battalions and 89 Squadrons were serving overseas.

on the Eastern, or Indian, side of the Administrative Border, whilst the trans-border tracts were held by irregulars. The exceptions to this rule were the garrisons* of Chitral, the Malakand garrisons (Dargai, Malakand and Chakdara) and two Indian battalions at Dardoni, one mile north of Miran Shah in the Tochi. This latter detachment dated from November, 1914, when the Bannu Independent Brigade had been called upon to meet an invasion of Afghan tribesmen from Khost, whom they had defeated with heavy loss on the 25th of March 1915. Subsequently a garrison of two battalions had remained, at first in an entrenched camp at Miran Shah, but later, in 1917, in the more healthy walled cantonment (Dardoni) which they occupied at the outbreak of hostilities with Afghanistan.

With these exceptions, the duty of policing independent tribal territory fell on Militia and Levies. Lord Curzon's idea was to give employment to the turbulent trans-frontier man by raising units which would provide a scope for their martial qualities, be a check on raiding and a protection to the main routes leading to Afghanistan. In case of actual hostilities they would act as an outpost zone behind which the Field Army could concentrate ready to strike a decisive blow. They were to be raised from the district they were formed to protect, but it was found to be impossible to carry out this idea in Waziristan, where the treachery and truculence of the inhabitants made it necessary to introduce mercenaries from other portions of the border. The then Commander-in-Chief, Sir William Lockhart, himself a frontier veteran, sounded a note of warning as to the possibility of these militias swelling the number of our enemies if their fellow tribesmen were in arms against us, but the system worked well from its inception till 1919.

The Militia were organized into battalions like the regular army, and were commanded and officered by selected officers of the Indian Army. They were divided into companies with a strength of 100 rifles, the number of such companies to a battalion varying with local requirements. In addition every battalion had one company of mounted infantry whilst the Kurram Militia maintained two 10 pounder mountain guns. Their uniform was the same as that of the Indian Army, with white metal buttons and shoulder numerals, and they were armed with a low velocity ·303 rifle with the short bayonet. The Militia units under the Chief Commissioner, North West Frontier Province, were:—

Chitral Scouts.
Mohmand Militia.
Khyber Rifles (2 battalions).
Kurram Militia.
North Waziristan Militia.
South Waziristan Militia.

The Chitral Scouts were a body of 2,000 Chitralis who differed from the other corps in that they were called up for training in batches for two months at a time and followed their normal vocations for the remainder of the year.

---

*See page 89.

The Mohmand Militia were a product of the War and were raised in 1917 to take over the line of posts along the Mohmand border from the regular units which had been blockading that tribe. Their functions more nearly approximated to those of the Frontier Constabulary (see below) by whom they were relieved on their disbandment in 1921.

The Khyber Rifles were an older corps and were formed in 1887 from the Khyber Jezailchees. They practically disappeared in 1897 for no fault of their own, but took over the Khyber from a regular brigade in 1899 contrary to the advice of the military authorities. They were raised locally from the tribes bordering on the Khyber, *viz.*, the Afridis, Shinwaris and Mullagoris.

The Kurram Militia were another local corps, recruited from the Turis and Bangash of the Kurram valley. The bulk of this unit were Shiah Mohammedans, and therefore, bitterly opposed to the orthodox Sunni tribes which surrounded them, *viz.*, the Orakazais, Wazirs and Chamkannis on the British side of the Durand Line, and the Jajis and Mangals of Afghanistan.

The North and South Waziristan Militia had few Wazirs and no Mahsuds in their ranks. The Mahsud companies in the South Waziristan Militia were disbanded in 1905 when they murdered their Commandant, Lieutenant-Colonel Harman. As already explained, the majority of the companies in both units came from other parts of the frontier.

Along the line of the Administrative Border for the prevention and interception of raids on the settled districts by the trans-frontier Pathans were a series of small posts. These were manned by the Frontier Constabulary, a force of armed civil police, who had been raised in 1913 to succeed the moribund and inefficient Border Military Police. The Constabulary had a quasi-military organization, being formed into battalions under selected civil police officers and they were armed with low velocity ·303 rifles.

In addition to the Militia and the Constabulary, there were certain local levies beyond our border armed with Martini-Henry rifles, who were employed by local political officers to garrison mud towers and to provide escorts. They had little value as fighting troops and may be left out of account.

In Baluchistan there were two corps of irregulars, the Zhob Militia and the Mekran Levy, the latter of whom do not come within the scope of this work. The Zhob Militia originally consisted of local Kakars and Sherannis, and was known as the Zhob Levy. In 1912 a proportion of Pathans from the North West Frontier Province was introduced into this corps and its name was changed to Zhob Militia.

Whilst the organization of the fighting forces had been arranged on a carefully thought out plan, the means of maintaining an army in the field were not adequate to meet the situation. As a result of the steady drain on the resources of India since 1914, stocks of electric and railway plant, and other stores, only procurable from the United Kingdom, had been reduced to the lowest ebb, and, owing to shortage of shipping, could not be replaced. Animal transport had been exploited to the uttermost and the reserve of animals left in the country had sunk very low. The supply of mules had been completely exhausted, and ponies, which are greatly inferior to mules in general utility and endurance, had to be employed as draught animals even in the Field Army. There was also a shortage of camels, due to heavy shipments overseas and to the ravages of *surra*.

Of supplies there was a reserve of 60 days for the Field Army: half of which was kept in stations west of the Indus, and half in Lahore, Bombay and Karachi. This proved ample during the campaign.

On the 6th of May general mobilization was ordered. Army Headquarters became General Headquarters, and the forces for the defence of the North West Frontier were organized as follows:—

North-West Frontier Force.

Commander.—General Sir A. A. Barratt, G.C.B., K.C.S.I., K.C.V.O., A.-D.-C.

Troops—

1st Cavalry Brigade.

10th Cavalry Brigade.

1st Division.

2nd Division.

Peshawar Area Troops.

Malakand Garrisons.

Chitral Garrison.

L. of C. Troops Northern.

Kohat Force (Kohat Independent Brigade).

Waziristan Force (Bannu and Derajat Independent Brigades).

Baluchistan Force.

Commander.—Lieutenant-General R. Wapshare, C.B., C.S.I.

Troops—

12th Mounted Brigade.

4th Division.

Zhob and Quetta Area Troops.

Meshed Force.

East Persian L. of C. Troops.

Central Reserve.

(To remain in peace stations till required.)

Commander.—

Nil. Under G. H. Q.

Troops—

4th Cavalry Brigade.

16th Division.

46th Mobile Brigade.

47th Mobile Brigade.

1st "Special Brigade" (in process of formation).

It will be seen that General Barratt's command was extensive, and its problems complex. Later, in June, Waziristan, with its own local issues to consider, was made into a separate command under General Headquarters.

To summarize the position, therefore, independent tribal territory was either not held at all or lightly held by Pathan Militia. The line of the Administrative Border was garrisoned by armed police. A striking force of two divisions and two cavalry brigades was available for offensive action on the Khyber front, and one division and one mounted brigade for operations on the Southern front. A defensive role was assigned to the troops in the Central area, and to the garrisons of Malakand and Chitral. A General Reserve of one division, two mobile brigades and one brigade of cavalry were ready for service wherever required. The units, however, were short of effectives and senior officers. Supplies were sufficient, but there was a shortage of transport.

Afghan Army and Fighting Force.

It should be borne in mind that the real military strength of Afghanistan depends on the armed population rather than on the regular forces. The army was, and is, regarded as a stiffening to the hordes of armed tribesmen whom fanaticism and love of plunder rally to the Afghan standard. The greatest number of these which have ever come together was in December 1879, when as many as 60,000 men assembled for the siege of Sherpur. The force which Amir Habibulla collected to suppress a rising in Khost in 1912 was composed of about 4,000 regulars and 18,000 tribesmen. These tribesmen, however, will rarely fight at any great distance from their homes. The difficulties of supply restrict the numbers which can be assembled and kept in the field. They come together, each man carrying his rifle, ammunition, knife and a supply of floor, the latter in a bag of undressed sheep skin. The flour is frequently spoiled by the action of rain or perspiration and is apt to become full of maggots. As it is used up or goes bad, the man goes off to his own home for more. It was generally considered that the largest body of tribesmen we should be likely to meet in the field at one place would be 20,000 and that usually the numbers would be very much smaller.

As an additional armament for them the Amir maintained in the Arsenal at Kabul 15,000 small bore rifles and over 400,000 Martinis.

The Afghan army comprised 78 battalions of infantry, 21 regiments of cavalry, 280 breech-loading guns and an equal number of muzzle-loaders, the latter chiefly on the Russian and Persian frontiers. The effectives totalled about 38,000 rifles, 8,000 sabres and 4,000 artillerymen. The country was divided into ten military districts, all of which, except Kabul, were in contact with one portion or another of the Afghan frontier. In Eastern Afghanistan, the districts which bordered on India were Jalalabad, Khost, Ghazni, Mukur and Kandahar. In these were stationed in normal times 35 battalions of infantry, 4¾ regiments of cavalry and 107 guns. In the Kabul district the garrison consisted of 17 battalions of infantry, 3 pioneer battalions, 7½ regiments of cavalry and 108 guns. In the remaining districts on the Russian and Persian borders were 23 battalions of infantry, 8¾ regiments of cavalry and 65 guns. Only breech-loading guns have been taken into account in this enumeration.

There was no staff and, except in Kabul, there was no attempt at even a brigade organization. In Kabul, four mixed brigades had been formed each consisting of one regiment of cavalry, one battery of field and one of pack artillery, three battalions of infantry and three machine guns.

The Afghan regulars lacked training, and could not be considered as first class troops, although their courage and endurance were undoubted. Weapon training was seldom carried out and tactical exercises were unknown. Their low power of manœuvre made them more liable to await than to initiate attack.

The infantry varied considerably in armament and equipment. Less than half the battalions were armed with small bore rifles, whilst the remaining units had Martinis and even Sniders. The battalions in Eastern Afghanistan had a higher proportion of ·303 rifles than those in the north and west. A bayonet was worn (and, in some cases, a sword as well) but no instruction in its use was given, and it was seldom used except to execute criminals and political prisoners. The officers and N. C. Os. were ignorant and deficient in the spirit of leading. All units had a ceremonial dress and in the case of the Kabul garrison, a service dress was issued. This consisted of a suit of khaki, puttees and ankle boots. The equipment was a leather belt with leather braces and three large leather pouches for ammunition. The head-dress was a round, black, lambskin cap with a metal badge representing a mosque on a crescent, the Afghan crest. In other districts the men frequently wore their national costume; a sheepskin coat (*poshtin*), wide trousers and native shoes. The strength of the battalions varied with the locality. In the Kabul and Jalalabad districts the authorised strength of some battalions rose to 1,000, but in other parts of the country it dropped as low as 500 rifles. When war broke out no battalion had more than 75 per cent. of effectives, although some of them made up their numbers by drafting in armed tribesmen to make up their establishment.

The cavalry were mounted on sturdy ponies, 14·2 and under, capable of great exertions, but unsuited to shock tactics. They were armed with a rifle and a sword, but they were little better than mounted infantry. Lances had been issued to the cavalry regiments in Kabul, but they were seldom carried. The number of sabres in a regiment varied from 600 in Kabul to 300 elsewhere.

The field artillery was under horsed and badly trained. The guns of the pack artillery were carried on ponies, which were badly looked after. Drills were infrequent, the guns being usually stored in sheds, range practices were seldom carried out and field practices and calibration unknown. The field guns had a maximum range of 4,500 yards and the pack guns of 3,500 yards. The guns actually employed against us in 1919 were a field howitzer 10 cm. Krupp, pack guns of Krupp manufacture with a calibre of 75 mm., and 7-pdr. pack guns.

Their machine guns were ancient, four barrelled Gardiners, operated by turning a handle.

The mechanical resources of Afghanistan were few. The only arsenal in the country was at Kabul, where guns, rifles, ammunition, shell (but not fuzes), equipment, boots, clothing, etc., were turned out. Smokeless powder was manufactured in small quantities, but cordite cartridges were usually imported from Europe through India. A smokeless powder plant had been imported in 1912, but owing to the ignorance of the agent employed, the machinery delivered was for nitro-cellulose for which the rifles were not sighted, so it was never used. A factory for black powder was situated at Bawali near Jalalabad which turned out sufficient for normal consumption.

Organized transport was practically non-existent, but an ample supply of camels was to be found in the country. A system of registration was in force, and machinery existed for the impressment of such privately owned animals as might be necessary. In 1912, 8,600 camels* were collected in 14 days for operations against the Khost rebels.

To facilitate the movement of troops, state granaries existed in the fortified posts which marked the stages every 12 miles or so along the main roads. The supplies in these posts varied considerably. On the main Kabul-Dakka road, where supplies were plentiful, rations for 12,000 men for two days were placed at nearly every stage. On other routes, where supplies were less easy to obtain, the stocks were greater.

In addition to the regular army, there were about 10,000 militia or "Khassadars". These men had no uniform, were armed with Snider rifles, and had no higher organization than a company of 100 rifles. They were usually scattered in parties of 10 to 100 men in small posts, or were employed in police, revenue, or other civil duties.

The position of the Afghan regular forces as shown on the map facing page 1 on the 6th of May, 1919, were:—

Kunar Valley—for operations against Chitral or Mohmand country—

6 battalions infantry.

8 pack guns.

Ningrahar and Khyber—

14 battalions infantry.

1 battalion pioneers.

1½ regiments cavalry.

44 guns.

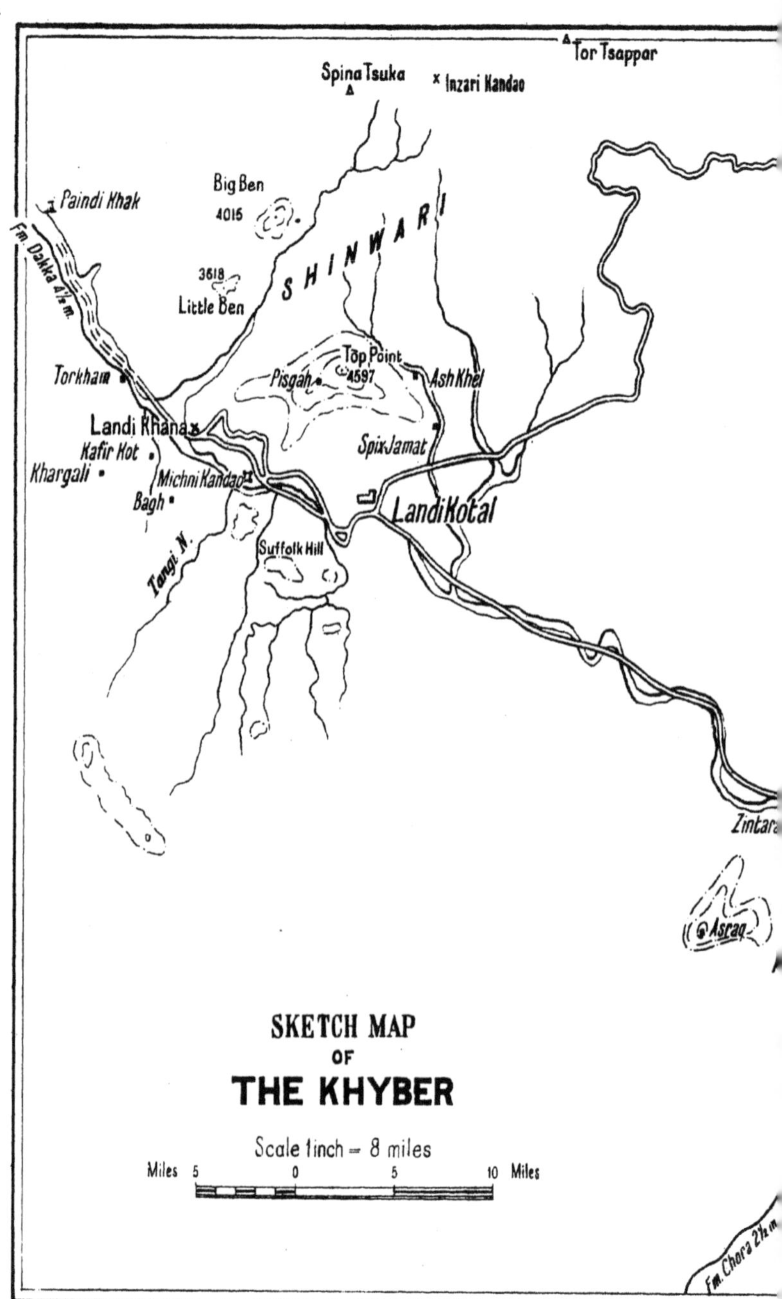

S.D.O. No. 4283 Sept. 1925.

No. 2

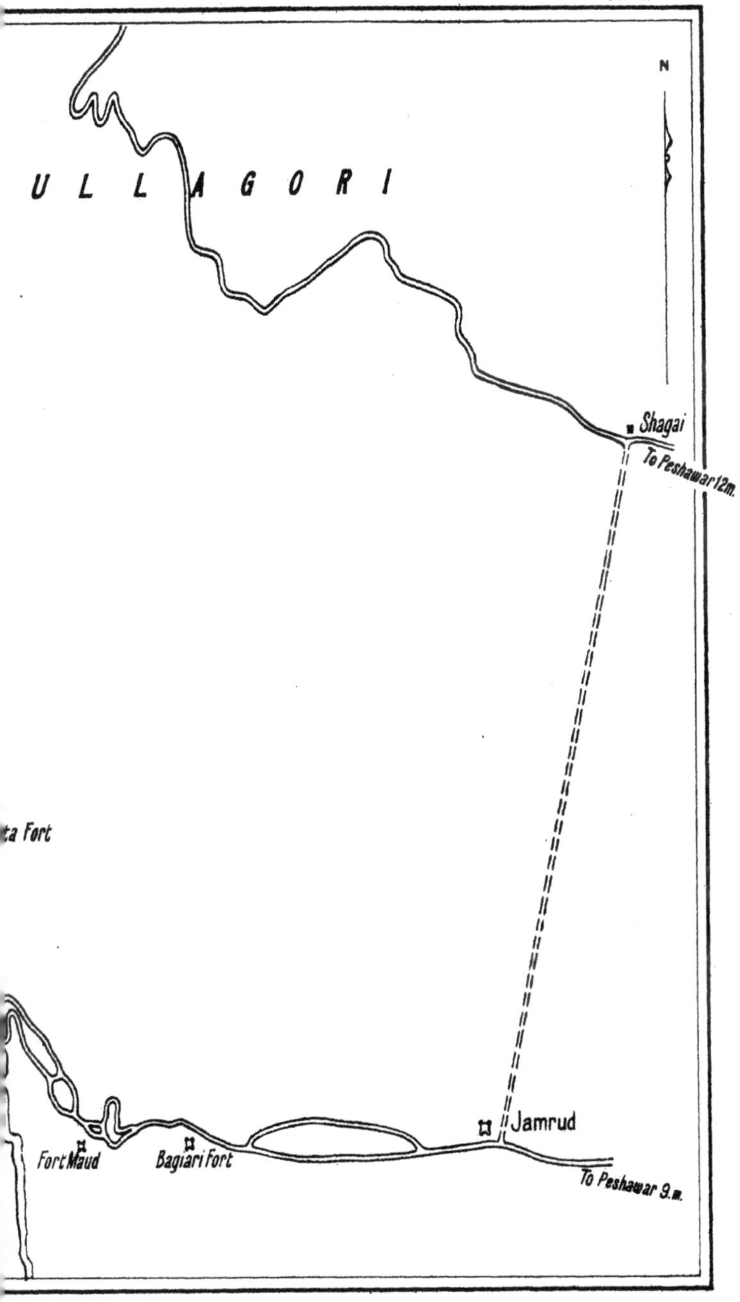

U L L A G O R I

N

Shagai

To Peshawar 12m.

ta Fort

Jamrud

Fort Maud

Bagiari Fort

To Peshawar 9.m.

Heliozincographed at the Survey of India Offices, Dehra Dun

Concentrating in Khost—in position to attack Kurram or Tochi—

16 battalions infantry.
2 battalions pioneers.
4 regiments cavalry.
60 guns.

Concentrating in Kandahar—

13 battalions infantry.
3 regiments cavalry.
60 guns.

General Reserve—Kabul—

11 battalions infantry.
5½ regiments cavalry.
43 guns.

Up to this date the call to a Holy War had not been received with general enthusiasm by the tribes. In the northern area the Afghan Pathans in Ningrahar (*i.e.*, between Jalalabad and Dakka) were eager for war, whilst the Afridis and Mohmands on the British side of the Durand Line were showing signs of restlessness, although they were not actively hostile. In the central area the Ghilzais also seemed to be taking up the Amir's cause with zeal. Along the rest of the frontier the proclamations seem to have had little, if any, effect. The movement was destined to spread eventually, but too late to be of practical value to the Afghans.

Phases of Operations.

The actual operations can be divided into three phases:—

Phase 1.—From the 6th to 25th May. Actions on the Khyber front and attempted Afghan penetration through the Mohmand country. Movement of British reserves to northern area and the formation of a further reserve by the creation of the 60th Brigade at Ambala, the 61st Brigade at Jubbulpore, the 62nd Brigade at Dhond, and the 63rd Brigade at Lucknow.

During this period there was little activity on the part of our border tribes.

Phase 2.—From the 26th May to the 2nd June. Invasion of central area by Nadir Khan and siege of Thal. Evacuation of Militia posts in Waziristan and mutiny of the North and South Waziristan Militias. Diversion of British reserves to Kohat and Bannu. The attack on Baldak. The Armistice.

During this period our border tribes were showing signs of hostility.

Phase 3.—From the 3rd June to 8th August. Cessation of hostilities on the part of the Afghan regulars, but general activity on the part of our border tribes.

CHAPTER IV.

THE KHYBER FRONT TO THE 13TH OF MAY INCLUSIVE.

Dispositions on 6th May 1919.

By the evening of the 6th May, the Afghan Forces near Bagh had increased to three battalions of infantry and two guns. A body of about 350 infantry and two guns had also moved from Dakka and occupied two prominent features, known as Tor Tsappar and Spinatsuka, about 5 miles north of Landi Kotal. Shinwaris and Mohmands from Afghan territory were gradually assembling and joining our enemies. At Dakka, 13 miles from Landi Kotal, there were another 5 battalions of infantry, 200 cavalry and 6 guns. The British garrison at Landi Kotal still consisted of 2 Companies Indian Infantry, 500 Khyber Rifles, one section sappers and miners and a section of mountain artillery, and an attack on this post was momentarily expected. Had the Afghans taken the initiative at this juncture, such action would have caused us serious embarrassment. The tribesmen on the British side of the Border would probably have risen, and the relief of the garrison through mountainous country, and harassed by an active and enterprising enemy, would have been a difficult operation. The Afghan commander, Mohammed Anwar Khan by name, was not equal to the occasion and let the opportunity slip.

British reinforcements arrive at Landi Kotal 7th and 8th May.

On the following day (7th May) the 2nd Battalion Somerset Light Infantry and the remaining two sections of No. 8 Mountain Battery, R. G. A. arrived in lorries from Peshawar and the crisis was over. On the same day Brigadier-General G. F. Crocker left Peshawar with the following force which reached Landi Kotal on the 8th of May:—

Headquarters 1st Infantry Brigade.

1/15th Sikhs less 1 Co.

1/35th Sikhs.

1/9th Gurkha Rifles less 1 Co.

2 troops, 30th Lancers.

No. 77 Battery R. F. A. (4·5″ howitzers).

No. 263 Company, Machine Gun Corps.

Afghans on Ash Khel Ridge.

Meanwhile the Afghans on Tor Tsappar and Spinatsuka, reinforced by bodies of tribesmen, had advanced and seized the Ash Khel ridge, 1 mile north of Landi Kotal. The enemy were now in a position from which they could either attack the fort or raid the Peshawar plain through Mullagori country. To meet any move in the latter direction, the 1st Lancers were ordered to move to Shahgai Thana, 12 miles north west of Peshawar.

Defence of Landi Kotal.

On arrival at Landi Kotal, the 1st Infantry Brigade brushed off the enemy detachments on the Ash Khel ridge, and established a strong piquet line from Spin Jamat, 2,500 yards north east of Landi Kotal, to Point 4,597 (now known as " Top Point ") and thence south west for 1,400 yards through " Pisgah " to a knoll overlooking the road. It was garrisoned by the 1/35th Sikhs, 1/9th Gurkha Rifles less 1 Company, and 100 men of the Khyber Rifles. To assist in further operations, Suffolk Hill (Point 4,147) and the feature 3,200 yards south east of it were seized and garrisoned, the former by 150 rifles of the 1/9th Gurkha Rifles, and the latter by 100 rifles of the 2nd Battalion Somerset Light Infantry. The 1/11th Gurkha Rifles arrived in lorries during the afternoon of the 8th, to be followed next morning by the 2/123rd Outram's rifles, who were making a forced march from Jamrud. These battalions belonged to the 2nd Infantry Brigade.

Description of Afghan position near Bagh.

General Crocker now decided to attack the Afghan regulars in their position at Bagh. They were holding a well defined ridge about 2,000 yards long, roughly shaped like a crescent, and facing north east. Their left was covered by the precipitous Khargali Nala, and their right rested on the equally difficult Tangi Khwar (stream). The approach from the north was abrupt but not too steep for laden mules. To the east and west were bold salients running down to Landi Khana, between which flowed the stream from Bagh springs. This ridge was held as an outpost line, the bulk of the Afghan troops being on the Khargali ridge, which was south west of, and roughly parallel to, the Bagh position. Here they could obtain water from the Khargali Nala, whilst the troops in the outpost position were obliged to obtain theirs from the Bagh springs *in front of their line*. Another curious feature was that the line of retirement ran parallel to their front.

Disposition of General Crocker's force on 9th May 1919.

General Crocker was still apprehensive of an attack from the north, whilst the operation was in progress. He, therefore, detached the two troops 30th Lancers, the machine gun company and the special 3·7″ howitzer section of No. 6 Mountain Battery, R. G. A. to support the already large force on the Ash Khel ridge. The troops at his disposal for operations on the 9th were:—

In protective positions covering Landi Kotal.	Striking force for attack on Bagh.
1-35th Sikhs.	2nd Bn., Somerset L. I.
1-9th Gurkha Rifles.	1-15th Sikhs.
100 Khyber Rifles.	1-11th Gurkha Rifles.
263 Co. M. G. C.	77th Battery, R. F. A.
2 troops, 30th Lancers.	No. 8 Mountain Battery, R. G. A.
1 section No. 6 M. B. R. G. A.	

In Reserve at General's Camp.

No. 7 Field Co. 1st S. and M.

2/123rd Outram's Rifles (to arrive during morning).

Strength of Afghan regulars.

The Afghan regular forces had increased and on Tor Tsappar, Spinatsuka and Bagh they totalled five battalions of infantry and six guns.

Objectives in the attack.

On the east side of the Tangi Khwar, and thus cut off from the main Afghan position, was a prominent feature known as Bright's Hill. It was decided to seize this hill and then to proceed west, to retake the water supply, then in the hands of the enemy, and to attack the main Afghan position (see map facing page 27).

Covering fire.

Of the forces available, the 2nd Battalion Somerset Light Infantry and one section No. 8 Mountain Battery R. G. A. were detailed to occupy Suffolk Hill to cover the advance. The range from Suffolk Hill to Bright's Hill was 800 yards, and from Suffolk Hill to the extreme right of the enemy main position 1,500 yards. No. 77 Battery R. F. A. were to come into action near Landi Kotal fort and No. 8 Mountain Battery R. G. A. less 1 section on the knoll held by the Khyber Rifles which marked the southwesterly extremity of the piquet line.

Attacking column.

The attacking force under Colonel C. N. MacMullen, C.M.G., D.S.O., 1/15th Sikhs, consisted of the 1/15th Sikhs and the 1/11th Gurkha Rifles.

First Battle of Bagh. 9th May 1919.

At 0445 hours on the morning of the 9th of May, the troops detailed to cover the advance moved out and occupied the positions assigned to them. The attacking column advanced down the main Landi Khana road. On reaching Digai Fort, Colonel MacMullen detached one company of the 1/15th Sikhs to attack the Bright's Hill. This was taken without opposition as the Afghans only occupied it by day and their piquet had not yet arrived in position. The remainder of the column passed round the north of Bright's Hill, leaving a Lewis gun in the Khyber Rifle post at Michni Kandao, and deployed in dead ground at the base of the western spur up which the attack was to develop. From here they pushed on up hill for 500 yards up to a point where the spur narrowed down to a neck 200 yards long leading to the crags in which the Afghan breastworks were erected.

Meanwhile enemy reinforcements were being pushed forward from Khargali ridge to oppose the attack. The Afghans developed a heavy and accurate rifle fire on the neck, and a further advance could not be made without heavy loss. The covering fire was insufficient, the attack lacked the weight necessary to exploit an initial success, and the numbers were small to meet a determined counter-attack. Bright's Hill had been taken, the water supply had been recovered and a position had been secured from which a further attack could be launched with every hope of success. No advantage was to be gained by a further advance, so the 1/15th Sikhs and the 1/11th Gurkha Rifles consolidated the ground gained by scooping out shallow trenches in the hard ground, and awaited the reinforcements which were on their way from Peshawar.

The advance checked, attacking troops dig in.

Half No. 7 Field Company Sappers and Miners were sent forward to assist them in this work, whilst the remainder of the company were employed in repairing the damaged water supply to relieve the acute shortage of water at Landi Kotal. In this forward position these two battalions remained for two days. The Afghans kept up a desultory fire on them, but they made no attack on the hastily prepared position. During the action the Afghans north of Landi Kotal remained inactive, and our troops in the Ash Khel ridge did not fire a shot during the day. Had fewer troops been employed on this protective duty the main attack would probably have been successful. During daylight, one battalion of infantry and the Khyber Rifles would have been ample to meet any demonstration from the direction of Spinatsuka. It would have been preferable for the machine guns to have been withdrawn from the covering force to provide overhead fire and the 2nd Battalion Somerset Light Infantry and one battalion from Ash Khel ridge might have joined the assaulting column. With four battalions making the actual attack, covered by properly organised gun and machine gun fire, it is possible that the operations might have resulted in the capture of the enemy position that day.

Attempted rising in Peshawar city.

Meanwhile the reinforcements which should have been reaching Landi Kotal had been detained by events elsewhere. On the 7th May, information was received by the Criminal Investigation Department that the Afghan Postmaster, who had been left at large although war was declared on the 6th May, and the Indian Revolutionary Committee in Peshawar city had arranged to collect a mob of 7,000 men in order to burn the Cantonments and Civil lines, damage the railway and destroy the mobilization stores. This rabble consisted of Afghan subjects, trans-border bad characters and bazar loafers. Two months' license in forming "volunteers," shutting down business ("Hartals") and holding seditious meetings had produced a contempt for authority among the disloyal elements, and they were ready for any mischief.

The following letter, written by the Afghan Postmaster on the 7th of May to the Amir, though somewhat vague and obscure in places, gives an idea of the state of affairs in Peshawar at the time. The idea of armed resistance being necessary to guard papers which might easily have been burnt is, of course, absurd.

Translation.

> "Hearing that the Post Office (*i.e.*, Afghan) was to be searched, I ordered armed resistance, as the whole of my correspondence went against the British Government. If necessary I would begin a Holy War in Peshawar City. Hearing of this, about 8,000 Peshawaris, both Hindus and Moslems, came to help me. That night 2,000 villagers from outside offered their assistance. I said that I would invite them when the time came. Sikh regiments have assured Hindus that they look on Moslems as brethren and will not fire on them. The (Indian) Government has not sufficient troops in India and often moves about one regiment consisting of 2 or 3 companies (sic) to make a display. In spite of many telegrams sent by the Chief Commissioner no regiments have arrived by train. British subjects will not supply recruits. There are disturbances throughout India, and troops, if sent from England, will not arrive in time. It has been given out at a public meeting that the Amir and Ghazis are ready to help Indians, and if war is delayed the public (Indian public) will be displeased with the Amir. The assembly cried with one voice that they could not forget the oppressions and tyrannies of the British Government. If after selected leaflets have been circulated and three Sipah

Salars (*i.e.*, Corps Commanders) have been appointed the Amir refrains from invading India, Hindus and Moslems will be much displeased. It is not expedient to delay and to give the English time to collect troops."

Of the five battalions of infantry which were allotted to the Peshawar Area for Internal Security, only two were actually in Peshawar. These were employed on guards and other duties. It was, therefore, decided to employ troops of the Field Army to deal with the fresh situation. The 2nd Infantry Brigade which was moving by rail from Nowshera to Jamrud during the night of the 7/8th of May was ordered to detrain two battalions at Peshawar, and one cavalry regiment was directed to march to Peshawar from Risalpur. Major-General S. H. Climo, C.B., D.S.O., was placed in command of the force which consisted of:—

Force for dealing with Peshawar City.

No. 1 Armoured Car Brigade.

1st King's Dragoon Guards.

2nd Battalion, North Staffordshire Regiment.

2/11th Gurkha Rifles.

They were ordered to surround Peshawar City, to block all exits and to demand the surrender of the Afghan Postmaster and 33 other malcontents and Afghans who had been the instigators of the plot.

Description of Peshawar City.

Peshawar City (see map facing this page) is shaped like a flattened " V ". Its length is about two miles, but its breadth is nowhere greater than 1,200 yards. The outer side of the " V " is encircled by the main line of the North Western Railway. The inner portion is filled with orchards and gardens. The city itself is surrounded by a high wall, in more or less good repair, which is pierced at intervals by 16 gates, most of which can be closed by a heavy door.

Plan of action.

It was decided to form four columns, each composed of cavalry and infantry. Each column was given a separate starting point along the railway, which was the starting line. Each column had certain gates for the closing of which they were responsible. The parties detailed for each gate were told off before leaving bivouacs, and one civil policeman with the name of the gate written on a slip of paper in English, Urdu and Nagri accompanied each party as a guide to avoid the possibility of troops losing their way. Mounted police accompanied the cavalry and foot constables the infantry. A Political Officer rode at the head of each column. The Ghor Khatri, the imposing fortress in the centre of the city, was reinforced by armed police and the remaining civil police posts were quietly evacuated during the course of the morning. It was decided to cross the starting line at 1400 hours, which gave ample time for all arrangements to be made, and this was also the portion of the day when the inhabitants indulge in a " siesta ". One armoured car battery preceded each of the two outside columns with orders to patrol the southeasterly wall of the city. No first line transport was available, so hackney carriages and municipal dust carts were requisitioned to carry ammunition and tools.

The investment of Peshawar City.

Precisely to the minute the columns with cavalry in front passed the starting line. The cavalry trotted out, and, without halting, dropped a detachment from the tail of the column at each successive gate. This detachment herded the few men then loitering about inside the city and prevented anyone from leaving it. The infantry following behind similarly, without halting, dropped a detachment from their own tail which shut or barricaded the gate. The Cavalry thus relieved trotted to join their column again. The operation was completely successful. The cavalry closed all the gates in eleven minutes, and in forty-four minutes they were shut or barricaded by the infantry, local reserves were in position, and the investment was complete. It was then announced that until certain specified men were handed up, no one would be allowed to enter or leave the city. The mob were thoroughly cowed by the completeness of these military measures, and the Afghan Postmaster and 22 of the revolutionary leaders were brought in by sunset (2000 hours). The remainder were accounted for, as they were proved to have left the city. The two battalions of the 2nd Infantry Brigade were relieved at 0600 hours on the 9th May and entrained for Jamrud, from whence they marched at 1430 hours for Ali Masjid, accompanied by No. 6 Mountain Battery R. G. A. and No. 285 Company, Machine Gun Corps.

2nd Infantry Brigade march for Ali Masjid.

Hardly had the 2nd Infantry Brigade commenced its march for the Khyber, when fire was opened on a company of the North Staffords within a mile of Jamrud fort. A party of tribesmen had laid an ambush inside the line of the Khyber Rifles piquets. The North Staffords, a fine shooting battalion, retaliated by killing three of the enemy and driving off the remainder. Warned by this General Climo determined not to trust the Khyber Rifles further, and placed his own piquets to cover the bivouac at Ali Masjid. The column arrived at Landi Kotal on the morning of the 10th May, having left one section No. 6 Mountain Battery at Ali Masjid.

The situation at Landi Kotal on the 10th May.

At Landi Kotal the situation had deteriorated. General Fowler, commanding the 1st Division, arrived at Landi Kotal on the evening of the 9th to see how matters stood, but he decided to remain there with his general staff officer and take over command of the operations. The Afghans were still holding on to their positions with great confidence, and the Afridis were showing signs of restlessness. The high hills to the south were covered with bodies of armed men who were watching the course of events round Bagh. Finally a piquet of the Khyber Rifles deserted with their rifles from near Landi Kotal. It was fully realized that if another unsuccessful attack was made, large bodies of Afridis would join the Afghans, and that our communications with Peshawar would be endangered. One and a half battalions of the 3rd Infantry Brigade were to arrive at Landi Kotal on the morning of the 11th of May to increase the numbers available for an assault, but it was considered that delay would have the same effect as a reverse. General Fowler chose the bolder alternative of relying on the troops he had in hand, and issued orders for an attack on the following morning, the 11th of May.

Plan of action.

The 2nd Infantry Brigade were ordered to carry out the actual assault, covered by the fire of every available gun and machine gun, and by rifle and Lewis gun fire of the 2nd Battalion Somerset Light Infantry. It was decided to force the enemy right and then to roll up his whole line. One battalion was withdrawn from the piquet line north of Landi Kotal and the defence of this sector was placed under General Crocker. The troops at General Fowler's disposal were—

In protective positions covering Landi Kotal.	Striking Force for attack on Bagh.
1st Infantry Bde. H. Q.	2nd Infantry Bde.
1-35th Sikhs.	2nd Bn., N. Staff. Regt.
400 Khyber Rifles.	2-123rd Outram's Rifles.
2 troops, 30th Lancers.	1-11th Gurkha Rifles.
	2-11th Gurkha Rifles.
	2nd Bn., Somerset Light Inf.
	1-15th Sikhs.
	77th Battery, R. F. A.
	No. 8 Mountain Battery, R. G. A.
	Special section (3·7″ howitzers), No. 6 Battery, R. G. A.
	1 Section, No. 6 Battery, R. G. A.
	263rd Company, Machine Gun Corps.
	285th Company, Machine Gun Corps.

Reserve at General's Camp.

1/9th Gurkha Rifles (to come under the orders of G. O. C. 2nd Infantry Brigade when relieved by):—

H. Q. 3rd Infantry Brigade.

4/3rd Gurkha Rifles.

2/1st Gurkha Rifles less 2 Companies.

The 2nd Infantry Brigade mustered 1,850 bayonets for the attack, whilst the machine gun companies were only able to man 22 out of their available 32 guns owing to shortage of personnel.

On the evening of the 10th May, a reconnaissance of the enemy position was made from Suffolk Hill, whence a clear view of the Bagh and Khargali ridges could be obtained. Officers commanding infantry battalions, machine gun companies and artillery batteries had the plan explained to them and objectives were pointed out. The task allotted to No. 77 Battery R. F. A. and two sections No. 263 Company Machine Gun Corps was to engage the enemy right, whilst No. 8 Mountain Battery R. G. A. and No. 285 Company Machine Gun Corps (10 guns) were to neutralize the remainder of the enemy front. The gun section and the special 3·7″ howitzer section No. 6 Mountain Battery R. G. A. were to be employed to engage targets as occasion offered (*i.e.*, superimposed). The 2nd Battalion, Somerset Light

Infantry and one section (4 guns) of No. 263 Company Machine Gun Corps were to bring enfilade fire to bear on the Afghan right from "Rocky Knoll", a hill 800 yards south-west of Bright's Hill.

At 0415 hours on the morning of the 11th of May, the 2nd Battalion Somerset Light Infantry, less piquets on Suffolk and Range Hill, and the section of machine guns left camp to take up their position. They failed to reach their objective under cover of darkness, and in reaching the position selected for them they sustained casualties from rifle fire directed from sangars on the high ground west and southwest of Tangi Khwar, the officer commanding, Lt.-Col. E. W. Worrall, being amongst those wounded.

Somersets take up their position.

At 0430 hours the 2nd Infantry Brigade marched from their bivouac to a position of assembly east of Bright's Hill. A further reconnaissance was carried out by battalion, company and platoon commanders from the summit of Bright's Hill where Brigade Headquarters was established. The 2nd Battalion North Staffordshire Regiment and the 2/11th Gurkha Rifles then moved forward and formed up in successive lines of two platoons extended to two paces in the dead ground in rear of the trenches held by the 1/15th Sikhs. The 1/11th Gurkha Rifles were already on the ground, and the 2/123rd Outram's Rifles were moved up immediately in rear of the latter unit.

The 2nd Infantry Brigade form up to attack.

At 0830 hours the artillery opened fire at the rate of two rounds a gun a minute. Two minutes later the machine guns opened on the enemy position. At 0838 the two leading platoons of the 2nd Battalion North Staffordshire Regiment left the cover of the trenches and advanced across the neck followed by the remainder of the battalion in lines of two platoons at a hundred yards distance. They came under enfilade fire from Bagh and Kafir Kot at once, and here most of their casualties occurred. On clearing the neck they were sheltered by the formation of the ground, which rose abruptly above them. They formed into lines of companies at 100 yards distance and continued to advance. "D" Company was temporarily moved to the right to keep down the fire of the Afghans in Bagh village, and this they did so successfully that the 2/11th Gurkha Rifles crossed the neck without loss, and moved direct on the enemy centre south of Bagh. The 1/11th Gurkha Rifles conformed to this movement, forming up on the right rear of the 2/11th and advancing against the Afghan left. The 2/123rd Outram's Rifles also crossed the neck and came into reserve in the centre.

The North Staffords lead the attack.

Meanwhile the 2nd Battalion North Staffordshire Regiment advanced steadily up hill to their objective. The heat of the day and the steepness of the slope made it necessary for them to halt at intervals to re-form and to get their breath. During these periods of immobility, the guns and machine guns would cease fire. After an interval they would re-open and the North Staffords would press on. Finally they reached a position so close to the bursting shells that the men of the leading platoons were stained yellow and many of them even vomited through inhaling the lyddite fumes. The artillery was then switched to the right. The North Staffords dashed forward and drove the Afghans out with the bayonet. Some of the enemy fled south and south-west where they were caught by the fire of the

Enemy right taken.

Somerset Light Infantry and of the four machine guns posted with them. The remainder retired to a series of small, round, closed works (sangars) which formed a second line. From these they were ejected by grenades, which were very effective in the confined space, and opposition on the enemy right ceased.

Enemy centre taken.

A few minutes later, the 2/11th Gurkha Rifles, who had moved rapidly over somewhat easier ground, burst through the Afghan centre. Their onslaught was so sudden that the Afghans were unable to remove their artillery, their guns being captured and the gunners bayonetted by the Gurkhas.

Enemy left taken.

The 1/11th Gurkha Rifles advanced through Bagh village, which they cleared. Pressing on, they captured on the ridge forming the right centre of the enemy position. One company swarmed up the precipitous side of Kafir Kot thus taking the extreme left of the Afghan line, and capturing a gun and a Gardiner machine gun.

Khargali ridge taken.

The 2/123rd Outram's Rifles were now pushed up behind the 2/11th Gurkha Rifles to take Khargali ridge. All resistance, however, was at an end, and the enemy were flying in all directions. On reaching the final objective the exhaustion of the troops, the rapid and complete dispersion of the Afghans, and the difficulties of the terrain prevented a pursuit being carried out. The Royal Air Force, however, followed the flying enemy and took toll of them by bombing and machine gunning groups of the fugitives. Our casualties during the day were:—

Killed—

British other ranks 7

Indian other ranks 1

Wounded—

Lt.-Colonel E. B. Worrall, 2nd Battalion Somerset Light Infantry.

Lieutenant Horseman, 2nd Battalion North Staffordshire Regiment.

British other ranks 26

Indian other ranks 3

Enemy losses.

The Afghans in this action lost over 100 killed and 300 wounded. Of their killed 66 bodies were buried next day. Our captures included:—

7·5 c.m. Krupp guns 2

7 pr. pack guns 3

Machine gun 1

with rifles, tents, horses, mules and a quantity of gun and small arms ammunition.

The success of the operation was due to the efficient co-operation of all arms; to the accurate shooting of the artillery and machine guns; and to the dash and energy of the infantry. This latter feature

No. 6

ROUGH SKETCH SHOWING
PICQUETS on LANDI KHANA—DAKKA Road as supplied by the 2nd. Inf. Bde. in May 1919

Scale 1 inch=1 mile (approx.)

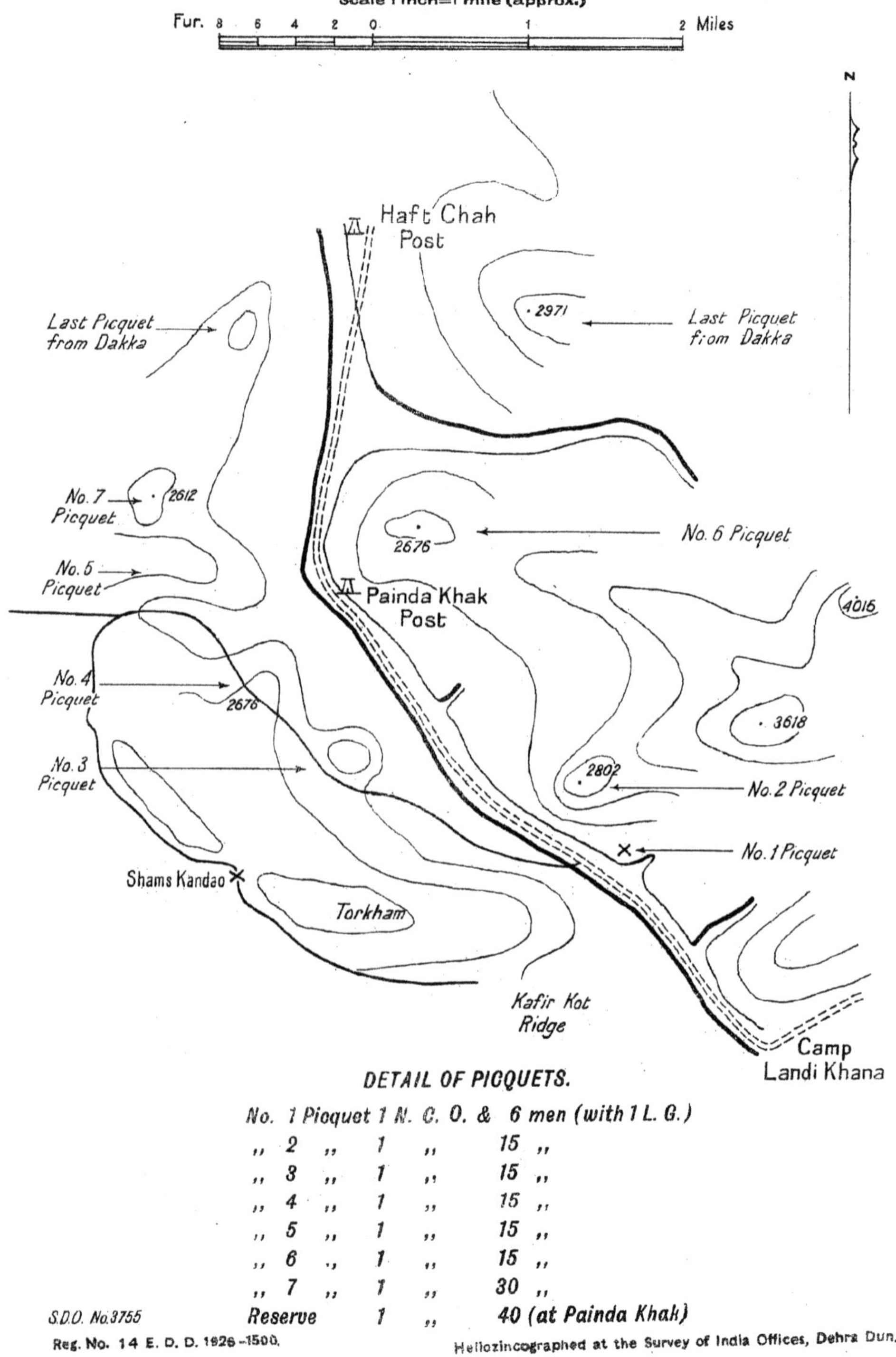

DETAIL OF PICQUETS.

No.	*1 Picquet*	*1 N. C. O. &*	*6 men (with 1 L. G.)*	
,,	*2* ,,	*1* ,,	*15* ,,	
,,	*3* ,,	*1* ,,	*15* ,,	
,,	*4* ,,	*1* ,,	*15* ,,	
,,	*5* ,,	*1* ,,	*15* ,,	
,,	*6* ,,	*1* ,,	*15* ,,	
,,	*7* ,,	*1* ,,	*30* ,,	
Reserve		*1* ,,	***40 (at Painda Khak)***	

S.D.O. No.3755

Reg. No. 14 E. D. D. 1926-1500.

Heliozincographed at the Survey of India Offices, Dehra Dun.

To face page 35

was the result of the careful and methodical training given to the 2nd Infantry Brigade by its commander, Major General S. H. Climo, C.B., D.S.O., who handled it during the action with skill and boldness. The keenness of the rank and file was very marked. Each battalion had been ordered to leave a platoon, brought up to a strength of 40 rifles, for the protection of the camp. The 2/123rd Outram's Rifles had, quite correctly, left a complete unit. The remaining three battalions had told off their weak and sickly men for the duty. It was afterwards found that most of these men had surreptitiously fallen in with their companies when they marched off from camp in the dark so as not to miss the fight. The action affords an example of a successful deployment outwards under fire.

Piquet line established.

At 1400 hours a piquet line was established, running from Kafir Kot, through Khargali village to the North Staffords objective. The remainder of the 2nd Infantry Brigade bivouaced near Bagh. The 1/15th Sikhs returned to Landi Kotal as did the 1/9th Gurkha Rifles who had arrived on the spur. The Headquarters of the 3rd Infantry Brigade with the 4/3rd Gurkha Rifles and the 2/1st Gurkha Rifles less two companies reached Landi Kotal during the day.

Reconnaissance towards Tor Tsappar and Spinatsuka.

On the morning of the 12th of May, General Crocker with a composite battalion made up from battalions of the 1st Infantry Brigade and No. 8 Mountain Battery R. G. A. moved north from Landi Kotal to reconnoitre the Afghan position on Tor Tsappar and Spinatsuka. These hills were found to be fortified with breastworks which were occupied by about 800 men. As the object of the reconnaissance had been attained and as no advantage was to be gained by attacking a strong position with the troops then available, the force returned to camp. The retirement was not pressed and the column reached Landi Kotal at 1730 hours, having lost four men wounded.

Royal Air Force about Dakka.

The Royal Air Force carried out reconnaissances during the day and bombed the enemy concentration at Dakka, causing the Afghans to evacuate their camp and retire hastily in the direction of Jalalabad. The Mohmands from the left bank of the Kabul river looted and carried away whatever they could lay their hands on.

Occupation of Dakka decided on.

It was now decided to take advantage of the demoralization of the Afghan army on this front and to seize Dakka, which offered facilities for the concentration of troops for an advance on Jalalabad and Kabul. There was ample space for camping grounds and for an aeroplane landing ground, whilst the Kabul river gave an unlimited supply of water. A cavalry force consisting of the 1st Cavalry Brigade, which had concentrated at Jamrud on the 11th May, and the 30th Lancers from Peshawar was placed under the command of Brigadier General G. Baldwin, D.S.O., and ordered to push forward to Dakka.

Plan for seizing Dakka.

The distance between Jamrud and Dakka is 33 miles. With the exception of the open stream in the gorge near Ali Masjid, the only place at which horses could be watered was in three long troughs half way between Landi Kotal and Landi Khana. It was arranged that General Baldwin's force should water at these troughs and it was calculated that they could do this in one hour. The second line transport was to be left at Landi Kotal under escort of the 30th

Lancers, whilst a mechanical transport convoy carrying two days' supplies (less fodder) should join the force at this place, and proceed with it to Dakka. The lorries were to be unloaded and returned to Landi Kotal the same afternoon. The road as far as the Dakka plain was to be piqueted by a mixed force drawn from all three infantry brigades, whilst the country north of the road, which had been occupied by the enemy for the past week, was to be secured by occupying Hill 3,618, 1½ miles north of Landi Khana.

Hill 3,618 captured.

At 0600 hours on the morning of the 13th May, the 2/123rd Outram's Rifles under Lt.-Colonel E. G. Byrne covered by the howitzer section of No. 6 Mountain Battery R. G. A. took Hill 3,618 without opposition. Pushing on to Hill 4,015 he established a piquet of 100 rifles of the 1/11th Gurkha Rifles and a party of the Divisional Signal Company on Hill 3,618 as a transmitting station to maintain communication between Landi Kotal and Dakka. When this piquet had completed its defences, the 2/123rd Outram's Rifles withdrew and returned to camp.

The force detailed to open and piquet the road to Dakka assembled at the ruins of the camp at Landi Khana, a relic of the Second Afghan War. It consisted of:—

Advanced Guard—

Commanding Major General S. H. Climo, C.B., D.S.O.

Troops in order of march—

1 composite battalion, 1st Infantry Brigade.

No. 285 Company Machine Gun Corps, less 2 sections.

No. 8 Mountain Battery, R. G. A.

Piquetting troops—

1/35th Sikhs.

Main body under Major General A. Skeen for march purposes only.

H. Q. 3rd Infantry Brigade.

4/3rd Gurkha Rifles.

2 sections 285 Co., M. G. C.

77th Battery, R. F. A.

250 Khyber Rifles.

1st Bn. Yorkshire Regt., less 1 Company.

Rearguard—

1 Company, 1st Bn., Yorkshire Regt.

The vanguard crossed the frontier at Torkham at 0600 hours and advanced without meeting with any opposition. The garrison of Haft Chah, a small Afghan post between Dakka and Landi Khana, fled without firing a shot, leaving 30,000 rounds of ·303 ammunition behind them. The 1/35th Sikhs were used up in piquets at this point and the 4/3rd Gurkha Rifles were sent on from the main body to piquet the remainder of the route. By 1000 hours the Dakka plain was

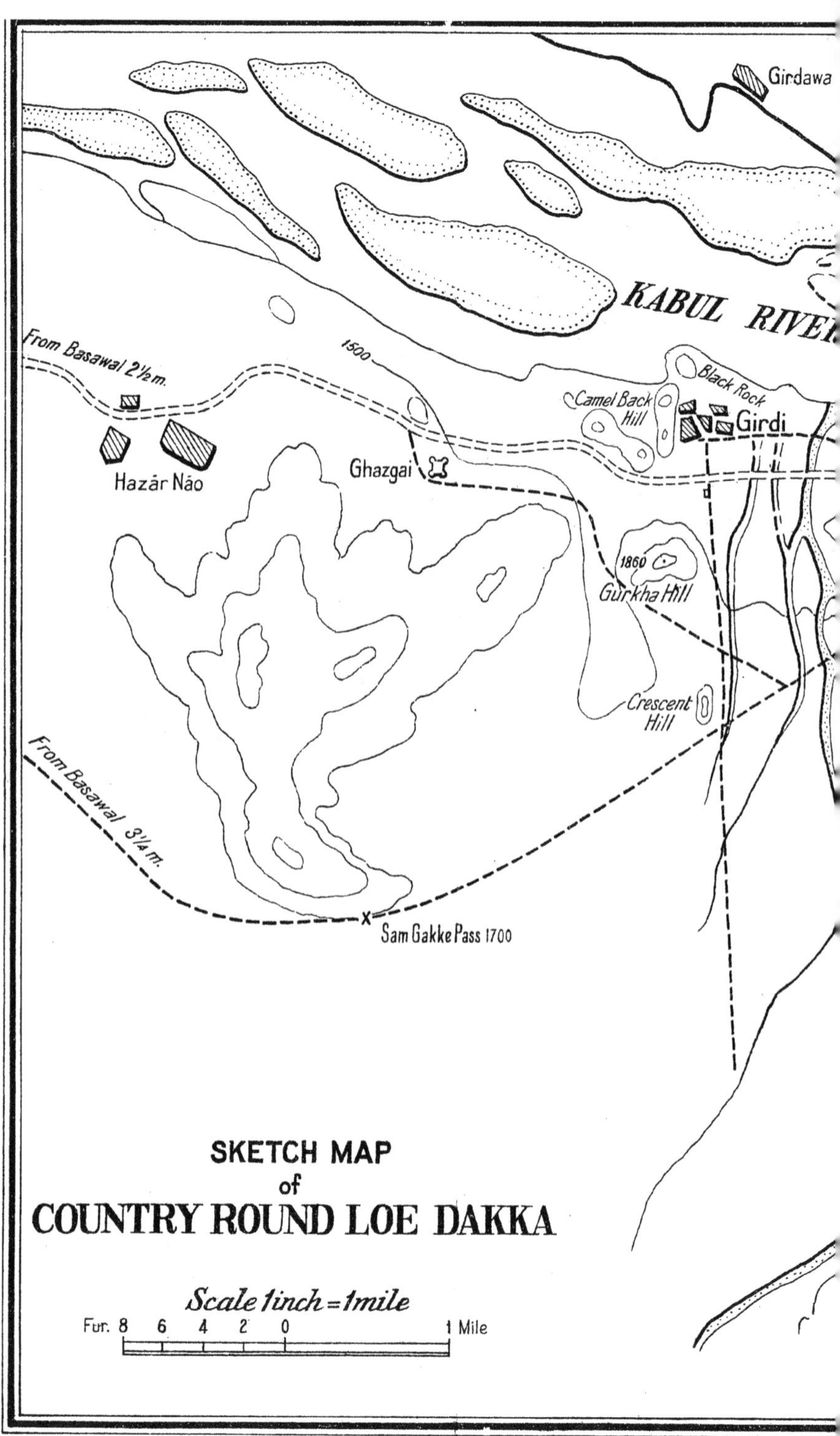

Reg. No. 14 E. D. D. 1926 –1500

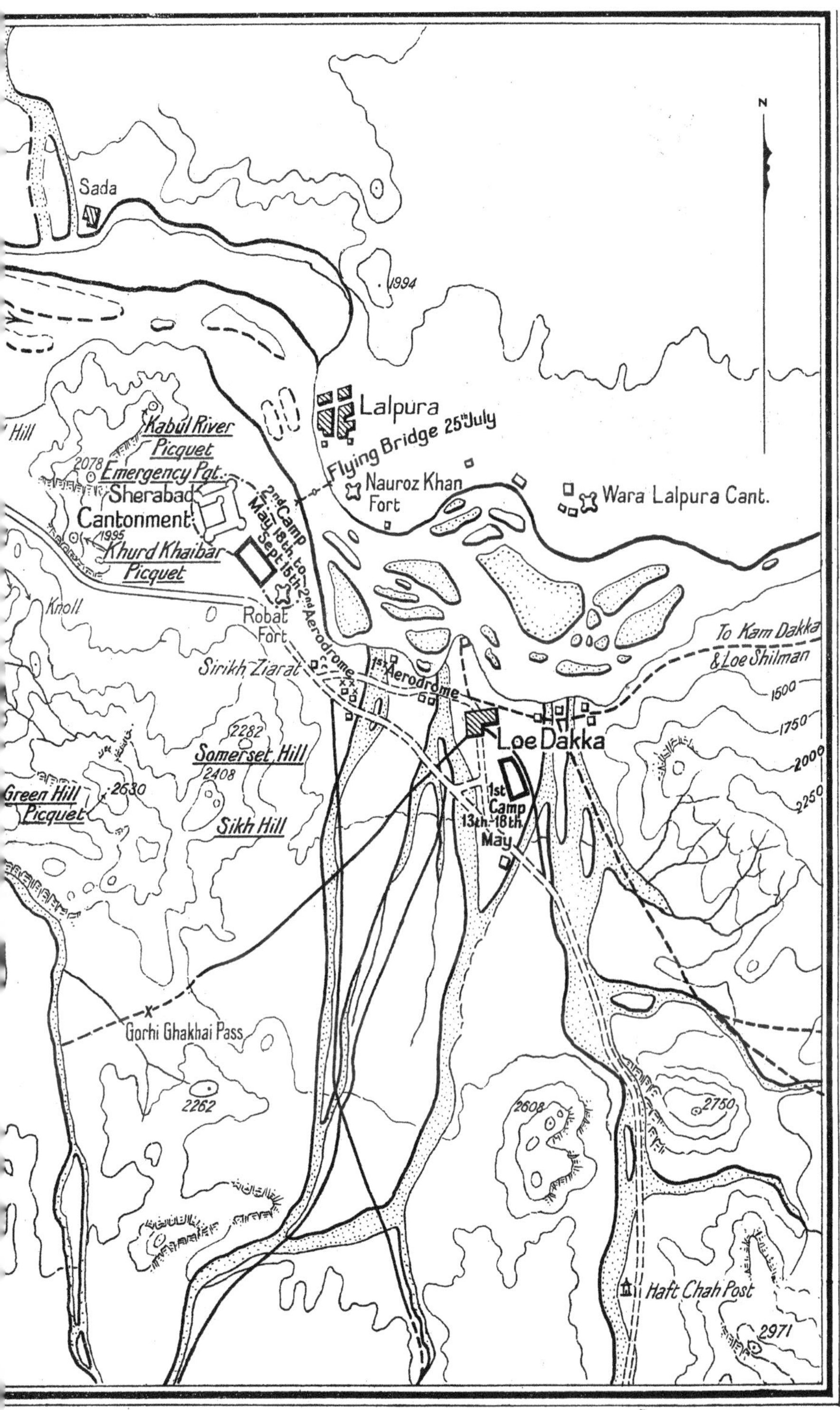

Heliozincographed at the Survey of India Offices, Dehra Dun.

reached without opposition and the men of the advanced guard not employed on protective duties commenced to improve the track for the passage of mechanical transport.

Cavalry march through the Khyber.

The cavalry were unopposed during their march through the Khyber. About a mile east of Ali Masjid, however, they found the road blocked with stones, and some delay was experienced before the obstacle was removed. They reached Landi Kotal at 0930 hours. Here, however, it was found that the watering arrangements were inadequate and it was not till 1230 hours that the last horse returned from the troughs. Realizing that no time was to be lost, General Baldwin sent forward the Advanced Guard, 1st Lancers and one section "M" Battery R. H. A. under Colonel Russell, followed by the Mechanical transport convoy with its escort of an armoured car battery, ahead of the Main Body. They reached Dakka and sent out patrols towards Sherabad and also east of the village. A few shots were fired at these patrols but no opposition was encountered. The lorries were unloaded and sent back to Landi Kotal with 41 Afghan subjects (mostly Hindu traders) who had been captured in Dakka.

Camp site at Dakka.

The site chosen for the camp was on the stony plain between two dry stream beds (nalas) just south of Dakka village. The main considerations in selecting a camp site are:—

(i) to be near the water supply,

(ii) to obtain protection for men and animals,

(iii) a good line of resistance,

(iv) observation of the enemy.

Although the first condition was fulfilled the more important tactical points had been ignored. The camp was within long range rifle fire from the hills to the east and west, men and animals were in the open, no good line of resistance existed, and the hills to the west shut out all observation. The most suitable place for a camp when engaged in operations of this description is directly under the hills, which should then be piqueted. Several suitable sites existed west of Dakka, notably those near Sirikh Ziarat and near Sherabad, and one of these should have been occupied. Piquets should then have been placed on the western ridge both for the security of the camp and also to facilitate a further advance into Afghanistan. On the contrary, with the camp placed where it was, if this ridge had been held there was nothing to prevent the enemy from working over the broken ground and interposing between these piquets and the camp. The only advantage possessed by the site chosen was that it could be re-inforced easily from Landi Kotal.

Criticism has been levelled at the employment of cavalry unsupported by infantry on such a mission on account of their vulnerability when at rest and their general unsuitability for work in hilly countries. On this occasion, however, no infantry was available and the Afghans were thoroughly demoralized. Further, the situation did not deteriorate until after the arrival of infantry at Dakka. The subsequent events occurred in consequence of faulty tactical dispositions and had little to do with the composition of the force.

CHAPTER V.

NORTHERN FRONT FROM THE 14TH OF MAY TO THE 3RD OF JUNE 1919.

1st Infantry Brigade, less 2 battalions, arrive at Dakka.

On the 14th of May the following reinforcements reached Dakka :—

Headquarters, 1st Infantry Brigade,

1/15th Sikhs,

1/9th Gurkha Rifles,

30th Lancers,

2 Indian sections, No. 6 Combined Field Ambulance.

The infantry commenced to build defences round the camp and to prepare a landing ground for aeroplanes.

Indian Infantry Brigade camp at Landi Khana.

On the same day, the 2nd Infantry Brigade left the bivouacs round Bagh, where they had remained after the action of the 11th of May, and went into perimeter camp at Landi Khana, where they were more suitably placed for piquetting the road to Dakka.

Cavalry reconnaissances at Dakka.

During the 14th and 15th of May, cavalry reconnaissances failed to locate any large bodies of Afghans, although occasionally shots were fired at the patrols. The aeroplanes also reported the country to the west to be clear of enemy concentrations. None of these cavalry reconnaissances, however, were pushed far afield, and therefore, though the enemy were gathering slowly, no news of their movements was received.

Troops at Dakka placed under 1st Division.

The troops at Dakka came under the orders of the General Officer Commanding the 1st Division on the morning of the 16th May, when General Baldwin and the headquarters of the 10th Cavalry Brigade left for Peshawar. General Fowler visited Dakka on the same morning and directed that the camp should be removed to a fresh site between Sirikh Ziarat and Robat on the morning of the 17th. He also gave orders that piquets for its protection should be placed on the ridge west of Dakka. General Crocker took over command of the troops actually in Dakka.

Reconnaissances towards Busawal.

Whilst the two generals were discussing the removal of the camp, events were happening which materially changed the outlook. Early that morning, Colonel C. N. Macmullen had left camp with orders to reconnoitre towards Busawal, 13 miles to the west. The troops under him were :—

3 squadrons, 1st King's Dragoon Guards.

1 section, " M " Battery, R. H. A.

1 section, No. 15 Squadron, Machine Gun Corps.

1/15th Sikhs, less 2 Companies.

1 section, No. 6 Combined Field Ambulance.

West of Dakka the road enters a semi-circle of hills and passes over a spur through a defile known as the Khurd Khyber pass. After descending from this spur, the ground is level for 1,000 yards when an isolated ridge is reached. Beyond this ridge lies the large Mohmand village of Girdi, which was not marked on the maps issued for the campaign.

Advance to Girdi.

The Khurd Khyber pass was secured with little opposition, and one company of the 1/15th Sikhs were posted on the heights overlooking it to secure the retirement of the force. Two troops of the 1st King's Dragoon Guards then galloped round the northern (or river) end of the second ridge, whilst the 1/15th Sikhs advanced across the plain and occupied it. The cavalry advanced on Girdi, but rifle fire was opened on them from the village and they were compelled to halt. The section of " M " Battery, R. H. A. and the machine gun section came into action 1,400 yards east of Girdi and opened fire on the village and on the hill 600 yards west of it. One troop of cavalry encircled the village from the north, one troop enveloped it from the south, whilst one troop, supported by a company of infantry moved on it direct. At 0930 hours, Girdi was secured, and the company of infantry advanced on to the ridge west of the village. Here it soon became evident that the Afghans had assembled in large numbers. The enemy opened artillery and rifle fire, and large bodies of mounted and dismounted men were seen advancing from the southwest on the left flank of the reconnoitring force. Colonel Macmullen had, in fact, become engaged with troops and tribesmen who had concentrated with the intention of re-capturing Dakka. The only course open to him was to disengage his troops as rapidly as possible and retire on the camp. This he did with complete success.

Heavy opposition encountered.

Retirement pressed by Afghans.

As is always the case in frontier warfare, this retrograde movement was the signal for increased activity on the part of the enemy. They pressed on with great boldness, and it was only by moving rapidly that the force reached the shelter of the company previously posted over the Khurd Khyber pass. From this point the retirement was laid out in successive lines, held alternately by the 1st King's Dragoon Guards and the 1/15th Sikhs. The enemy still advanced with determination and near Robat fort they came within 400 yards of the Horse Artillery guns. The pressure was relieved by one squadron of the 1st King's Dragoon Guards, who charged and rode through the Afghans, and inflicted many casualties on them. The relief thus gained was sufficient for the force to reach the camp without much difficulty, but they were followed up closely by the enemy. The broken nature of the ground assisted the Afghans to approach the camp, on which they opened a heavy fire with rifles and artillery. The animals, which offered a conspicuous target, were hastily removed, the horses to the nala to the east of the perimeter, and the transport animals to the shelter afforded by the houses in Dakka village. Many followers deserted and fled in the direction of Landi Khana.

Afghans advance on camp.

Enemy pushed back from vicinity of camp.

The 2nd Bn., Somerset Light Infantry and the 1/35th Sikhs had just arrived from Landi Kotal. The latter battalion was ordered to move to the west to prevent any further advance of the enemy, whilst the 1/9th Gurkha Rifles (less two companies who were on piquet duty, towards Landi Khana), supported by one company of the 1/15th Sikhs, were sent to take up a position to the south-west. Two squadrons of the 1st Lancers were also sent out to seize the foothills to the south. These measures kept the Afghans back, but they occupied the hills to the west and dragged their artillery to the summit. A heavy fire was kept up till dark, when it slackened, and the covering troops returned to camp.

Our casualties.

Our casualties during the day were:—

Killed—

Captain T. N. C. Kemp, 1/9th Gurkha Rifles.

2nd Lieutenant H. Hunt, 1/15th Sikhs.

British other ranks, 5.

Indian other ranks, 3.

Wounded—

Major E. J. H. Haughton, Brigade Major, 1st Infantry Brigade.

Captain W. R. T. Cooper, 1st King's Dragoon Guards.

Lieut. R. I. Ward, 1st King's Dragoon Guards (died of wounds 26th May).

Lieut. C. G. Harraway, "M" Battery, R. H. A.

Rissaldar Ganga Man, 33rd Cavalry.

British other ranks, 38.

Indian other ranks, 46.

making a total of 10 killed and 89 wounded. In addition 58 animals were killed and 30 wounded.

Stampede of horses.

During the night, small parties of the enemy prowled round the camp, and snipers fired into the horses sheltering in the dry stream bed. This caused a stampede and many of the horses broke loose and made for the hills.

Enemy position.

The Afghans, who numbered 3,000 men and 7 guns, were holding the hills (see map facing page 39) from the Khurd Khyber to the Ghori Ghakhai pass, with a total frontage of 4,000 yards. Their position bulged in the centre, and receded on both flanks. The hills rose abruptly for about 1,100 feet from the Dakka plain, and terminated in a razor-backed escarpment, from which they sloped away more gently to the west. As long as these hills were held, the camp site was untenable. It was essential that the enemy should be dislodged as soon as possible, and, although the guns were short of ammunition as a result of the day's action, General Crocker decided to advance to the foot of the hills under cover of darkness and to attack at dawn.

Plan of action.

The 1/35th Sikhs, supported by the 1/9th Gurkha Rifles, less 2 companies, were to attack Somerset Hill, then known as Stonehenge. On their left, the 1/15th Sikhs were given the feature subsequently known as "Sikh Hill" as their objective. The 2nd Bn. Somerset Light Infantry were to remain in camp as a general reserve. Two companies of the 1/9th Gurkha Rifles had stayed in their piquet positions towards Landi Khana during the night. One squadron of the 1st Lancers were to guard the right flank by moving to the vicinity of Robat fort, whilst one squadron of the 30th Lancers was to watch the Gorhi Ghakhai pass on the left. A message was sent to Landi Kotal asking for reinforcements and more gun ammunition, both of which were promised by the General Officer Commanding the 1st Division.

Attack on Somerset Hill.

The 1/35th Sikhs and the 1/9th Gurkha Rifles reached the foot of the hills before dawn. The two companies of the 1/9th Gurkha Rifles took up a position to cover the advance with rifle fire, and the 1/35th Sikhs worked upwards till by 0530 hours they had reached within a hundred yards of the crest without a shot being fired at them. Here the leading platoons were met by a heavy fire at short range. The three senior officers of the battalion were wounded, and three Indian officers were killed, almost at once. The enemy fire increased in intensity and accuracy. The guns from camp opened fire on the Afghans, who could be seen standing on the crest and firing on our men, but they were too late to save the situation. More and more casualties occurred, and the 1/35th Sikhs retired rapidly through the 1/9th Gurkha Rifles. One company was rallied, but the remainder took refuge in the ruins at the foot of Somerset Hill, which they were unable to leave owing to the heavy fire brought on them by the enemy.

Our troops retire.

19th Gurkha Rifles advances.

The 2 companies of the 1/9th Gurkha Rifles and the company of the 1/35th Sikhs which had re-formed then advanced, working up converging spurs, up to a point half way up Somerset Hill. From here Lieut. Tungate and two platoons of the 1/9th Gurkha Rifles worked forward, covered by infantry and artillery fire to within 20 yards of the crest, where they hung on, unable to move further.

1-5th Sikhs advance up Sikh Hill.

Meanwhile the 1/15th Sikhs (three companies) reached the foot of Sikh Hill as dawn was breaking. One company was posted on the foothills to cover the advance with rifle fire. One platoon also took up a position on a low hill 800 yards to the south to cover their left flank. The remainder advanced by two converging spurs, one company on each, and reached the point where these ridges met about 300 yards from the summit. Here a false crest screened them from the heavy fire which had been opened on them. A further advance would necessitate moving on a narrow front up a steep slope, under fire from three sides, and could only be made if adequately supported by artillery which was not available. It was decided, therefore, to hold the position they had taken until further developments took place.

Advance checked.

Situation at 1000 hours.

At 1000 hours the fight had definitely come to a standstill. The artillery had run out of ammunition. Two companies of the 1/9th Gurkha Rifles, one company of the 1/35th Sikhs, and one company and three platoons of the 1/15th Sikhs were clinging on to positions on the sides of the slopes. The enemy guns were endeavouring, without much success, to search the nala where the cavalry horses were taking cover, and Dakka Village, where the transport was hidden. Our advanced troops were ordered to hold their positions at all costs, and water and ammunition was pushed up to those troops within reach. At 1030 hours three lorries arrived with gun and small arms ammunition and our artillery again became active. Orders were issued for the 2nd Bn. Somerset Light Infantry to attack Somerset Hill, but at 1130 hours, before this movement could begin, the expected reinforcements arrived at the mouth of the defile leading to the Dakka plain under Major General A. Skeen, C.M.G., who took command of the operations. The troops with him were:—

Headquarters, 3rd Infantry Brigade.
1st Bn. Yorkshire Regt.
2/1st Gurkha Rifles.
Howitzer section, No. 6 Mountain Battery, R. G. A.
One section, No. 77 Battery, R. F. A. (Howitzer).
No. 285 Company, Machine Gun Corps.

General Skeen's dispositions.

General Skeen quickly made his dispositions. The howitzers came into action on the open ground west of the mouth of the defile, where they were able to bring enfilade fire to bear on Somerset Hill and oblique fire on Sikh Hill. The machine gun company were posted on a small mound 1,000 yards north of the howitzers in an equally favourable position. The 2/1st Gurkha Rifles were formed up on the left of the machine guns, and the 1st Bn. Yorkshire Regiment were ordered to form on the right of the mound. These two battalions were the general reserve. Unfortunately, the 1st Bn. Yorkshire Regiment mistook the verbal orders given to them and moved off to participate in the attack. Owing to the broken nature of the country, their advance was not noticed by General Skeen, who had ridden on to camp to confer with General Crocker. As they approached Sikh Hill, the Yorkshire opened fire on the two companies of the 1/15th Sikhs, who were in position on the slope. Before this fire could be stopped, two officers, one Indian officer and seven men of the headquarters of the 1/15th Sikhs had been hit.

Enemy Retirement begins.

The attack was timed to start at 1400 hours. The fire of our howitzers, however, was so accurate and deadly that the Afghans commenced to retire soon after 1300 hours. Colonel Macmullen perceived this and decided to advance. He placed himself at the head of his men, firing his Very pistol as he went to inform the artillery of the progress of his advance, and reached the summit at 1355 hours. The 2nd Bn., Somerset Light Infantry then moved forward, and, carrying the 1/9th Gurkha Rifles with them, took Somerset Hill without difficulty. The enemy dispersed so rapidly that the 1/35th Sikhs, who had been sent round the northern spur of Somerset Hill to intercept the retreat, were unable to inflict any loss on them.

Sikh Hill captured.

Somerset Hill captured.

Our casualties during the day were:—

Killed—

Lieut. R. P. L. Adams, 1/35th Sikhs.
Lieut. T. P. Mugford, 1/35th Sikhs.
Lieut. A. C. Henderson, 1/9th Gurkha Rifles.
Indian Officers, 3.
British other ranks, 3.
Indian other ranks, 20.

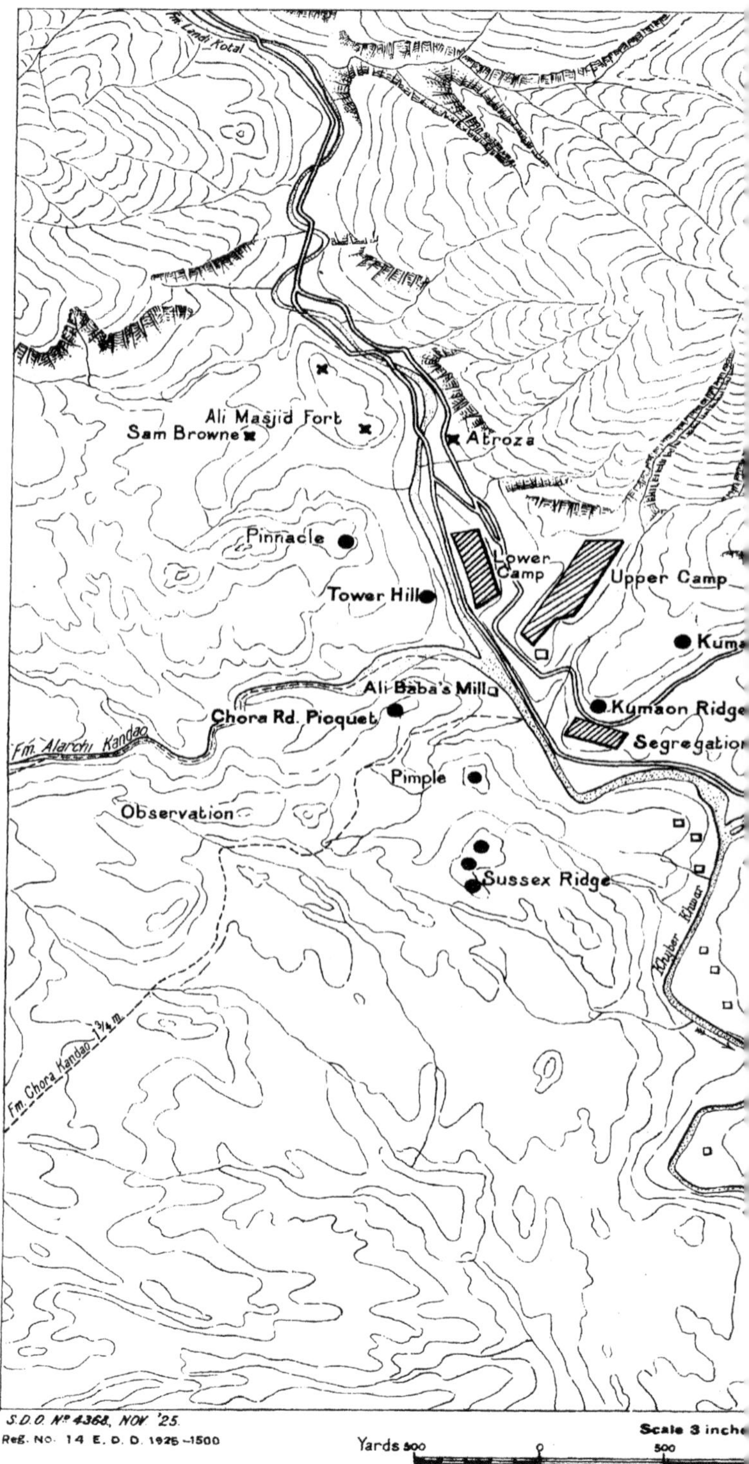
Fm. Lendi Kotal
Ali Masjid Fort
Sam Browne
Atroza
Pinnacle
Lower Camp
Upper Camp
Tower Hill
Kuma
Ali Baba's Mill
Kumaon Ridge
Chora Rd. Picquet
Fm. Alarchi Kandao
Segregation
Pimple
Observation
Sussex Ridge
Khyber Khwar
Fm. Chora Kandao 1¾ m.
S.D.O. No. 4368, NOV. '25.
Reg. No. 14 E. D. D. 1925-1500
Scale 3 inche
Yards 500
0
500

No. 8

SKETCH MAP
of
ALI MASJID.

REFERENCE

Masonry Blockhouses.........✖

Open Picquets......................●

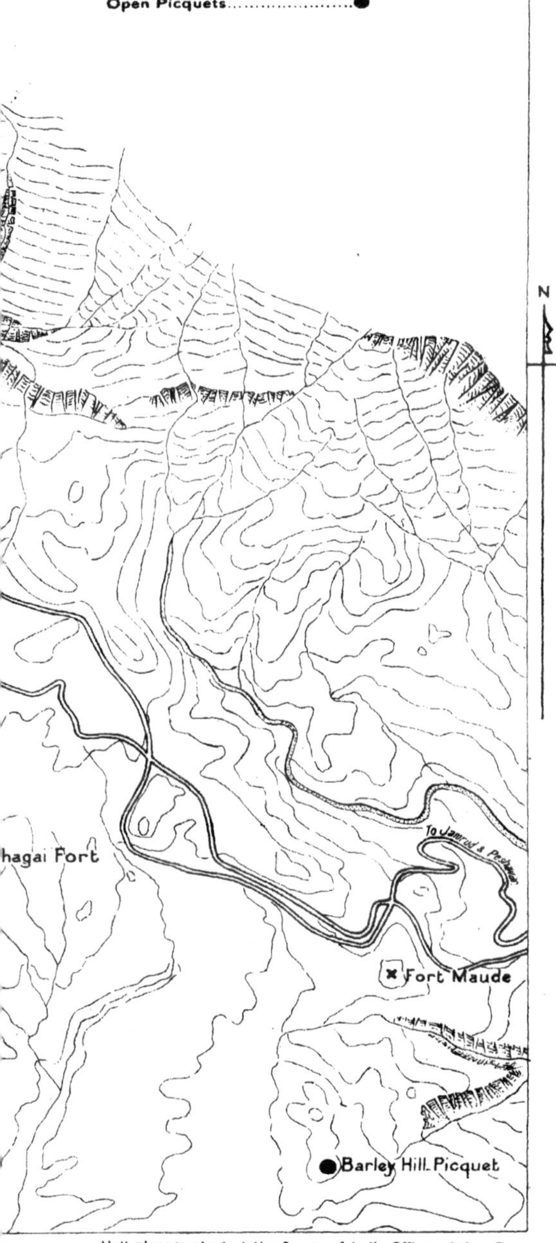

Heliozincographed at the Survey of India Offices, Dehra Dun.

To face page. 43

Wounded—

Lt.-Col. S. K. B. Rice, 1/35th Sikhs.

Captain T. F. S. Burridge, 1/35th Sikhs.

Captain C. W. W. Ford, 1/35th Sikhs.

Lieut. C. Briard, 1/35th Sikhs.

Captain G. H. Hawkins, 1/15th Sikhs.

Lieut. D. W. Dinwiddie, 1/15th Sikhs.

Captain A. W. F. Brown, 1/9th Gurkha Rifles.

Captain G. W. E. Maude, 1st Bn., Yorkshire Regt.

Indian officers, 4.

British other ranks, 12.

Indian other ranks, 133.

Total Killed 22, Wounded, 157.

The enemy casualties were about 200 killed and over 400 wounded, whilst they left 5 of their 7 Krupp guns behind them.

Once again the Afghans let slip the opportunity which had been given to them. Determined counter-attacks on the isolated bodies of men, who were hung up close to their position and unsupported by artillery fire, would have succeeded through weight of numbers. Their lack of training, their low power of manœuvre and their want of confidence in the bayonet prevented them from taking advantage of their initial success, and from wiping out the weak forces sent out against them in detail.

Our cavalry were spectators in this action. They could not be sent round the enemy flanks until Somerset and Sikh Hills had been captured, and the enemy retirement was so rapid that even if they had been pushed through the Khurd Khyber pass after the Afghans had been dislodged, it is doubtful whether they could have inflicted serious damage on the fugitives. They might, however, have been organized as an infantry unit for camp defence, and as a general reserve, and thus freed the 2nd Bn. Somerset Light Infantry to take part in the first assault.

The value of howitzers firing high explosive shell from an angle on to the razor-backed ridges so commonly found on the north-west frontier and in Afghanistan was fully demonstrated in this action. The susceptibility of Pathan and Afghan to any threat to their flanks was also very marked. This action also brought out the need for personal reconnaissance and the organisation of covering fire.

The Afridis show signs of hostility.

Whilst the 1st Division and the cavalry were engaged in the operations related above, the Afridis in the Khyber began to show signs of restlessness. Although the British victory of the 11th of May seemed to have had a settling effect on the tribe as a whole, certain malcontents in Afghan pay were busily engaged in raising a religious agitation against us. At Chora, 7 miles southwest of Ali Masjid, an influential headman (malik) of the Malik Din Khel Afridis named Yar Mohammed had built himself a large fort At one time he had received the title of " Khan Bahadur " from the Indian Government, but he had been deprived of this honour for various acts of hostility against us. Early in May this individual collected a body of 30 or 40 Afghans, and on the 11th of May he sent a defiant letter to the Political Agent, Khyber, Sir Abdul Khayyum, saying that he was going to cut our communications. He first showed his hand on the 13th of May, when, as has been described before, he caused an obstruction to be placed in the road to delay the march of the cavalry column. After this, small bodies of Afridis sniped the road near Ali Masjid and cut the telephone wire by night. The number of these malcontents began to increase and the road became unsafe. Moreover, the Khyber Rifles began to be affected by their kinsmen joining the ranks of our enemies, and started to desert. The only regular troops between Jamrud and Landi Kotal were two companies of the 3/11th Gurkha Rifles and a section of No. 6 Mountain Battery, R. G. A. belonging to the 1st Division. On the 14th May, the lines of communication through the Khyber were placed under the General Officer Commanding the 2nd Division, who directed Br. General G. Christian, C.B., D.S.O., to clear up the situation. The troops at General Christian's disposal were the 2/33rd Punjabis and the 2/8th Gurkha Rifles, less 250 men, of his own Brigade (the 6th Infantry Brigade), the 1/61st Pioneers and an armoured motor battery.

Events near Ali Masjid.

On the morning of the 14th of May, the daily convoy left Jamrud with No. 7 Combined Field Ambulance, and escorted by the 2/8th Gurkha Rifles (less 250 rifles) and by re-inforcements for the 1st Division consisting of the 2/34th Sikh Pioneers and details of the 36th and 47th Sikhs, and of the 2/9th and 4/11th Gurkha Rifles, whilst the road was piquetted by the 1/61st Pioneers. No opposition was offered to the main body, but when the transport reached a point 2 miles from Ali Masjid it was fired on and several casualties occurred among the animals and personnel. The rearguard became heavily engaged, and was only extricated by sending back a reinforcement of 50 rifles from Ali Masjid. The two companies of the 3/11th Gurkha Rifles and the 2/34th Sikh Pioneers marched on to Landi Kotal the same day, but the convoy and the drafts were retained at Ali Masjid. Six piquets were posted on the heights to the southeast and southwest for the protection of the camp. During the night the camp and the piquets were subjected to heavy rifle fire, and two men were killed and four wounded.

On the following morning the convoy with No. 7 Combined Field Ambulance, escorted by the details of the 36th and 47th Sikhs and the 4/11th Gurkha Rifles left for Landi Kotal, whilst the posts between Ali Masjid and Jamrud were taken over from the Khyber Rifles by regular troops. The 1/61st Pioneers again piquetted the road to within two miles of Ali Masjid, whilst the 2/8th Gurkha Rifles secured the remainder of the route. Detachments of the 2/33rd Punjabis were placed in the towers which guarded the road, and the garrisons supplied by the Khyber Rifles joined the column. The remainder of the 2/33rd Punjabis moved on to Ali Masjid, whilst the 1/61st Pioneers and the Khyber Rifles returned to Jamrud. As soon as the piquets of the 2/8th Gurkha Rifles attempted to withdraw from Orange Patch ridge, 2,000 yards south-west of the fort, they were attacked by large bodies of Afridis. One company of the 2/33rd Punjabis was sent out from Ali Masjid and succeeded in extricating the piquets who lost one man killed and four men wounded.

Khyber Rifle Posts taken over.

On the morning of the following day, the 16th of May, it was again necessary to take Orange Patch ridge to ensure the safe passage of the convoy, as this feature dominated the road at a range of 400 yards. One company of the 2/33rd Punjabis, supported by 200 rifles of the 2/8th Gurkha Rifles, accordingly left camp to take up a position there. They found it occupied by a body of 250 tribesmen, who opened a heavy fire and the troops were unable to advance. Reinforcements of 100 rifles of the 1st Battalion Sussex Regiment and 100 rifles of the 2/8th Gurkha Rifles, however, arrived in mechanical transport from Peshawar at this time, and of these 60 rifles of the Royal Sussex and 40 of the 2/8th Gurkha Rifles were sent to their assistance. The combined force, covered by the fire of the section of No. 6 Mountain Battery, R. G. A. advanced and captured the ridge after a stiff fight. Our casualties amounted to:— Action on Orange Patch Ridge.

Killed.—

British other ranks	2
Indian other ranks	3

Wounded.—

British other ranks	9
Indian other ranks	13

During the day, the 2/33rd Punjabis took over the posts of Katakushta and Zintara from the Khyber Rifles, who were thus completely relieved of their duty of keeping the road open.

In spite of the fighting of the past three days, the situation showed no signs of improvement. In fact a heavy fire was kept up on Fort Maude all night long. Matters were so unsatisfactory that Brigadier-General Peebles, C.B., C.M.G., D.S.O., was ordered to move up the Khyber with a strong force to clear up the situation and to attack any force of the enemy which had gathered between Jamrud and Ali Masjid. His own Brigade, the 4th Infantry Brigade, was at Peshawar under orders to march to Landi Kotal the following morning (17th). To gain time, the transport of the brigade was sent on to Jamrud under escort of the 3/5th Gurkha Rifles less 2 Companies on the evening of the 16th whilst the troops followed next morning, two battalions proceeding by rail and two on Mechanical Transport. At 0900 hours, the following troops left Jamrud for Ali Masjid:— 4th Infantry Brigade march into the Khyber.

No. 2 Mountain Artillery Brigade less two sections.

One battery, No. 1 Armoured Motor Brigade.

One section, No. 222, Company, Machine Gun Corps.

4th Infantry Brigade.

1st Battalion, Durham Light Infantry.

1/33rd Punjabis.

40th Pathans.

2/54th Sikhs, F. F.

No. 41, Combined Field Ambulance.

No bodies of the enemy were met, and the column arrived at Ali Masjid thoroughly exhausted by their exertions in the great heat. The transport, however, was fired on and five men were wounded. Although no defeat had been inflicted on the Afridis, the presence of such a large body of troops relieved the situation considerably. The tribesmen still indulged in sniping and cutting the telephone wire, but the Khyber was comparatively quiet for a month.

Disbandment of the Khyber Rifles.

On the evening of the same day, the Khyber Rifles were paraded at Jamrud and were informed that those men who wished to take their discharge might do so at once. About 100 men, amongst whom were a large proportion of Indian Officers and Non-Commissioned Officers, elected to remain in the service, but the rest availed themselves of the offer and left for their homes the same evening. The Khyber Rifles thus ceased to exist.

The situation on the evening of the 17th of May on the Northern front was distinctly favourable. The Afghans had been defeated in two decisive engagements, and no formed body of regulars was met with again in this area during the campaign. The march of the 4th Infantry Brigade into the Khyber had had the effect of quieting the Afridis for the time being. The distribution of the troops of the Field Army on this date was as follows:—

Distribution of troops, 17th May.

Dakka—

1st Cavalry Brigade.

30th Lancers.

No. 24 Squadron, Machine Gun Corps less 2 sections.

One battery and one section, mountain artillery.

1st Infantry Brigade.

3rd Infantry Brigade less 2 battalions.

1 Company Machine Gun Corps.

Landi Khana—

2nd Infantry Brigade.

1 Company Machine Gun Corps.

Landi Kotal—

Headquarters, 1st Division.

One battery, VIIth Brigade, R. F. A.

No. 1 Mountain Artillery Brigade less one battery and two sections.

2 battalions, 3rd Infantry Brigade.

1 battalion, pioneers.

Ali Masjid—

4th Infantry Brigade.

2 battalions, 6th Infantry Brigade.

No. 2 Mountain Artillery Brigade less 2 sections.

One section, machine guns.

Jamrud—

6th Infantry Brigade less 3 battalions.

VIIth Brigade, R. F. A. less one battery.

2 sections, No. 2 Mountain Artillery Brigade.

SKETCH MAP MOHMAND BORDER No. 9

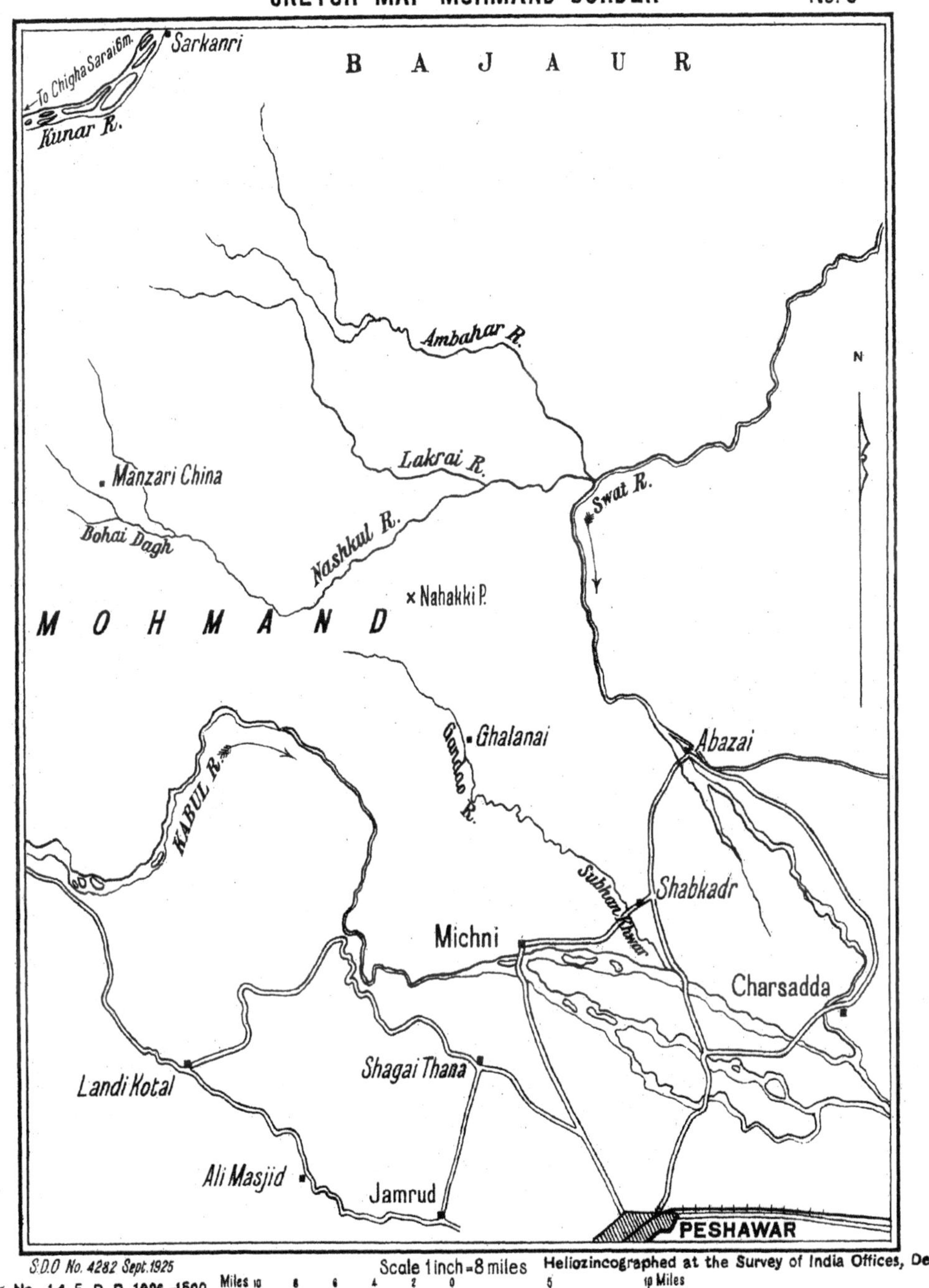

To face page.

Kacha Garhi—

One battalion, 5th Infantry Brigade.

Peshawar—

10th Cavalry Brigade less 2 regiments.

Headquarters, 2nd Division.

2 companies, Machine Gun Corps less 1 section.

1 section, No. 24 Squadron, Machine Gun Corps.

One battalion, 5th Infantry Brigade.

One battalion, 6th Infantry Brigade.

Nowshera—

XVIth Brigade, R. F. A.

5th Infantry Brigade less 2 battalions.

No. 23 Indian Mountain Battery.

(The latter two in quarantine for cholera which first made its appearance here).

Risalpur—

1 regiment, 10th Cavalry Brigade.

1 section, No. 24 Squadron, Machine Gun Corps.

Position on the Mohmand border.

During the Great War, the Mohmands, who live to the north of the Kabul River, had been particularly troublesome, and from 1915 to 1917 they had given plenty of occupation to the 1st Peshawar Division. Four general actions had been fought near Subhan Khwar against the Mohmands and their allies the Bajauris, *i.e.*, in April, in September and in October, 1915, and in November, 1916. In October 1916 a strict blockade of their country had been instituted. A chain of posts had been erected about 400 yards apart between Abazai, where the Swat River leaves the hills, and Michni on the Kabul River. Between these posts a double apron barbed wire fence had been constructed, thus shutting the Mohmands into their own country. In front of the barbed wire fence was a curtain of live wire, supplied with electric current from the power house at Abazai. During the winter of 1916 and 1917 and the spring of 1917, this blockade line was garrisoned by one brigade of the 1st Division, each of the three brigades in turn taking a tour of two months' duty there. In May 1917, rough country towers were built in place of the open works in use up to that time, the live wire was removed and the garrison reduced to two battalions. In July, the Mohmands made terms with the Government and the Mohmand Militia were raised to relieve the regular troops on this portion of the border. The towers and the wire were still in the hands of the Mohmand Militia in 1919.

Afghans enter Mohmand territory.

In accordance with their plan of raising the tribes on both sides of the border against us, a small force of Afghans consisting of two infantry battalions and six guns which were stationed at Sarkanri and Chigha Sarai on the Kunar River entered the valley of the Bohai Dagh in Mohmand territory on the 14th of May (see map facing this page). Five days later (19th of May), they reached Ghalanai on the Gandao stream, 13 miles northwest of Shabkadr. Their slow progress of less than 6 miles a day was due to the tribesmen not joining them in anything like the numbers they anticipated. On the contrary, the Mohmands had had quite enough of fighting since 1915 and they were still feeling the effects of the long blockade. They were loud in their protestations of loyalty to the British, and even offered to co-operate with us if we advanced to give the Afghans battle in the Gandao valley. They were probably influenced in their expressions of good-will towards us by the condition of the Afghan troops who had penetrated their territory. One battalion, the Turki, was in a fair state of training and discipline, but the other, the Wardaki, was little better than an armed rabble. They were both much under strength, and the total of effectives including artillerymen was under 1,200 men. However, a band of 4,000 tribesmen eventually gathered together, a few being Mohmands and the remainder Bajauris, and prepared to invade British territory.

At the time there were not sufficient troops in Peshawar to meet the threatened attack. On the evening of the 20th of May, however, the 44th Infantry Brigade arrived from Lahore, and this reinforcement was utilized to form two columns, one of which was sent to Shabkadr and one to Michni.

The Shabkadr column under Brigadier General W. M. Southey, C.M.G., commanding the 44th Infantry Brigade consisted of:—

½ squadron, 19th Lancers.

1 squadron, 23rd Cavalry, F. F.

XVIth Brigade, R. F. A. less 1 battery.

No. 15 Motor Machine Gun Battery.

1 Battery, No. 1 Armoured Motor Brigade.

4th Infantry Brigade less I battalion.

1/1st Kent Battalion.

1/30th Punjabis.

2/30th Punjabis.

The Michni column was composed as follows:—

½ squadron 30th Lancers.

1 section No. 24 Squadron, Machine Gun Corps.

1 section No. 286 Company, Machine Gun Corps.

1/6th Jat Light Infantry.

The Shabkadr column went into the old perimeter camp at Subhan Khwar, as there was every indication that the enemy would advance by this route. The posts along the Mohmand blockade line were reinforced by infantry and machine guns, but beyond burning some empty towers on the night of the 22/23rd of May, the enemy showed no signs of activity. On the 24th their stock of provisions ran out. The tribesmen dispersed to their homes and the Afghan regulars returned to their stations on the Kunar River. On the 25th of May orders were issued for all troops to be withdrawn from Michni and Shabkadr, and they were all concentrated in Peshawar by the 30th of May.

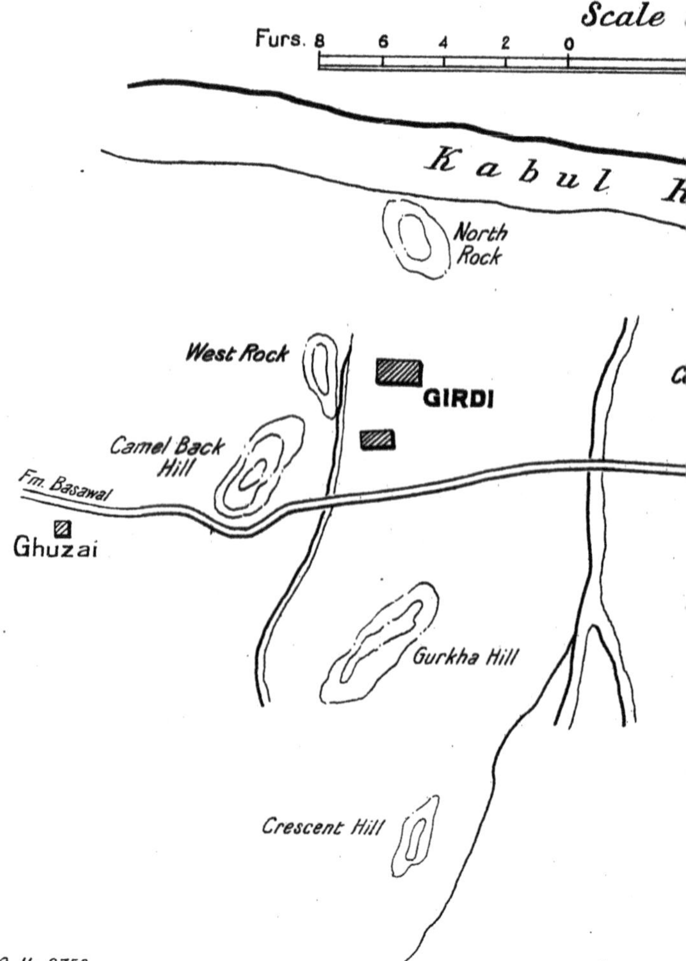

S.D.O. No. 3756

Reg. No. 14 E. D. D. 1926–1500

N. 10

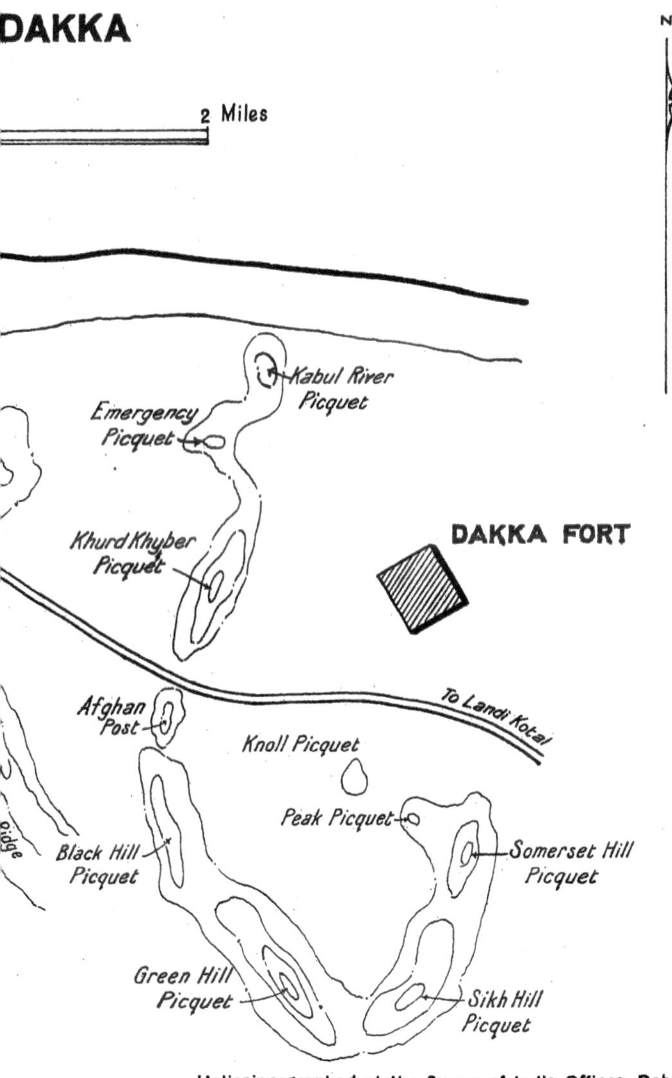

Heliozincographed at the Survey of India Offices, Dehra Dun.

To face page. 49

Whilst these events were taking place on the Mohmand border, arrangements were being made for an advance from Dakka to Jalalabad. It was decided to employ the 1st Division and the 1st Cavalry Brigade to carry out this operation, and as a preliminary measure, 30 days' supplies were to be collected at Landi Kotal and Dakka. The shortage of transport of all kinds, however, was so acute that the carriage of such a large amount of stores through the Khyber presented a difficult problem. The Mohmand operations also, short as was the period they lasted, proved a strain on the limited resources of the transport services. To ease the situation, foraging expeditions were carried out from Dakka and an average of 400 maunds of unthreshed grain was collected daily from the Afghan villages to the west. On the 24th of May the Mohmands from the north of the Kabul River, whilst still hostile to us as a tribe, began to bring in fresh vegetables for sale, and a plentiful supply of these continued to come into Dakka as long as our troops remained in Afghanistan. Even counting in these local supplies it was found that it would be necessary to leave the 16th Division almost entirely without transport, and thus quite immobile. Nevertheless, it was calculated that the supply situation would be such that a forward move could be made on the 1st of June.

Preparations for an advance on Jalalaba d

Troops were steadily concentrated in the forward area. On the 18th of May, the camp at Dakka was moved to the plain between Robat and Sherabad. Piquets were placed on the hills to the south and west, and the location of these is shown on the map facing this page. The usual dry stone wall defences (sangars) were built for these posts, and barbed wire fences were erected later, when wire became available. Similar posts were constructed to guard the road to Landi Khana and these latter were garrisoned, first by dismounted cavalry, and, later, by infantry. On the 18th of May, also, two battalions of the 4th Infantry Brigade and one section of No. 6 Mountain Battery, R. G. A. from Ali Masjid and No. 38 Battery R. F. A. from Jamrud arrived in Landi Kotal. On the following morning (19th) the two remaining battalions of the 3rd Infantry Brigade moved from Landi Kotal to Dakka. On the 31st of May the whole of the 4th Infantry Brigade were concentrated at Landi Kotal. As the 30th Lancers were now no longer required in the forward area, they were sent back to Peshawar on the 22nd of May to rejoin the 10th Cavalry Brigade. The Headquarters of the 1st Division still remained at Landi Kotal so a fresh staff was organized for the force at Dakka, which was now known as "Dakka Force".

The Royal Air Force, though handicapped by the inferior quality of their machines (B. E. 2-C.s.), actively bombed enemy cantonments and concentrations on or near the line of advance. They paid particular attention to Jalalabad, the winter capital of Afghanistan, where one ton and eight hundredweights of explosives were dropped in a single day. At the time deputations of Afridis were staying there for the purpose of receiving money and ammunition from the Governor to encourage them to harass our communications. True to their predatory traditions, these tribesmen took advantage of the confusion which ensued and plundered the town. They then made off to their own country with much booty, to the disgust of the Afghan officials.

Assistance of Ruling Chiefs.

The ruling chiefs of India showed their loyalty in this war, just as they did in the days of the German menace. His Highness the Maharajah of Patiala, His Highness the Raja of Rutlam, the Nawab of Loharu and Prithi Singh of Jodhpur volunteered for active service, whilst the following States placed their armed forces and resources at the disposal of the Government of India:—

Alwar.	Kashmir.
Bahawalpur.	Khairpur.
Bhopal.	Maler Kotla.
Dhar.	Nagar.
Faridkot.	Patiala.
Gwalior.	Rampur.
Hill Tippera.	Rutlam.
Hunza.	Sirmur.
Idar.	Sunth.
Indore.	Tehri.
Jaipur.	

together with the Governors of Yasin, Panial, Ishkoman and Ghizr in the Gilgit Agency. The allied State of Nepal also promised a contingent of their forces for service against the Afghans.

By the 26th of May all was ready for an advance on Jalalabad. On that date, however, Afghan forces appeared in the Kurram. Reinforcements were hurried to Kohat, and the transport which should have been employed for the invasion of Afghanistan was diverted to meet the new inroad into our territory.

This dislocation of the arrangements for a forward movement was followed by an armistice. Since the 15th of May there had been unofficial negotiations carried on through the medium of Sardar Abdur Rahman Khan the Afghan envoy in India for a cessation of hostilities. On the 31st of May the Amir asked for an armistice which was granted on the 3rd of June. The terms are given in the following extract from a letter from the Viceroy to the Amir, dated the 2nd of June 1919:—

Terms of Armistice.

(1) That you should at once withdraw all your troops from the frontier. No Afghan troops are to be located within 20 miles of the nearest British Force.

(2) That the British troops should remain where they now are in Afghan territory, with freedom to continue such military preparations and precautions as may be deemed necessary. The troops will, however, take no offensive action whatever, so long as the terms of the armistice are observed by your side.

(3) British aircraft will not bomb or machine gun Afghan localities or forces so long as the armistice is observed, but they will have freedom of movement in the air to reconnoitre and observe the positions of Afghan forces in order to ensure against any concentration or collection of Afghan forces or tribesmen in contravention of the armistice.

Further, that you undertake that your people will not fire on or molest British aircraft and will return without delay, unhurt, any British aircraft and airmen who may have been forced to land in Afghan limits and use your utmost endeavour to ensure the safety of any British airman who may be forced to land in tribal territory.

(4) That you should at once send urgent messages to the tribes both on your own side and on our side of the Durand frontier, into whose limits your troops have advanced, or who have been excited by your agents and proclamations, stating that you have asked the Government of India for a cessation of hostilities and that you will not countenance further aggressive action on their part against the British Government; and if they take such action it will be at their own risk and they will receive from you and find no asylum in Afghanistan, from which they will be ejected if they come.

CHAPTER VI.

THE CENTRAL FRONT—EVENTS IN THE KURRAM AND TOCHI IN MAY AND JUNE.

Position on 6th of May.

On the 6th of May, the only signs of enemy activity on the Central Front was the building of "sangars" on the Peiwar Kotal. Afghan agents had had little success in their endeavours to rouse the Orakzais, the Wazirs and the Mahsuds. Nadir Khan, the ex-Commander-in-Chief, was known to be approaching Matun, where he would be in a position to strike at the Kurram or the Tochi. The obvious thing for us to do was to assume the offensive, and to pinch out the Khost salient from the south and west; but for this there were not sufficient troops and there was practically no transport. Our commanders, then, were forced into a defensive attitude, and compelled to await an attack wherever Nadir Khan chose to make this blow with the 14 battalions of infantry and 48 guns at his disposal.

Problems in the Kurram and Tochi.

The problems in the Kurram and in the Tochi were diametrically opposed to each other. In the Kurram we were called upon to defend a brave, but numerically weaker, people from their enemies, whilst the appearance of an Afghan force in the Tochi would be the signal for the less well disposed Wazirs to rise against us. The Mahsuds might also be expected to take the field, but the traditional enmity between these two kindred tribes precluded the possibility of concerted action on their part against us. On the Kurram front, General Eustace, who commanded at Kohat, was committed, therefore, to the defence of the Kohat district and of the Kurram Agency right up to the Afghan border at the Peiwar Kotal and Kharlarchi. On the other hand, it was decided that if the Afghans invaded the Tochi valley, the posts along that river above Miran Shah should be evacuated, and their garrisons withdrawn to the Lower Tochi.

Reinfor ements.

The point immediately threatened was Parachinar. As has been mentioned already in Chapter III, one battalion of infantry, one squadron of cavalry and one section of mountain artillery had been sent to reinforce the Kurram Militia at Parachinar, and these reinforcements, which arrived on the 7th of May, allayed the alarm of the inhabitants. More troops were also sent to Kohat, as shown in the table below:—

Unit.	From	Date of arrival in Kohat.
3rd Bn. Guides Infantry F. F.	Mardan	12th May.
22nd Motor Machine Gun Battery.	Rawalpindi . . .	15th May.
H. Q. 60th Infantry Brigade.	Ambala	19th May.
2-26th Punjabis . .	Ambala	19th May.
4-39th Garhwal Rifles . .	Ambala	19th May.

No. 11

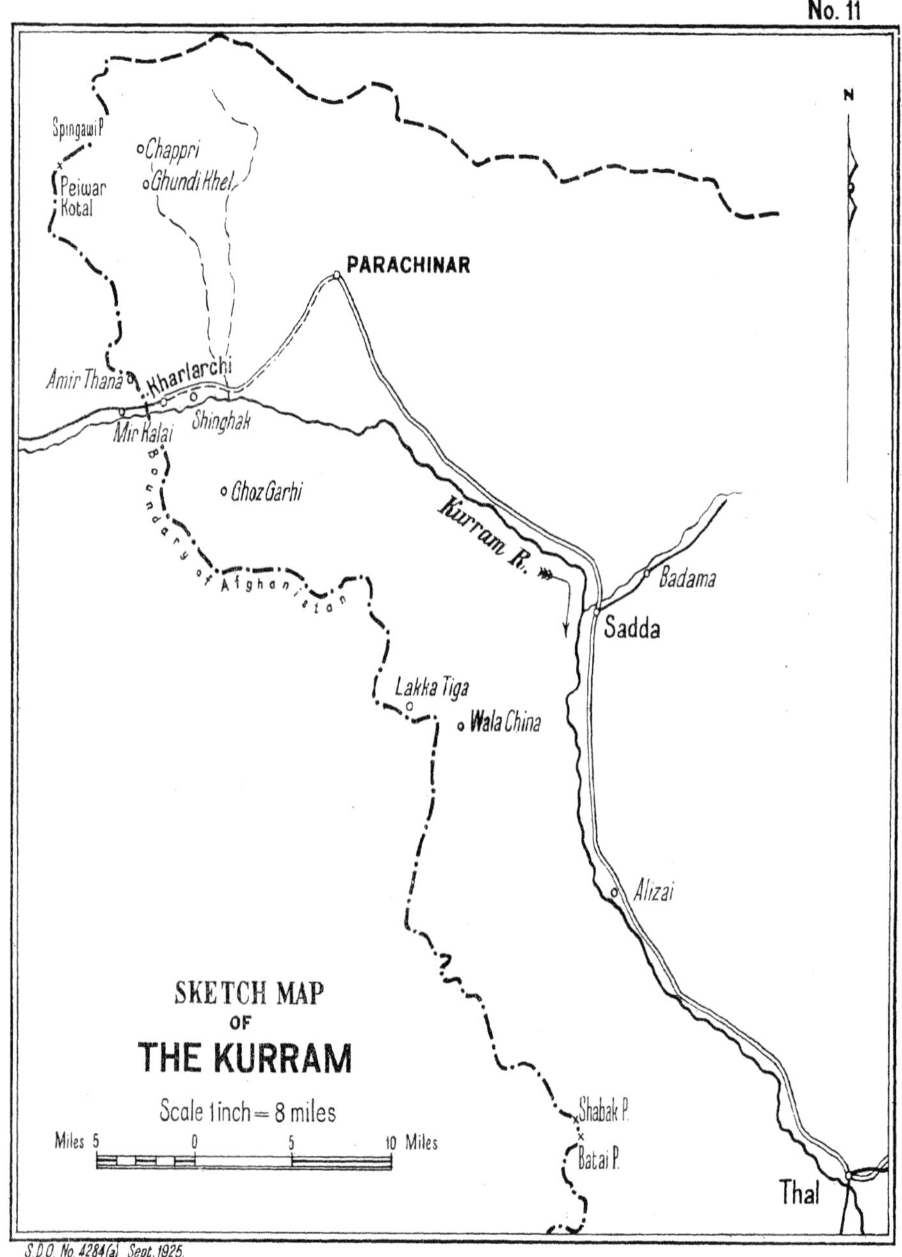

S.D.O. No. 4284(a) Sept. 1925.

Reg. No. 14 E. D. D. 1926-1500

Heliozincographed at the Survey of India Offices, Dehra Dun.

To face page. 53

Of these the 3rd Guides and No. 22 Motor Machine Gun Company were sent forward to Parachinar, where they arrived on the 22nd and 15th of May respectively. Sanction was also obtained to enlist 300 ex-sepoys of the Kurram Militia for temporary depot duty in Parachinar, thus releasing the whole militia for active operations.

Dispositions of the Kurram Militia

As early as the 2nd of May, Major Dodd, commanding the Kurram Militia, had sent one piquet of 60 men under Lieutenant Farwell to Ghundi Khel to watch the Peiwar Kotal, and another of 45 men to Shinghak to secure the route along the Kurram River through Kharlarchi. On the 14th of May, information was received that Nadir Khan had arrived at Ali Khel, 11 miles west of the Peiwar Kotal, and that an attack from this direction was to be expected. Major Dodd accordingly moved out from Parachinar with a column consisting of 450 infantry, 50 mounted infantry and the two guns of the Kurram Militia and bivouaced near Peiwar village. The rumour proved to be incorrect, so the guns were brought back to Parachinar on the 16th, but the force remained in the vicinity and, aided by the local Turis, prevented the enemy from advancing on the Peiwar villages. The post of Lakka Tiga, 16 miles south by west of Parachinar, was also reported to be threatened by the Afghans, so a column of 200 infantry and 60 mounted infantry of the Kurram Militia marched there under Captain Champion on the 16th of May. The latter found few enemy, but was able to carry off 60 head of cattle. In fact, though the Afghan regulars and tribesmen on the Peiwar Kotal were reinforced, and a desultory rifle and artillery fire was kept up on our post of Teri Mangal, little of importance took place during the first three weeks of the campaign. The conduct of the Orakzais and Zaimukhts was satisfactory, whilst that of the Wazirs between the Kurram and the Tochi was not yet definitely hostile. On the 22nd of May, the distribution of our troops in this area and of the Afghans by whom they were threatened is as shown below:—

Column to Lakka Tiga.

Distribution by British and Afghan forces, 22nd May.

British.	*Afghan.*	*British.*
Bannu-Tochi Area.	Gardez, Ali Khel and Matun Area.	Kohat-Kurram Area.
Dardoni.	*Matun District.*	*Parachinar.*
1 sq., 31st Lancers.	1¾ cavalry regts.	1 sq., 37th Lancers.
33rd Mountain Battery.	48 guns.	2 sections, No. 28 Mountain Battery.
No. 55 Co. 1st Sappers and Miners.	14 battalions infantry.	No. 22 Motor Machine Gun Battery.
1-41st Dogras		1-57th Rifles, F. F.
2-112th Infantry.		3rd Guides, F. F.
		Kurram Militia.

British. Bannu-Tochi Area.	*Afghan.* Gardez, Ali Khel and Matun Area.	*British.* Kohat-Kurram Area.
Miran Shah.		*Thal.*
N. Waziristan Militia.		H. Q. 60th Infy. Bde. (left for Parachinar on 23rd).
Saidgi (for Dardoni).		1 sq., 37th Lancers.
3-6th Gurkha Rifles.		1 section, No. 28 Mountain Battery.
Bannu.		1-109th Infantry.
		3-9th Gurkha Rifles.
Nos. 5 and 6 Armoured Motor Batteries.		*Hangu and Samana.*
31st Lancers, less 2 squadrons.		3-8th Gurkha Rifles.
		Kohat.
1 section trench howitzers.		
1-103rd Mahratta L. I.		37th Lancers, less 2 squadrons.
55th Coke's Rifles.		No. 23 Mountain Bty.
		1-151st Sikh Infy.
		2-26th Punjabis.
		4-39th Garhwal Rifles.

Nadir Khan leaves Matun. On the 23rd of May, Nadir Khan left Matun and marched down the Kaitu River. It was impossible to foretell the direction he would take, but his movement caused excitement among the Wazirs of the Tochi Agency. **Column to Mohammed Khel.** A column was sent from Dardoni on the 24th of May to Mohammed Khel, a distance of 14½ miles, to reassure the militia in the posts west of that place and to overawe the local inhabitants who were beginning to give trouble. **Nadir Khan advances Spinwam.** On the evening of that day, however, it was ascertained that Nadir Khan was directing his march on Spinwam, a Militia post on the Kaitu where the road from Thal to Idak crosses that river. **Evacuation Spinwam and Shewa.** It was therefore decided to withdraw the garrison of Spinwam, and also that of Shewa, a post on the Kurram river, 8 miles north-east of Spinwam, to Idak. To assist the retirement of these detachments, Colonel Ellwood assembled two squadrons of his regiment, the 31st Lancers, at Khajuri, and advanced across the Sheratulla plain on the morning of the 25th of May. The garrison of Shewa first retired on Spinwam, and then the combined force commenced its march of 21 miles on to Idak. Hardly had they left Spinwam than the Afghan regulars took possession of the fort. With them came large numbers of Wazirs who had joined Nadir Khan as soon as the latter had crossed our border. These

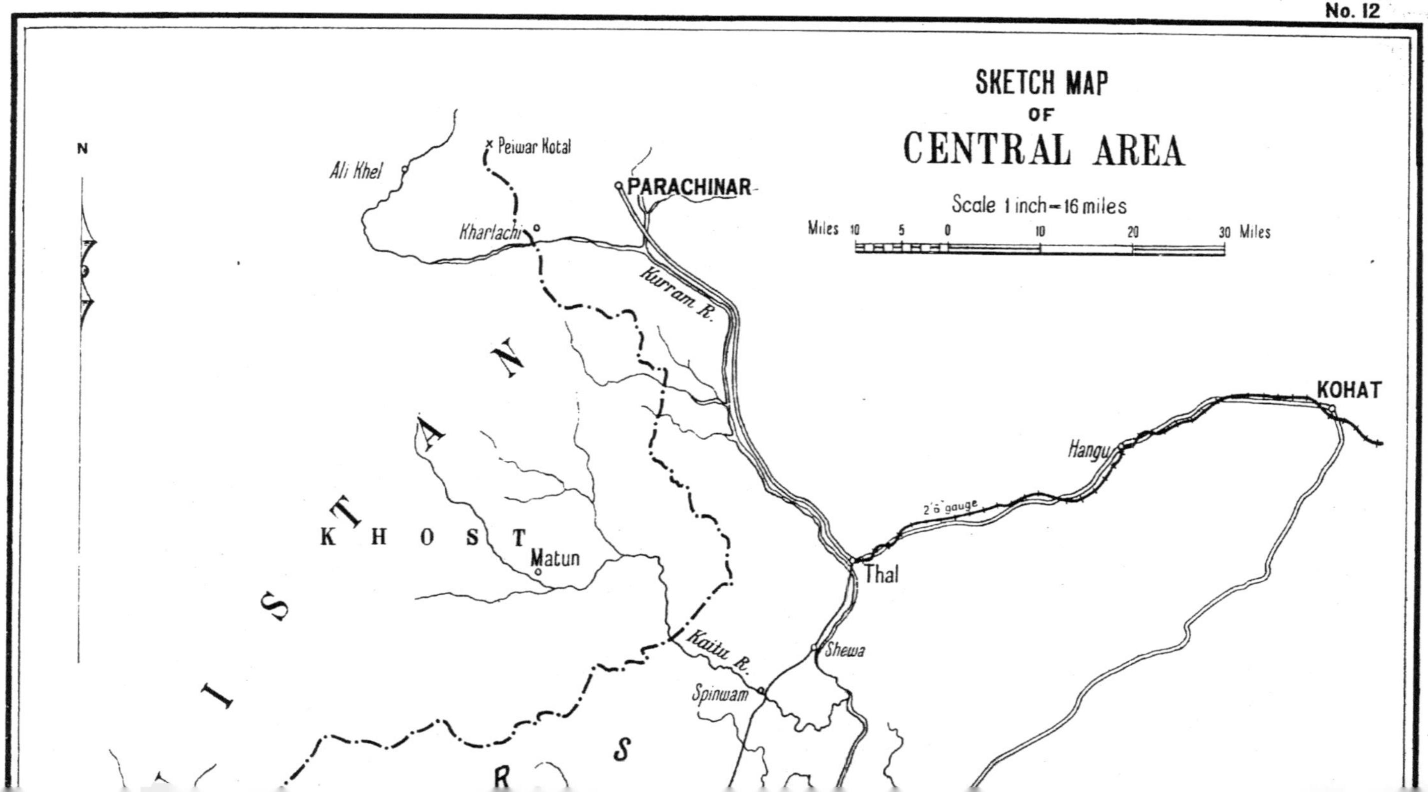

No. 12

SKETCH MAP OF CENTRAL AREA

Scale 1 inch = 16 miles

Miles 10 5 0 10 20 30 Miles

N

Ali Khel

Peiwar Kotal

PARACHINAR

Kharlachi

Kurram R.

KOHAT

Hangu

2'6" gauge

Thal

Shewa

Kaitu R.

Spinwam

Matun

KHOST

AFGHANISTAN

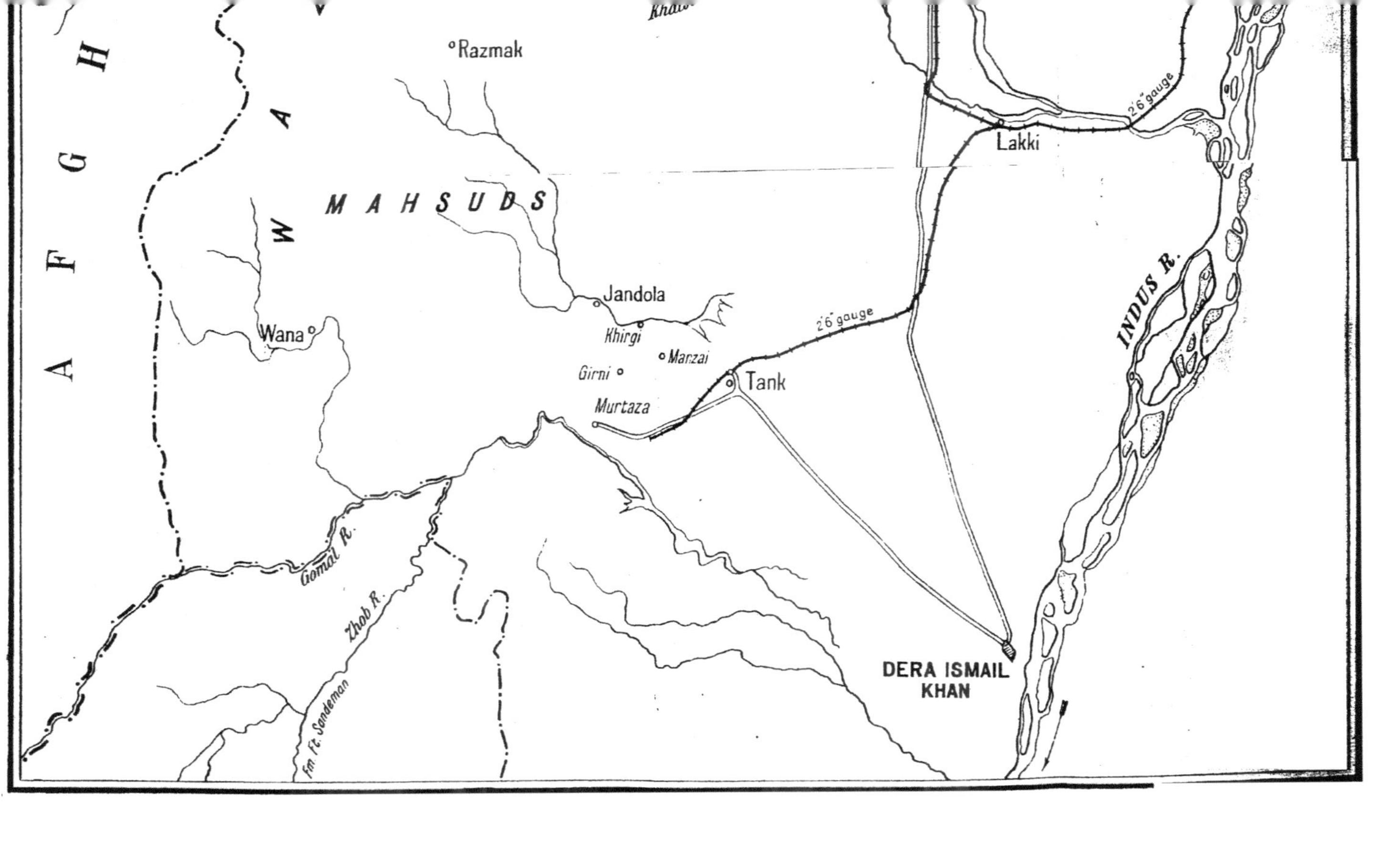
Razmak
A F G H
W A
M A H S U D S
Jandola
Wana
Khirgi
Manzai
Girni
Tank
Murtaza
2'6" gauge
2'6" gauge
Lakki
INDUS R.
Gomal R.
Zhob R.
Fm. Ft. Sandeman
DERA ISMAIL KHAN

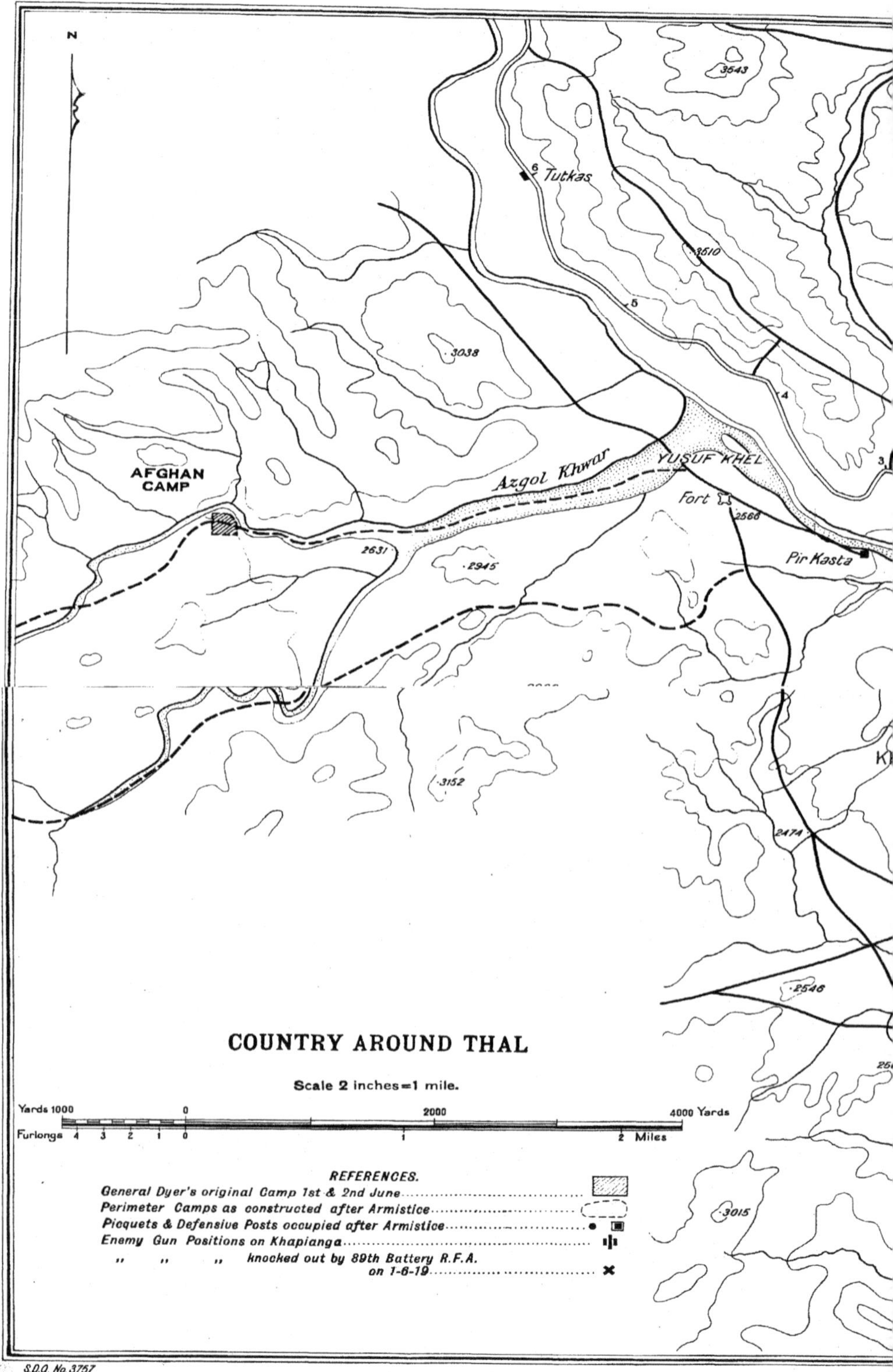

S.D.O. No. 3757
Reg. No. 14 E. D. D. 1926–1500

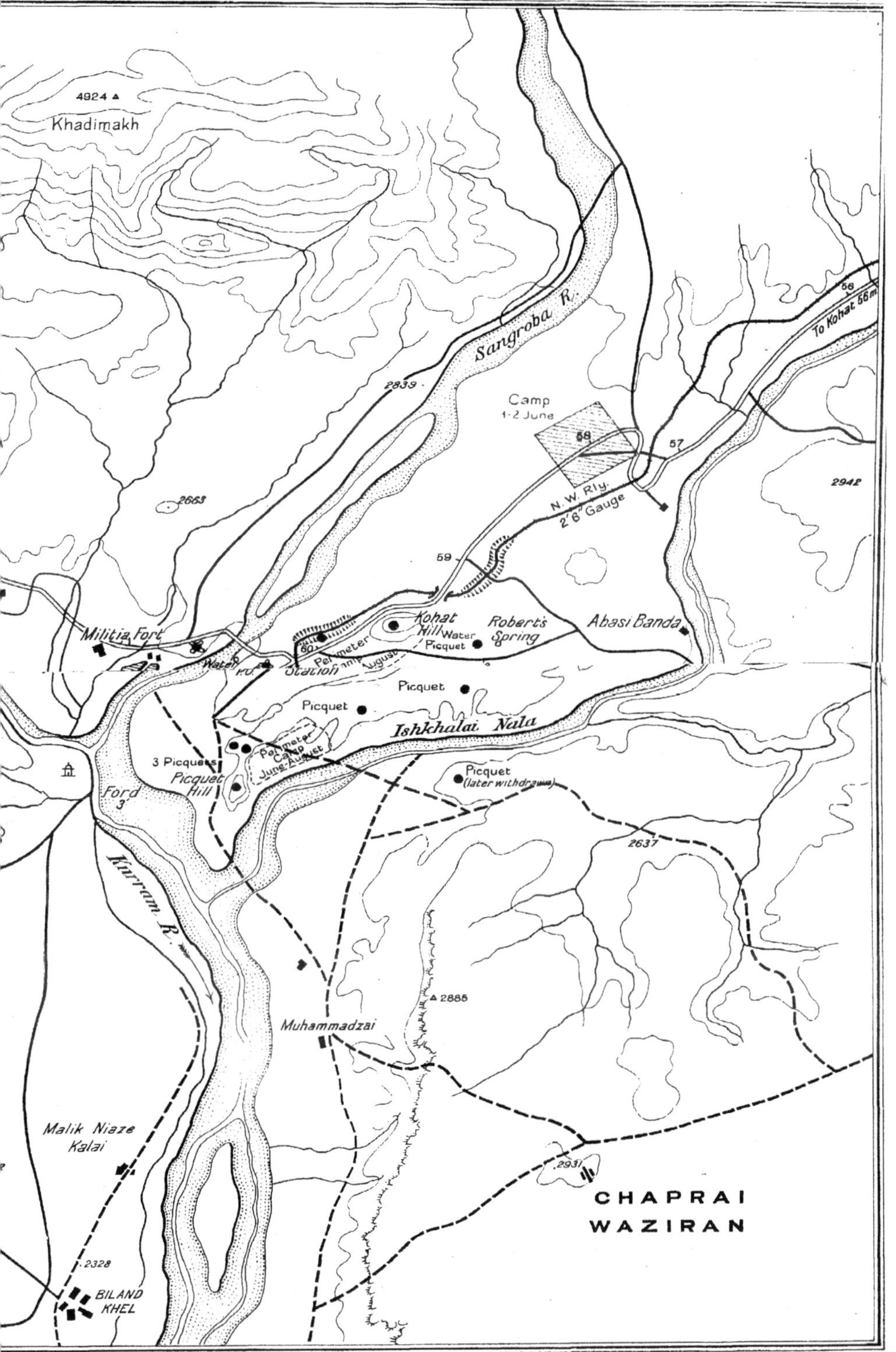

Heliozincographed at the Survey of India Offices, Dehra Dun.

Wazirs immediately took up the pursuit of the militia, and cut off one Indian officer and 15 men whom they made prisoners. They were unable to do further damage, and the party arrived at Idak on the evening of the 25th of May.

Evacuation of upper Tochi posts.

Whilst these posts were being evacuated, the officer commanding the column at Mohammed Khel had been ordered to bring in the garrisons of Spina Khaisora, Datta Khel and Tut Narai in the Upper Tochi, and to return to Dardoni. These posts were successfully evacuated and the stores in them which could not be carried away were burnt. Boya was handed over to an influential chief of the Daurs, a small tribe who live in the Tochi valley. This individual was either unable or unwilling to hold the fort, and it was looted and burnt by the local tribesmen. The column and the militia garrisons returned to Miran Shah and Dardoni about midnight. About 150 of the Militia were found to have deserted during this retrograde movement. By now it was realised that not only were the Tochi Wazirs hostile, but that the Wazirs in the North Waziristan Militia were thoroughly disaffected. It was found necessary to place 200 men of the 1/41st Dogras in Miran Shah fort to cope with the growing spirit of unrest. On the 26th of May these Wazirs broke into open mutiny, and, headed by Subedar Pat and Jemadar Tarin, they escaped from the fort by digging a hole through the wall to join their fellow tribesmen who were now in arms against us.

Mutiny of Wazirs in N. Waziristan Militia.

Evacuation of Wana and Gomal posts.

In Southern Waziristan, also, the militia posts were evacuated with even more disastrous results. Shahwali, the brother of Nadir Khan, was reported to be contemplating an invasion of the Wana plain from Urgun. It was decided that Wana and the Gomal posts should be evacuated before the events in the Tochi should become known. On the 26th of May arrangements were being made to leave Wana, when the Wazirs and Afridis seized the keep and turned on the officers and the men of the battalion who remained loyal. Major Russell made his way to Fort Sandeman with the remnant of his command after a running fight of over 60 miles with the mutineers and the local Wazirs. During this retirement he lost five officers killed and two wounded. A full account of these and subsequent occurrences in Waziristan are given in "Mahsud Operations, 1919-20" and will not be dealt with in this book.

Hardly had the Militia garrison been withdrawn from Spinwam, than Nadir Khan appeared before that post with 3,000 Afghan infantry, two 10 cm. Krupp field howitzers, seven 7·5 cm. Krupp pack guns and a large force of tribesmen. He was now 20 miles distant from Thal, Bannu and Idak on the Tochi. The route over which he had advanced was an unexpected one, as it had been reported as being unfit for the passage of large bodies of troops. It was still uncertain as to the direction he would take, so a column consisting of 2 companies 2/10th Jats, 1 squadron 31st Lancers, 1 section No. 33 Mountain Battery, and 1 section Trench howitzers from Bannu moved to Kurram Garhi, 4 miles north west of Bannu, to guard the defile of the Kurram River. General Eustace, also on the 25th of May sent the 1/151st Sikh Infantry, the 4/39th Garhwalis and one section of No. 23 Mountain Battery followed on the 26th by No. 57

Bannu Movable column at Kurram Garhi.

Thal reinforced.

Company, 1st Sappers and Miners, to reinforce Thal. The garrison then consisted of:—

Thal Garrison.

1 squadron, 37th Lancers.

1 section, No. 23 Mountain Battery.

1 section, No. 28 Mountain Battery.

No. 57 Co., 1st Sappers and Miners.

4/39th Garhwal Rifles.

1/109th Infantry.

1/151st Sikh Infantry.

3/9th Gurkha Rifles.

Two 3 ins. trench howitzers.

Plan of defence.

General Eustace himself took command of the force, and made arrangements for the defence. An inner and outer line were taken in hand, and the sections were allotted as follows. (See map facing page 55):—

Outer line—

From Sangroba Nala inclusive to Kohat Hill exclusive, 4/39th Garhwal Rifles. From Kohat Hill inclusive to Piquet Hill exclusive, 1/151st Sikh Infantry. From Piquet Hill inclusive to Sangroba Nala inclusive together with the hornwork of the fort, 1/109th Infantry, less 1 company.

Inner line—

Fort, Railway station and Civil Rest House, 3/9th Gurkha Rifles, less 2 companies.

General Reserve—

In diagonal trench near Rest House, dug by Lord Roberts in 1879, 2 companies, 3/9th Gurkha Rifles; 1 company, 1/109th Infantry.

Afghans invest Thal.

Work proceeded on the strengthening of these lines during the whole of the 26th of May. At 0900 hours on the 27th, Afghan troops appeared and the investment of Thal was begun.

That fort is situated on a plateau a mile broad between the Sangroba and Ishkalai Nalas. It is 100 feet above the Kurram River which flows a mile to the west of the fort. Half a mile to the west is the large village of Thal which contains 372 houses and which is inhabited by Bangash Pathans. To the north-west, beyond the Sangroba Nala, is the bold peak of Khadimakh, which rises 2,300 feet above the plateau. To the east the ground slopes gently upwards for 20 miles to the watershed between the Kurram and the Miranzai valleys. To the south of the Ishkalai Nala are a series of hills running east and west, which rise in height as they recede from Thal till they culminate in the fantastically shaped peaks of Kafir Kot. To the west of the Kurram is an isolated hill known as Khapianga, 800 feet above the river. The administered territory is here merely a slip five miles broad. The Zaimukht border runs north of Khadimakh, whilst to the south and southwest a line following the course of the Kurram river to within half a mile of Thal village and then trending to the west, marks the limits of the Wazirs. Water was obtained from a well in the Sangroba Nala, 300 yards north-east of the fort, whence it was pumped up for the use of the troops and of the railway.

The Afghan headquarters were established at Yusaf Khel on the Kurram river, 3 miles north-west of Thal. Their artillery came into action on Khapianga and at "Black Rock" a small conical hill near Yusaf Khel. From these places they opened fire on Thal fort at ranges of 3,500 and 5,500 yards respectively, and did much damage to the parapet and to the buildings in the fort. Several shells burst in the barrack used as a hospital. Communication trenches were dug inside the fort to keep down the number of casualties there. Thal village was occupied by parties of Afghan infantry, whilst bodies of tribesmen crossed the Kurram and seized the hills overlooking Mohammedzai, 3,500 yards south of the fort, and also the lower spurs of Khadimakh.

Bhoosa, Petrol and rations set alight by shell fire.

On the 28th of May the fire of the 10 cm. howitzers became more accurate and intense. The petrol dump and the *bhoosa* stacks outside the fort and the rations in the railway station yard were set on fire, and the wireless station was hit and put out of action for a time. Our artillery were outranged by these howitzers and were unable to reach them. This was the only occasion during the campaign when we were definitely inferior to the Afghans in artillery. An attempt was made to keep down the Afghan bombardment by two machines of the R. A. F. which bombed the enemy gun emplacements. This was effective for the time being, but the relief was temporary. At 10-30 hours, Afghan regulars debouched from Thal village and made a half-hearted attack towards the fort. This was easily repulsed by the combined fire of guns, Lewis guns and rifles, and was not repeated.

Frontier Constabulary post abandoned.

On the night of the 28/29th of May, the Frontier Constabulary evacuated the militia post on the right bank of the Sangroba Nala which they were holding, and made off towards Hangu. This was occupied by the enemy, who were thus in a position to threaten the water supply. On the 29th, the garrison began to dig pits, which they lined with tarpaulins for the storage of water. Owing to the burning of the ration dumps, food began to run short, so troops and animals were placed on half rations. During the night of the 29/30th of May, attacks were made on Piquet Hill, the spur to the south of the fort held by the 1/109th Infantry. The section of No. 28 Mountain Battery opened fire on the enemy, one gun using star shell and the other shrapnel. This combined with the rifle fire and the grenades of the piquets quickly drove the enemy back. Our losses were Lieutenant S. C. Scott, and five men wounded.

Attack on Piquet Hill.

On the 30th of May the aeroplanes were employed elsewhere and the Afghan artillery kept up a heavy fire all day. By this time they had conveyed a 7·5 cm. gun across the Kurram south of Thal and were firing on our piquets from point 2931. Considerable damage was done to the parapet of the fort and to our gun emplacements. On the following day (31st) both sides were aware of the approach of the relieving column, which reached Thal on the 1st of June, and little activity was shown.

Preparation for the reliefs of Thal.

The news of Nadir Khan's invasion, and of his investment of Thal, put an end, for the time being, to the preparations which were being made for an advance on Jalalabad. It was realised that Thal should be relieved without delay, otherwise the Orakzais and Zaimakhts who, up to this time, had not shown signs of actively supporting the Afghans, would be driven into the ranks of our enemies. Energetic measures were at once taken to concentrate a force sufficient for this purpose at Kohat. The first difficulty was transport and 62 lorries were sent by road from Peshawar to Kohat to supply the deficiency there.

The 2/69th Punjabis had already arrived from Ambala on the 24th, and the 1/69th Punjabis from Lucknow on the 25th of May. Reinforcements were hurried into Kohat as is shown in detail in the table below:—

Unit.	From	Date of arrival in Kohat.
89th Battery, R. F. A. with 150 rifles, 2-4th Border Regiment.	Peshawar	28th May.
45th Infantry Brigade—		
1-25th London Regiment	Peshawar	28th May.
2-41st Dogras		
2-72nd Punjabis		
3-150th Infantry		
2-6th Royal Sussex Regiment	Lahore	30th May.
1-124th Baluchistan Regiment	Do.	
H. Q. 16th Division	Do.	Do.
No. 66 Fd. Co. 2nd S. and M.	Bangalore	31st May.
287 Co. Machine Gun Corps	Do.	1st June.
2-7th Gurkha Rifles	Ambala	Do.
46th Mobile Brigade—		
1-5th Hampshire Regiment	Ambala	Do.
2-151st Infantry		
2-9th Gurkha Rifles		
10-96th Battery, 218th Bde. R. F. A., less 1 section.		
No. 3 Motor Machine Gun Bty.		
46th Bde., Ammn. Column		

A Mobile Column was formed at Hangu, 26 miles west of Kohat, consisting of:—

1 squadron, 37th Lancers.
89th Battery, R. F. A.
1 section, No. 23 Mountain Battery,
20 men, No. 57 Coy., 1st S. & M.
265 rifles, 57th Rifles, F. F.
1/69th Punjabis.
1 company, 2/4th Border Regiment.

Brigadier-General R. F. H. Dyer, C.B., Commanding the 45th Infantry Brigade, was placed in command of the operation for the relief of Thal, and the Mobile Column at Hangu came under his orders. In addition to these troops he had his own brigade. As he considered that more artillery was required, he took four of the six 15 pounders of the Frontier Garrison Artillery from Kohat fort. These guns had no horses, but by utilizing seven motor lorries he was able to drag the guns and to carry the ammunition and gunners. These four guns were sent to Hangu by road on the 29th of May, whilst the 3/150th Infantry proceeded to the same place by rail. The 1/25th London Regiment and the 2/41st Dogras were to be railed on to Hangu early on the 30th of May. Finding that there were no engines, and that the first train could not start till 1000 hours, General Dyer ordered these two battalions to be railed direct to Togh, and set off for Hangu by car. At Hangu he made arrangements for the troops there to move to Togh, also, the same day. They marched at 1730 hours but the rear-guard did not arrive in camp till 0100 hours. The "Thal Relief Force" thus concentrated at Togh was composed of:—

Composition of Thal Relief Force.

H. Q. 45th Infantry Brigade.
1 squadron, 37th Lancers.
89th Battery, R. F. A.
Four 15-prs., Frontier Garrison Artillery.
1 section, No. 23 Mountain Battery.
½ section, No. 57 Co., 1st Sappers and Miners.
1 section, Pack Wireless.
1 armoured motor battery.
1/25th London Regiment.
2/41st Dogras.
1/69th Punjabis.
3/150th Infantry.
250 rifles, 57th Rifles, F. F.
1 company, 2/4th Border Regiment.

Advance on Thal.

Most of the troops had had no food all day. They were able to cook at Togh, but few of them had any sleep. At 0400 hours on 31st, the column left Togh, and marched to a camp just south of

Darsamand village by the 51st milestone, a distance of 18 miles. The heat was great and there was no breeze to temper it. The march discipline was good but the troops suffered from the heat and the lack of water. The rear guard arrived in camp at 1300 hours. After a short rest the camp was entrenched, and piquets were placed on the neighbouring heights to secure it. Communication was opened with Thal through the visual station at Fort Lockhart on the Samana Ridge, which was visible from both places.

At 0500 hours on the 1st of June the force left camp to cover the last nine miles to Thal, and to fight the enemy for the relief of this post. To guard the left, or southern, flank, the 250 rifles of the 57th Rifles F.F. were pushed across the Ishkalai Nala, which here runs parallel to the road and railway, and this unit placed piquets along the low features immediately south of the nala.

On reaching the aeroplane landing ground, two miles north-east of Thal, General Dyer was met by Major G. G. E. Wylly, V.C., D.S.O., General Staff Officer to General Eustace, and obtained from him a full description of the enemy dispositions. On the left, or east, bank of the Kurram River, a body of 2,000 tribesmen with a few regulars and four guns were holding the low spurs of Khadimakh running towards Thal. To the south of the Ishkalai Nala, on the Wazir hills, was a force of 4,000 tribesmen under one Babrak, an influential Zadran chief. This body was composed of Pathans from Khost, known collectively as Khostwals, and of Wazirs from British territory, between whom there was a certain amount of friction. The main force of Afghan regulars, with the field howitzers was near Yusaf Khel and on Khapianga on the right, or west, bank of the Kurram, which was, at the time, between two and three feet deep. To the north, the Orakzais and Zaimukhts were gathering, but they were waiting for Nadir Khan to capture Thal before they definitely threw in their lot with the Afghans. General Dyer decided to attack those detachments east of the Kurram and to deal with Babrak's command first. To give the impression that both were to be attacked simultaneously, fire was opened by the 89th Battery, R. F. A. and by the four guns of the Frontier Garrison Artillery both on Thal village and on the heights overlooking Mohammedzai, which were held by the Wazirs and Khostwals.

Enemy dispositions.

Plan of attack.

The infantry were then deployed for the attack. The 1/69th Punjabis, supported by the 3/150th Infantry, were directed to take hill 2657, whilst one section of No. 23 Mountain Battery, the 1/25th London Regiment, the 2/41st Dogras and the half section of No. 57 Company, 1st Sappers and Miners, moved forward to cover the advance to a position half way between Thal and Abasi Banda. The suddenness of the attack and the accuracy of the artillery fire proved too much for the heterogeneous and undisciplined followers of Babrak, and they scattered in all directions. The 1/69th Punjabis seized the heights with the trifling loss of four men wounded by 1600 hours. 200 men of the 3/150th Infantry were left to occupy the captured position, whilst the remainder of the troops were withdrawn to a camp on the road near the 58th milestone. One section of the 89th battery, R. F. A., then trotted forward to Thal where they engaged and silenced the enemy guns on Khapianga.

Barbrak's position captured.

On the following morning, 2nd of June, General Dyer assumed command of all the troops in Thal, whilst General Eustace returned to Kohat. An attack was launched on a two battalion front against the enemy on the lower slopes of Khadimakh north-west of Thal. The leading infantry consisted of two battalions of the Thal garrison, the 1/151st Sikh Infantry on the right and the 3/9th Gurkha Rifles on the left. They were followed by the 1/25th London Regiment and the 2/41st Dogras. As the attack was developing, General Dyer received a letter from Nadir Khan saying that he had been ordered by the Amir to suspend hostilities, and asked for an acknowledgment to this communication. General Dyer, whose knowledge of the Oriental was profound, gave him a characteristic answer. "My guns will give an immediate reply, and a further reply will be sent by the Divisional Commander to whom the letter has been forwarded". Khadimakh spurs captured.

It soon became evident that Nadir Khan and his forces were retiring with all possible speed. The spurs were rapidly occupied with little opposition, our casualties being only five men wounded. The Royal Air Force who were operating on the right flank of the infantry, dispersed a body of 400 Zaimukhts on the northern flopes of Khadimakh with bombs and Lewis gun fire. The heat was now very great and General Dyer considered that he had made sufficient calls on the energy of his infantry. The armoured cars and one squadron of the 37th Lancers were, however, pushed up the left bank of the Kurram to harass the retiring Afghans, whilst two sections of the 89th Battery, R. F. A., moved forward to Mulla Rasul, 1½ miles north-west of Thal fort, to shell the camp at Yusaf Khel. A reconnaissance of the Royal Air Force discovered that the Afghan headquarters had been removed to a spot in the foothills, 3 miles west of its former location. Nadir Khan retreats.

On the following morning, the 3rd June, a column left Thal at 0700 hours to seize the Afghan camp at Yusaf Khel. It consisted of:— Afghan camp captured.

2 troops, 37th Lancers.

1 section, 89th battery, R. F. A.

60 rifles, 1/25th London Regiment, with 4 Lewis guns.

2 armoured cars.

They forded the river at Pir Kasta, and reached Yusaf Khel at 1100 hours. It was found that the Afghan camp had been hastily abandoned, and that gun ammunition and stores were lying about everywhere in disorder. The troops were unable to remove these with the means at their disposal, but a column with camels went out next morning to bring the booty back to Thal. The local villagers, however, made good use of the opportunity given them and stole practically everything of value during the night.

Preparations were now made to exploit the victory, and to follow Nadir Khan to Matun. These plans, however, had to be abandoned owing to the signing of the armistice on the 3rd of June. It was Preparations for an advance on Matun.

abandoned owing to armistice.

still possible to take measures against our own tribesmen, and, on the 4th of June, a column set out to destroy the large Wazir village of Biland Khel as a punishment for the active assistance given by its inhabitants to the Afghans during the seige. The Kurram was in spate so the force had to return. On the following day, *i.e.*, the 5th of June, the attempt was renewed. The troops employed were:—

Destruction of Biland Khel.

2 sections, No. 57 Co., 1st Sappers and Miners.

1 Company, 2/41st Dogras.

1 Company, 2/72nd Punjabis.

1 Company, 3/150th Infantry.

The advance was covered by the fire of the four 15 pounders which came into action near the civil rest house, half-way between the fort and the railway station. The advanced guard, consisting of the company of the 2/41st Dogras, moved round and through the village, and took up a position on the nala 900 yards south of Biland Khel to cover the actual destruction of the village. As there was a large quantity of supplies in Biland Khel, 300 camels were sent out from Thal in answer to helio message to carry them away. Half the village was allotted to the 3/150th infantry and half to the 2/72nd Punjabis whilst the Sappers and Miners prepared the six largest towers for demolition. These latter were found to be so solid that a charge of 50 pounds of guncotton was required for each of them. As much grain, *bhoosa* and wood as could be taken away was carried out of the village, and dumped to the north clear of the houses, where it was loaded on camels. At 1645 the signal for retirement was given and the towers were blown up. The retirement was not pressed and the column returned to Thal unmolested, having lost two men wounded, who were hit by snipers firing at long range.

Whilst the village was being cleared, a deep cave was discovered with an underground stream (*karez*) running through it. It was known to be occupied, but it was uncertain whether there were armed men in it or not. Bugler Narain Chand, No. 57 Coy., 1st S. & M., volunteered to go in and see who were inside. He entered the cave unarmed, and found six women there. They came out, and were allowed to go away. The bugler then entered the cave again, accompanied by sepoy Puran Singh, 2/72nd Punjabis, and explored it thoroughly, but no enemy were found. This affords a good example of the lonely courage required of the rank and file during campaigns on the North-West Frontier.

In the seige of Thal we again see the failure of the Afghans to take advantage of an initial success. The advance of Nadir Khan down the Kaitu was a masterly stroke, and the movement of his comparatively large force, encumbered with gun elephants, over bad roads is a tribute to his forcefulness and personality. On reaching Thal, however, his lack of experience and military training were very evident. He had the advantage of the initiative, for the garrison never assumed the offensive against him. His artillery was superior in number of guns and in shell power. The troops opposed to him were mostly new battalions, composed of young soldiers without sufficient training. The extent of the perimeter was nearly five miles, and vulnerable nearly everywhere. There was every prospect that a well organized and determined assault, adequately covered by artillery and rifle fire, would have pierced the hastily constructed defences, and swept away the small garrison. A victory would have had far-reaching effects. The Orakzais and Zaimukhts would have risen, and General Fagan's force in the Upper Kurram would have been isolated. General Dyer's column would have had to fight its way from Hangu to Parachinar, instead of advancing through a friendly country. This reluctance to attack, which was so characteristic of the Afghans during this campaign, was possibly due to a number of causes in this instance. Nadir Khan expected to be joined by the Orakzais and Zaimukhts, as well as by the Wazirs. He was probably waiting for the two former tribes to join him before launching an attack. The various jarring elements of which his force was composed may have made a concerted attack an impossibility. His ignorance of modern warfare made him confident that his artillery alone would reduce the garrison of Thal to submission, and he was apparently unwillingly to sustain the losses which an assault would entail. When confronted by the bold and energetic tactics of General Dyer, Nadir Khan made no attempt to collect his scattered forces, and to fight even a defensive action on ground of his own choosing, although his numbers exceeded those of the Thal garrison and the Thal Relief Force combined. In this he may have been prompted by personal motives. A defeat would have meant political extinction. His partial success was remembered, whilst his disorderly flight was conveniently forgotten. On the conclusion of hostilities he became Commander-in-Chief and War Minister, whilst a column was erected at Kabul with a chained lion representing Britain at the base, to celebrate this feat of arms, which is described as an Afghan victory. As will be seen from the foregoing pages, he was within easy reach of victory, which he and his subordinates lacked the experience, ability and energy to seize.

Our casualties during the siege were:—

Killed—

Captain A. G. Wakefield, 114th Labour Corps.
Indian other ranks, 7.

Died of wounds—

Indian other ranks, 4.

Wounded—

Lieut. S. C. Scott, 1/109th Infantry.

British other ranks, 5.

Indian other ranks, 76.

Whilst these events were happening at Thal, fighting was going on in the Upper Kurram. The Afghans, operating on outer lines, had four large groups on a frontage of 29 miles. Of these, three were kept under observation by small detachments of our troops, whilst the central reserve at Parachinar was in a position from which it could strike in any direction. The disposition of the British and Afghan Forces in this area on the 26th of May is given below.

	Lakka Tiga.	Ghoz Garhi.	Kharlarchi.	Peiwar Kotal.
Distance between forces.	13 miles.	6 miles.	10 miles.	
Afghan.	400 regulars.	800 Maqbils, (tribesmen).	100 regulars.	2,000 regulars.
	600 tribesmen.		900 tribesmen.	4 mountain guns.
	2 mountain guns.		1 mountain gun.	1 machine gun.
			1 Machine gun.	1,000 tribesmen.
British.	Kurram Militia.		Kurram Militia.	Kurram Militia.
	80 mounted infantry.		200 infantry.	400 infantry.
	200 infantry.			2 mountain guns.
Distance from Parachinar.	19 miles.		11 miles	15 miles.

In reserve at Parachinar.

"A" Squadron, 37th Lancers.
2 sections, No. 28 Mountain Battery.
No. 22 Motor Machine Gun Battery.
57th Rifles, F.F.
3rd Bn. Guides Infantry, F.F.
400 Rifles, Kurram Militia.

Garrisons of the Kurram Militia between Parachinar and Thal.

Alizai, 50 rifles.
Sultan Kot, 15 rifles.
Badama, 80 rifles.
Chapri, 12 rifles.
Arawali, 25 rifles.
Shakardara, 15 rifles.
Uchdara, 40 rifles.

Afghan attack on Peiwar villages.

On the 26th of May, the date before Nadir Khan appeared at Thal, the Afghans attacked the outposts protecting the Peiwar villages. Afghan regulars and tribesmen, covered by artillery fire, advanced from the Spingawi pass, 2 miles north-east of the Peiwar, on Chapri village. Captain Wilson moved out from Ghundi Khel with 200 men of the Kurram Militia, passed through the outpost line, and counter-attacked the enemy, who were driven back to the hills with loss. The attempt was renewed on the following day, but the Kurram

Militia, who had been reinforced by one section of No. 22 Motor Machine Gun Battery, drove off the attack with considerable loss to the enemy.

Alizai occupied by troops from Parachinar.

On the same day (*i.e.*, 27th) news was received in Parachinar of Nadir Khan's move on Thal. It was reported that Alizai was threatened by a gathering of tribesmen from the Batai Pass, 14½ miles west of Thal Fort and 10 miles south by west of Alizai. Brigadier-General A. E. Fagan commanding the 60th Infantry Brigade at Parachinar therefore sent out a detachment of one section No. 22 Motor Machine Gun Battery and 200 men of the 3rd Guides in motor lorries to Alizai to replace the garrison of the 1/109th Infantry, which had been withdrawn to Thal on the previous day. He also sent a proposal to the General Staff of the Kohat District that he should operate from the vicinity of Lakka Tiga against Nadir Khan's lines of communication with Matun, but the despatch rider carrying the message found that the road near Tutkas was held by the enemy, and was obliged to turn back. An attempt was made to send a wireless message to the same effect on the following morning but it failed to get through. Nothing, therefore, came of the suggestion, but Captain Champion, who was at Wala China, 3 miles east of Lakka Tiga, with 80 mounted infantry, was ordered to move south and worry the flanks of the force near Batai Pass. Captain Champion reached the Shabak Pass two miles north-west of the Batai on the evening of the 28th of May. He found that the information regarding an enemy concentration was incorrect. He remained in the vicinity of the Shabak till the 31st, when he was fortunate enough to get in rear of an Afghan convoy returning to Matun, and killed 9 of the escort. The unfriendliness of the villagers and the lack of supplies, however, compelled him to retire to Wala China the same evening, and thus he was deprived of the chance of harassing the Afghans retiring from Thal.

Captain Champion advances on Shabak Pass.

Kharlarchi attacked by Afghans.

On the 28th of May, a force of Afghans surrounded Kharlarchi post, which was held by a detachment of 75 men of the Kurram Militia. A small force was sent from Parachinar to their assistance, consisting of:—

2 troops, 37th Lancers.

1 section, No. 22 Motor Machine Gun Battery.

25 mounted infantry, Kurram Militia.

50 Infantry, Kurram Militia.

The machine guns under Major Malony arrived first, and opened fire on the enemy. The cavalry considered the ground unfavourable for mounted attack, so they and the militia advanced on foot. The enemy driven back with a loss of 29 killed and many wounded, whilst our losses were two killed and one wounded. The cavalry and machine guns were withdrawn to Parachinar after dark.

Lieut. Beamish attacks Afghans near Lakka Tiga.

The Afghans now decided to invade the Kurram from Jaji Maidan through Lakka Tiga with the intention of joining hands with the Orakzais and Zaimukhts, whose borders run close to the Kurram between Sadda and Alizai. The Jaji tribesmen had an old-standing feud with the villagers on our side of the border. Numbers of the former joined the Afghans west of Lakka Tiga, whose forces were thereby increased to 3,000 men and five guns. If this invasion had been successful, Parachinar would have been cut off from the Lower Kurram and the Orakzais and Zaimukhts would probably have risen against us. To prevent this movement, Lieutenant Beamish, who was at Lakka Tiga with 200 men of the Kurram Militia, was ordered to engage the Afghans. In spite of his inferiority in numbers, he moved out and attacked the Afghans on a front of four miles on the 28th and 29th of May. Although he failed to inflict a decisive defeat on them, he kept them fully occupied and prevented them from invading the Kurram.

Garrison of Alizai reduced.

As it was evident that the concentration of tribesmen on the Batai Pass was a myth, lorries were sent to Alizai on the 29th, and 150 out of the detachment of 200 men of the 3rd Guides, together with the section of the motor machine guns were brought back to Parachinar. On the same day, the 29th, another half-hearted attempt was made to attack Peiwar village from the direction of Spingawi, but it was beaten off by the Militia, supported by one section of mountain artillery and one section of the motor machine gun battery from Parachinar.

Subedar Gul Khan defeats Orakzais near Badama.

Hitherto the Orakzais had given no active assistance to the Afghans, in spite of the exertions of Mulla Mahmud Akhundzada, the most influential of the religious leaders of the tribe. On the 29th and 30th of May, however, parties of the Masuzai, Alisherzai and Koni Khel sections of the Orakzais gathered in the Khurmana valley and attacked the post of Badama, 3½ miles north-east of Sadda on the main Kurram road. Subedar Gul Khan of the Kurram Militia collected 60 men from Badama and 40 from Sadda. With these and the local villagers he boldly attacked the invaders and drove them back to the mountains with a loss of 20 dead, whilst only one of his men was killed in the fight.

Raid on Amir Thana.

News was now received that General Dyer's column was marching to the relief of Thal. General Fagan decided to carry out two raids on the Afghans on the 2nd of June, one on the Peiwar, and one on Amir Thana, 1¼ miles west of Kharlarchi. After thus striking the enemy west of Parachinar, he intended to organize a column to harass Nadir Khan when the latter retired on Matun. General Dyer's advance was so rapid, and the Afghans retreat from Thal was so precipitate, that this move into Afghanistan was never carried out. The raid on the Peiwar, also, was found to be impracticable, as the troops would have to march 18 miles during darkness over bad roads before they reached the position from which they could commence operations. That from Kharlarchi on Amir Thana duly took place and was completely successful.

At 1830 hours on the 2nd of June, Major Dodd left Parachinar with the following troops, and reached Kharlarchi after dark:—

1 squadron, 37th Lancers, less 2 troops.
1 section, No. 28 Mountain Battery.
1 section, No. 22 Motor Machine Gun Battery.
1 company, 3rd Guides, F.F.
1 troop, mounted infantry, Kurram Militia.
100 infantry, Kurram Militia.
2 light trench howitzers manned by 57th Rifles, F.F.

The company of the Guides Infantry F.F. moved out during the night, and occupied a low ridge 1,000 yards west of Amir Thana and the section of No. 22 Motor Machine Gun Battery took up a position which covered the door of the fort. At dawn, the section of No. 28 Mountain Battery came into action against Amir Thana, and under cover of their fire the trench howitzers of the 57th Rifles, F.F advanced to within 500 yards of the fort. After a 15 minutes' bombardment, the infantry of the Kurram Militia assaulted the post and attempted to climb the walls. In this they were unsuccessful, but soon afterwards, at 0900 hours, the garrison of 50 men surrendered and the fort was then burnt. The shooting of the trench howitzers was disappointing owing to defective cartridges. Meanwhile, the cavalry and mounted infantry advanced along the river on Mir Zaman Kalai, $1\frac{1}{4}$ miles south of Kharlarchi, covered by the fire of the guns and machine guns. As the mounted force approached Mir Zaman Kalai, the guns stopped firing, and the cavalry and mounted infantry rushed the village and burnt it. Our troops then pressed forward to Mir Kalai, $1\frac{3}{4}$ miles south-west of Amir Thana, and captured the breastworks erected by the enemy between these two places. The Afghan General, whose headquarters were in Mir Kalai, fled hurriedly with his whole force. In all, six villages of the Jajis were burnt. Our casualties were two Indian other ranks killed, and Lieut. Carter, Kurram Militia, and four Indian other ranks wounded. The enemy lost 60 killed, of whom 32 were counted on the ground.

Motor lorry column from Parachinar to Thal.

On the 3rd of June, news of the relief of Thal was received at Parachinar. The enemy were still reported to be holding the road at Tutkas, 6 miles north-west of Thal, so General Fagan sent 70 men of the 57th Rifles, F.F. in motor lorries with a section of the motor machine gun battery from Parachinar to open the road to Thal. It was found that the Afghans had disappeared. The motor lorries and machine guns went through to Thal and returned to Parachinar on the same evening without firing a shot.

This was the day of the armistice, and after this no offensive action was taken against the Afghans. Although the terms granted to the Afghans stipulated that Afghan forces should be withdrawn 20 miles from the nearest British force, their regulars still remained on the Peiwar Kotal and in the neighbourhood of Kharlarchi and Lakka Tiga.

Afghan break armistice and attack Teri.

Nor did they scruple to break the terms by carrying out offensive movements. On the 5th of June, bodies of Afghans descended from the Peiwar, drove in our outposts and threatened Teri post. A force of 100 infantry and 30 mounted infantry of the Kurram Militia with 2 machine guns arrived from Parachinar, and checked the attackers. The action, however, continued all night, and the Turi villagers were forced to abandon breastworks (sangars) which they were holding on the flanks of the Militia. The latter were now in danger of being enveloped from their left. To prevent this, an attack was made on the ridge between Teri and Sursurang to the south from which our troops had been driven on the previous day. Although this was captured with little loss, the enemy continued to press. One company of the 57th Rifles, F.F. and a section of trench howitzers were sent from Parachinar to reinforce the Militia and General Fagan proceeded to the spot and made a personal reconnaissance. He then ordered the remainder of the 57th Rifles, F.F. and a section of mountain artillery to Teri from Parachinar. The left flank had been secured, but bodies of Afghan regulars and Mangal tribesmen now moved along the lower slopes and threatened the right flank and the large village of Shalozan. The company of the 57th Rifles, F. F. took over the protective line held by the Kurram Militia, and the latter were able to extend to the right and to check this enveloping movement. Several attacks were made by the enemy during the night, but on the following morning, the 7th of June, the Afghans began to retire, and by 1200 hours they had all returned to the Peiwar Kotal.

General Beynon's protest.

On the 7th of June, whilst this fighting was still in progress, General Beynon, commanding the Kohat-Kurram Force, arrived in Parachinar. He sent a letter to the Afghan Commander, Shah Mahmud, a younger brother of Nadir Khan (and better known in 1919 by his title of Sar Sar-i-os, or Master of Horse) in which he informed Shah Mahmud that an armistice had been signed, and demanded the withdrawal of the Afghan troops. He further stated that unless this was done within 48 hours, the British would attack him. A few days later, the Afghan commander replied apologizing for the attack on Teri, and excused himself by saying that he was unaware of the armistice until the morning of the 7th of June. He took no steps, however, to withdraw from the Peiwar, and General Fagan was not permitted to carry the threat into execution.

As soon as Thal was relieved, a reorganization of the troops in the Kohat-Kurram Force was carried out. The 4/39th Garhwal Rifles and the 1/109th Infantry marched from Thal to Parachinar where they arrived on the 8th of June, to become part of the 60th Infantry Brigade. The 65th Infantry Brigade was formed at Thal under Brigadier-General C. O. O. Tanner. It consisted of:

1/69th Punjabis.
2/69th Punjabis.
2/151st Infantry.
3/9th Gurkha Rifles.

At Kohat Brigadier-General C. E. F. K. Macquiod, D.S.O., assumed command of the 47th Infantry Brigade composed of:—

2/26th Punjabis.
2/7th Gurkha Rifles (relieved by 1st Kashmir Rifles, 7th July 1919).
3/8th Gurkha Rifles (on the Samana).
2/9th Gurkha Rifles (relieved by 1/152nd Infantry, 9th July 1919).

Troops not belonging to the Kohat-Kurram Force, were gradually removed to other stations. The Headquarters of the 16th Division proceeded to Nowshera, where they were needed to deal with the expecting rising in the Swat Valley. On the 24th of June, Major-General A. Skeen took over command of the Kohat-Kurram Force, and formed a fresh headquarters. The movement of troops out of this area is given in the attached table.

Table showing withdrawal of additional units from Kohat.

Unit.	Date of leaving Kohat.	For.
H. Q. 16th Division	12th June	Nowshera.
2-6th Royal Sussex Regiment	16th June	Peshawar.
1-124th Baluchistan Regiment	19th June	Do.
45th Infantry Brigade	17th, 18th, 19th June	Nowshera.
1096th Battery, R. F. A.	19th June	Ambala.
1-151st Infantry	20th June	Chaklala.
1-5th Hampshire Regiment	22nd June	Simla Hills.
No. 3 Motor Machine Gun Battery	29th June	Ambala.
1 Section, Trench Howitzers	29th June	Ambala.
46th Brigade Ammunition column	29th June	Ambala.
2-7th Gurkha Rifles	7th July	Dehra Dun.
2-9th Gurkha Rifles	9th July	Do.

Two small operations were carried out against the Wazirs of the Kurram south of Thal by the 65th Infantry Brigade. The first took place on the 10th of June, when Lieut.-Colonel A. D. Strong with a force of one squadron of cavalry, one section of mountain artillery and one and a half battalions of infantry carried off a large quantity of grain, *bhoosa* and building material from Biland Khel.

The second was undertaken to punish the Wazirs south of Biland Khel. It was intended that the column should leave Thal on the 13th of July, but a spate in the river necessitated its departure being postponed till the 16th of July. On the latter date, the following troops left Thal under the command of Brigadier-General Tanner:—

Headquarters, 65th Infantry Brigade.
1 Pack Wireless Section.
"B" Squadron, 37th Lancers.
1 section, No. 3 Mountain Battery, R. G. A.
No. 23, Mountain Battery, less 1 section.
No. 57 Field Co., 1st S. and M., less 2 sections.
2 platoons, 1/81st Pioneers.
1/69th Punjabis.
2/151st Infantry.
3/9th Gurkha Rifles.
2 platoons, 1/90th Punjabis.
2 platoons, 1st Patiala Infantry.
1 section, No. 60 Combined, Field Ambulance.
Brigade Ammunition Column.

The column marched to Shewa (10 miles) which was reached on the same day, and a perimeter camp was formed. Parties were sent out to the surrounding villages and *bhoosa* grain and firewood were brought in without opposition. The sappers, assisted by infantry working parties, demolished Shewa itself. On the following morning, the 17th, a detachment was sent across the river, where they destroyed all the villages between Gulpir and Umar Khan, and burnt the *bhoosa* and grain there. On the 18th, the column commenced to withdraw by easy stages to Thal, destroying all the villages on the right bank of the Kurram River as they went. Dadar was reached on the 18th, Biland Khel on the 19th and Thal on the 20th. During these operations 54 villages were burnt and their towers destroyed.

The long drawn out negotiations which were taking place at Rawalpindi between the Afghan delegates and the representatives of the Government of India, were very unsettling to the tribesmen. They were convinced that the Amir was not in earnest, and that he was merely gaining time with a view to resuming hostilities. Two unsuccessful attempts were made by the Orakzais to tamper with the railway between Kohat and Thal. A party of some 400 tribesmen also attacked the Frontier Constabulary post at Shinawari, 18 miles north-west of Hangu, on the night of the 21/22nd of July, but they dispersed on the following day when columns from Fort Lockhart and Hangu marched out to its relief.

On the 30th of July, a report was received that a large body of Orakzais and Zaimukhts were collecting in the Khurmana Valley to raid the Kurram, and to attack the posts of Badama and Sadda. Reinforcements of regular troops were sent to Sadda, whilst four aeroplanes flew over the Khurmana to locate the gathering. On their way back, the last machine was shot down at short range by a party concealed on the hill side, and the pilot and observer were both wounded. A race for the wrecked machine then took place between the tribesmen and the Militia from Badama. The Militia just won, and the wounded airmen, who had roughly dismantled their machine, were brought in. The engine was brought in intact the following morning by a party of Kurram Militia from Badama, assisted by a detachment of regular troops from Sadda.

On the 8th of August, peace was signed at Rawalpindi and all activity in this area ceased.

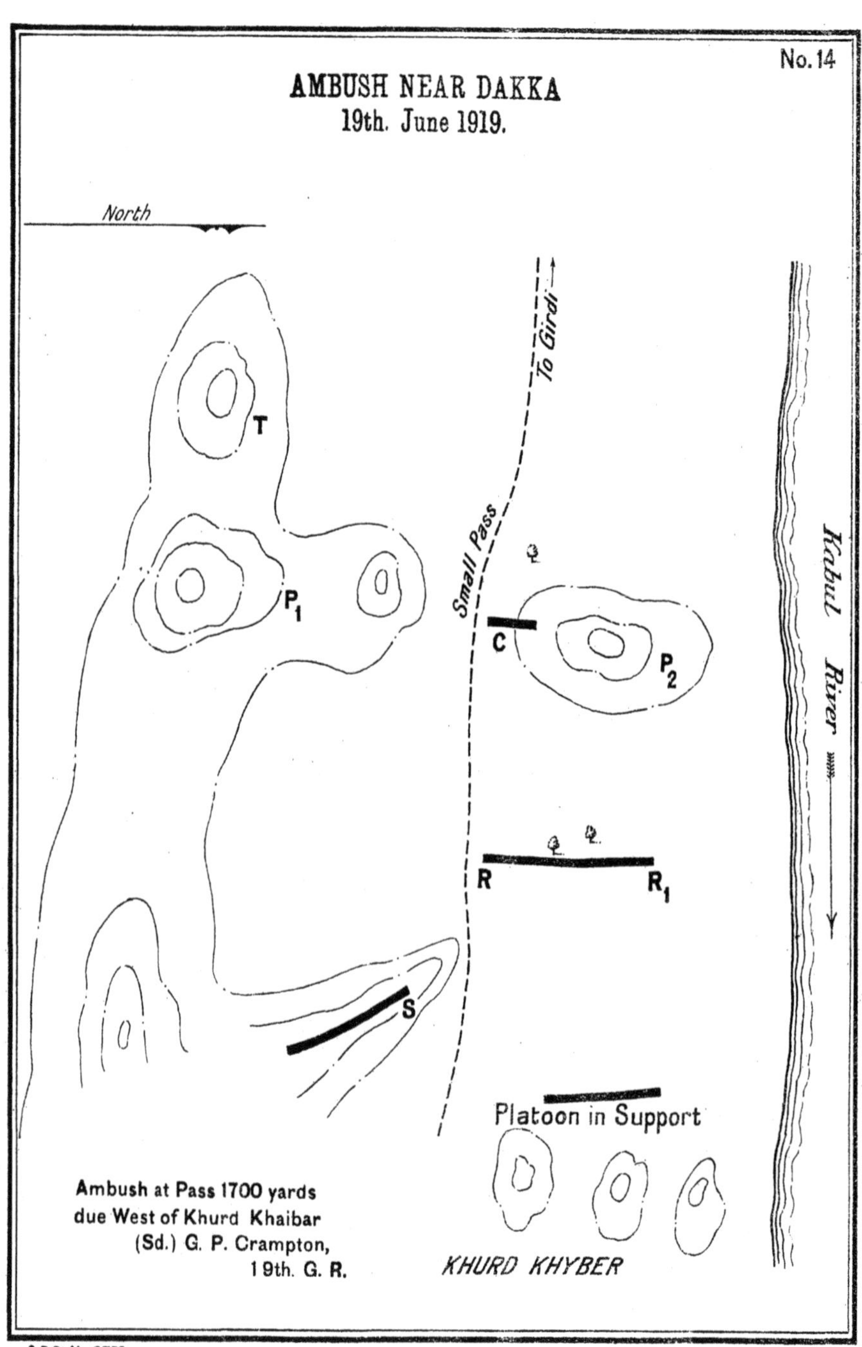

S.D.O. No. 3758

Heliozincographed at the Survey of India Offices, Dehra Dun.

Reg. No. 14 E. D. D. 1926 -1500

To face page 71

CHAPTER VII.

NORTHERN FRONT.—EVENTS BETWEEN THE 3RD OF JUNE AND THE 8TH OF AUGUST AND THE DESTRUCTION OF CHORA.

Although the armistice of the 3rd of June put an end to hostilities with Afghanistan, the inactivity to which our troops were condemned produced a rapid deterioration in the situation as regards the Pathan tribes. The Amir still continued to incite the tribes on both sides of the Durand Line to wage war on us, and his efforts met with considerable success. The Afghan Mohmands and Shinwaris, stirred up by the local priesthood, harassed our reconnoitring and foraging parties, sniped our camps at Dakka and Landi Khana and attacked our piquets. In the Khyber and in the Peshawar districts, bad characters of the Afridi tribe were active against our lines of communication, and raided the plains. The various actions fought during this period are better described by localities than in chronological order, and this chapter is therefore divided into three portions dealing with events:—

(*a*) West of Landi Kotal.

(*b*) In the Khyber.

(*c*) In the Peshawar Area.

WEST OF LANDI KOTAL.

Camp at Dakka. At Dakka, the new camp site proved to be much more suitable than the one originally selected. It was easy to protect, the sanitary conditions were good, and there was ample room for the whole force. The ground at first appeared to be a level stretch of turf, but it was soon found that the grass wore off and the surface was friable. The traffic passing over it quickly reduced it to powder, and the dust became intolerable. It soon became necessary to cover the roads with shale from the surrounding hills to prevent the camp from being smothered with dust. Even then dust storms were frequent, whilst the heat was very great. On the whole, however, the health of the troops was good.

In addition to physical trials, the tribesmen round Dakka never ceased to annoy our troops. The Mohmands from the north (left bank) of the Kabul river fired into camp nearly every night. This sniping was kept within bounds by the artillery and machine guns, who registered during the day on spots where the enemy were likely to conceal themselves, and opened fire when the flash of the rifle disclosed the position of the sniper.

The country to the west in the direction of Girdi was kept under observation by daily reconnaissances carried out by cavalry supported by infantry. It was seldom that these reconnaissances were not interfered with and that their retirement on camp was not followed up. To deal with this, General Skeen laid two ambushes, which were quite successful.

Special measures had to be devised to conceal the number of troops employed. All movements across the plain west of the Khurd Khyber were clearly visible to the enemy patrols on the north bank of the river, and the tribesmen at Girdi and Hazarnao to the south of the Kabul were informed of our movements by a series of signals. Thus, a single rifle shot indicated that the usual daily reconnaissance by a squadron of cavalry supported by infantry piquets was in progress. Two or more shots meant that a larger force was being employed. The enemy thus had the initiative, and could accept or decline action as they chose.

Tribesmen ambushed, 19th June.

The first of these ambushes was carried out on the 19th of June by a company of the 1/9th Gurkha Rifles under Captain G. P. Crampton. About 1 mile west of the Khurd-Khyber Pass (see map facing page 71) the road passes between two small features known as Conical Hill and Twin Peaks. The company assembled behind the Khurd Khyber and sent out two piquets, each of one section, to occupy these hills. One platoon then advanced through the Khurd-Khyber with 150 transport mules. Under cover of the dust raised by the animals, two platoons moved forward and concealed themselves behind Twin Peaks and Conical Hill. The mules under their escort then proceeded to graze in the open country between Conical Hill and the river. Seeing this, a party of 200 to 300 tribesmen advanced to within a thousand yards of the piquets. A squadron of the 1st King's Dragoon Guards then moved forward to the gap between the hills, and sent out a patrol to engage the enemy and to lure them on. The mules were then sent back to camp, whilst their escort remained to act as a reserve. As soon as the mules had disappeared through the Khurd Khyber, the cavalry also retired, and the two infantry piquets moved down just below the crest to give the impression that they also had evacuated their position. The enemy immediately began to follow up what they thought was the retirement. When the tribesmen had approached within 200 yards, the piquets rushed back to their previous position, the two platoons in hiding occupied the gap, and the whole opened fire. It was a complete surprise, and the enemy lost from 10 to 15 men killed before they could take cover. Meanwhile a party of tribesmen had moved towards Gurkha Hill and threatened to envelop the left flank of the company. The retirement to camp was, therefore, begun, which was cautiously followed by the enemy. We had no casualties in this engagement.

The tribesmen were much annoyed at having been outmanœuvred like this. A large body of Mohmands, who had been collected by the Haji of Turangzai and the Chaknaur Mulla, crossed to the south (right) bank of the Kabul river, and joined forces with the Shinwaris there. The camp piquets were fired on during the night of the 19/20th of June, and it was reported that an attempt would be made to attack the camp at Dakka on the evening of the 20th. General Skeen decided to forestall the enemy and to draw them into a fire ambush before the proposed attack could take place. Accordingly the following troops

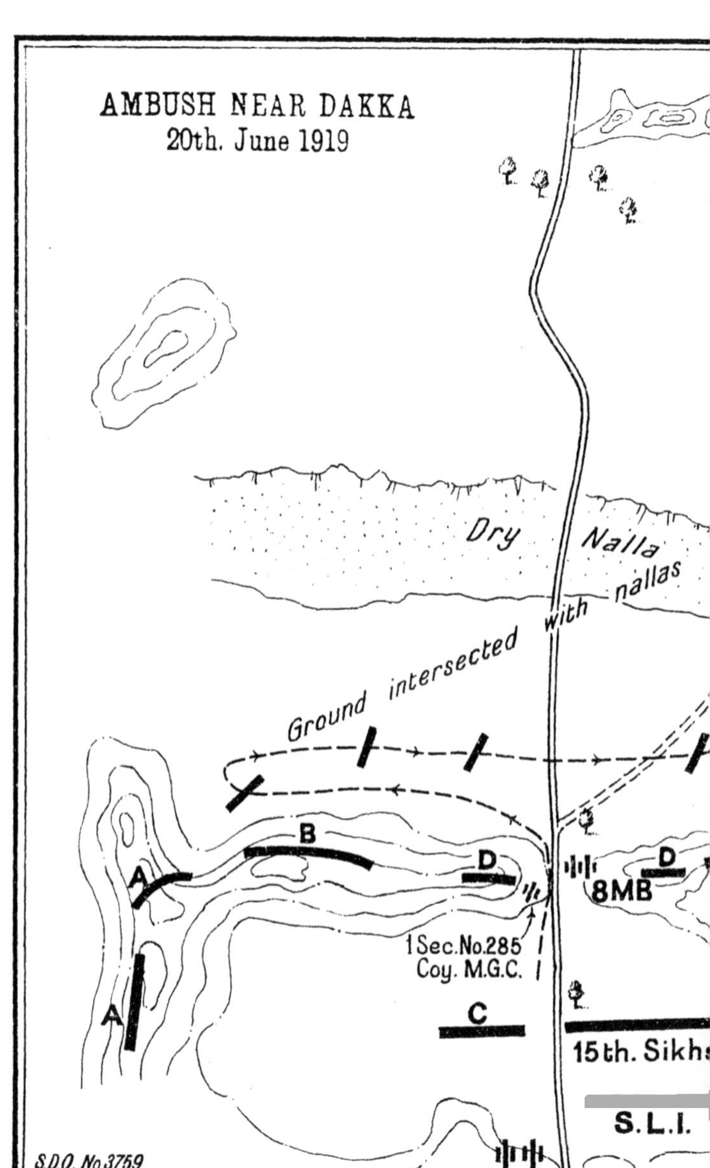

Reg No. 14 E. D. D. 1926 -1500.

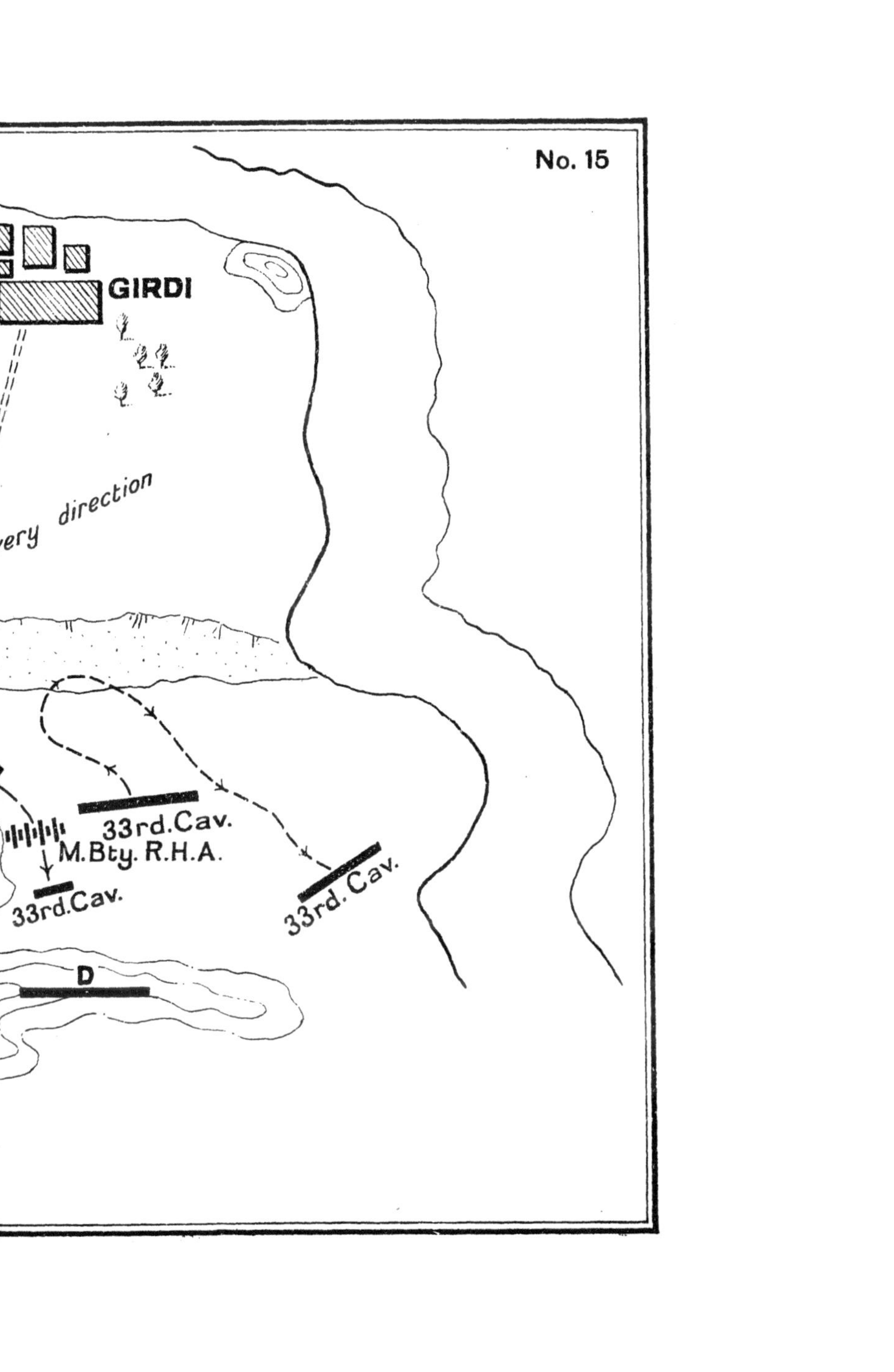
No. 15
GIRDI
very direction
33rd. Cav.
M. Bty. R.H.A.
33rd. Cav.
33rd. Cav.
D

were placed under Lieut.-Colonel Freeland, commanding the 1st Infantry Brigade, for this purpose:—

Headquarters, 1st Infantry Brigade.
2 squadrons, 33rd Cavalry.
2 sections, "M" Battery, R. H. A.
No. 8 Mountain Battery, R. G. A.
1 section, No. 285 Company, Machine Gun Corps.
2 companies, 2nd Bn., Somerset Light Infantry.
1/15th Sikhs, less 2 companies.
1/9th Gurkha Rifles.
2 sections, No. 6 Combined Field Ambulance.

Fire ambush, 20th June.

At 1300 hours, the 1/9th Gurkha Rifles left camp, and at 1430 hours, they occupied Conical Hill and Twin Peaks with 3 companies, whilst 1 company was kept in reserve to the south of the road and 500 yards east of Twin Peaks. As soon as these positions had been taken up, the headquarters of the 1st Infantry Brigade moved forward with No. 8 Mountain Battery, R. G. A., the section of No. 285 Company Machine Gun Corps and the 2 companies of the 1/15th Sikhs. One section of No. 8 Mountain Battery, R. G. A., was left on the Khurd Khyber Pass, whilst the 1/15th Sikhs came up level with the reserve company of the 1/9th Gurkha Rifles on the north of the road. The remaining four guns of No. 8 Mountain Battery, R. G. A. and the machine guns moved forward to the col. between Conical Hill and Twin Peaks. These troops were in position by 1515 hours. The enemy then started to leave their breast-works on Camel Hump Hill, west of Gildi, and to advance towards our piquets. Orders were issued for the remainder of the force to leave camp. The two squadrons of the 33rd Cavalry and the two sections of "M" Battery, R. H. A., moved through the Khurd-Khyber to a concealed position under the northern spur of Conical Hill, whilst the 2 companies of the 2nd Bn., Somerset Light Infantry, came up into reserve on the road between the Khurd Khyber and Conical Hill.

At 1645 hours, one squadron of the 33rd Cavalry advanced through the col. towards the west to draw the enemy on. Under cover of the dust, No. 8 Mountain Battery, R. G. A., took up a concealed position on the north side of the road to the west of the col., and the machine guns came into action in line with them on the south of the road. The tribesmen then advanced and opened fire on the cavalry. At 1720 hours the squadron in front reported that they were unable to advance further without sustaining casualties. They were then withdrawn rapidly across the front of the 1/9th Gurkha Rifles on to the other squadron, which was on the right of the line. Both squadrons then moved forward to tempt the tribesmen to advance still further, but it soon became evident that the ambush of the previous day had made them cautious. At 1840 hours, it was apparent that they could not be enticed nearer the piquets, so Colonel Freeland ordered No. 8 Mountain Battery, R. G. A., to fire one round from the col., which was the preconcerted signal for the action to commence. Guns, machine guns, Lewis guns and rifles kept up a concentrated fire for 15 minutes, and the enemy scattered in all directions. Their losses on this occasion were 30 killed and 25 wounded, whilst on our side Lieut. Hari Das, I.M.S., the medical officer of the 1/9th Gurkha

Rifles, was the only man wounded. On the following day the tribesmen dispersed to their homes and the troops at Dakka were not molested for a week.

Shinwaris attack piquet near Landi Khana.

Two days later, a party of Shinwaris under Zar Shah attacked the piquets near Landi Khana. Between the latter place and Dakka, two methods were in force for the protection of the road. Dakka Force had a system of permanent piquets up to a point half way between Haft Chah and Paindi Khak (see map facing this page), whilst the 2nd Infantry Brigade used to link up with Dakka Force by posting piquets daily before the convoy passed through. On the 22nd of June the battalion piquetting the road was the 2nd Bn., North Staffordshire Regt. The first three piquets were posted without any opposition. Nos. 4, 5 and 7 were then sent out together, whilst two platoons were in the valley ready to open covering fire should it be required. No. 4 piquet took up its allotted position, and No. 7 reached a point half way up the hill they were to occupy. The hill on which No. 5 piquet was to be posted had a double crest, from which two spurs ran, one to the north-east and one to the south-east. On this occasion the piquet was advancing in successive lines from the north-east. On reaching the false crest, the leading line of 6 men were fired on from the main crest, 30 yards to the south-west. Two men were killed out-right, two were mortally wounded, one was severely wounded, and the sixth man had a shot through his helmet. Without a moment's delay the covering party opened fire on the crest with Lewis guns and rifles. The remainder of No. 5 piquet moved to the right round the shoulder of the hill, and attacked the enemy up the reverse slope. Lieut. Bevill and 10 men from the reserve advanced up the south-easterly spur, and attacked from that side. This was too much for the tribesmen, and they made off to the south-west, where they came under the fire of No. 4 piquet. This drove them back in front of No. 5 piquet which was now in position. Here they suffered more casualties from the fire of No. 5 and No. 7 piquets. They then broke and fled to the high hill north of Shamas Kandao. From here they were dislodged by a section of No. 6 Mountain Battery, R. G. A., who had been pushed forward from Landi Khana as soon as the action commenced. The enemy lost 16 men killed or severely wounded whilst the casualties in the North Staffordshire were:—

Killed or died of wounds, 4.

Wounded—

Lieutenant Bevill.

British other rank, 1.

This affords a good example of troops taken at a disadvantage extricating themselves by their own courage and initiative. The covering fire was well organized, and ready when it was required. The shooting of the Lewis guns and rifles was good. This, combined with the promptness with which the piquet changed the direction of the attack whilst still continuing to advance, converted an awkward situation into a creditable victory.

As a result of this action, day piquetting in the Landi Khana section was discontinued, and permanent piquets were established. Although the tribesmen occassionally sniped the piquets and the road at long range, they never came to close quarters with the troops at Landi Khana during the remainder of the campaign.

Early in July, the tribesmen began to gather again west of Dakka, and to harass our foraging parties. On the 5th of July, a special reconnaissance was made as far as Hazarnao, 6½ miles west of Dakka. The tribesmen had constructed sangars north and south of the road near Girdi, but these were captured without much difficulty. A running fight was carried on from this point to Hazarnao, and many casualties were inflicted on the enemy. The retirement was followed up but a few rounds from the 77th Battery, R. F. A., soon discouraged the tribesmen, and the troops returned to camp with a loss of two men wounded.

Enemy attack piquets near Dakka.

On the 12th of July, a body of 800 tribesmen attempted to cut off the day piquets of the 2/1st Gurkha Rifles west of the Khurd-Khyber by advancing up the nala leading to Black Hill (see map facing page 49). It so happened that this company had placed additional piquets on West Ridge right in the path of the advancing enemy. The tribesmen attacked these piquets but they were beaten off after severe fighting. The tribesmen retired towards Gurkha Hill and towards Girdi. Our artillery obtained good targets, and were able to inflict casualties on the enemy during their flight. Our losses amounted to 5 killed and 7 wounded, whilst of the tribesmen 25 were killed and 21 were wounded.

A further attempt was made to ambush our piquetting troops on 23rd of July by a body of 500 to 600 tribesmen, who seized Twin Peaks early in the morning. The 1st Bn., Yorkshire Regiment, which was supplying the piquets, occupied West Ridge and Conical Hill without opposition, but the platoon detailed to hold Twin Peaks was held up. They were reinforced by a second platoon, and another attempt was made to seize the hill. A few men succeeded in reaching the summit, but they were unable to maintain their position and were compelled to retire. One company of the 2/1st Gurkha Rifles now arrived from camp, and the hill was attacked for the third time. The troops succeeded in reaching the summit but the enemy opened a heavy fire on them under cover of which a body of tribesmen charged and drove our men off the hill. The remaining three companies of the 2/1st Gurkha Rifles now came up, and a fourth attack was prepared. At 0915 hours, fire was opened on Twin peaks by 2 guns of No. 8 Mountain Battery, R. G. A., from Green Hill, and by 2 howitzers of the 77th Battery, R. F. A., and one howitzer (3·7″) of No. 8 Mountain Battery, R. G. A., from camp. The infantry then advanced and took the hill without much opposition.

Our losses in this engagement were:—

Killed—

Lieutenant H. E. Hare, Dublin Fusiliers, attached 1st Battalion, Yorkshire Regiment.

Subedar Tula Gurung, 2-3rd (attached 2-1st) Gurkha Rifles.

British other ranks, 4.

Indian other ranks, 3.

Wounded—

British other ranks, 9.

Indian other ranks, 5.

Of the enemy, 30 dead were counted on the spot, and their total casualties probably amounted to 150.

Peace signed. On the 24th of July, the Afghan peace delegates arrived in Dakka, and after this date the tribesmen on this front showed little activity. On the 25th of July, a flying bridge was put up across the Kabul River, and a bridge head was established on the left bank. After this, the sniping, which had been particularly irritating, practically died down.

Peace was signed at Rawalpindi on the 8th of August, but Dakka was not handed over to the Afghans until the 17th of September, when the troops of the 1st Division and the 1st Cavalry Brigade marched back to their peace stations.

KHYBER.

During June there was little activity on the part of the Afridis against our troops in the Khyber. Raiding gangs were active in the Peshawar plain, and the period of inactivity enforced on us by the armistice produced the usual unrest. Afghan agents in the Tirah and in the Bazar valley were active in formenting trouble and they found plenty of inflammable material in the men who had served in the Khyber Rifles. These *ex*-militia men were adventurous spirits, and their training made them dangerous. The focus of discontent was Chora, 7 miles south-west of Ali Masjid, where Yar Mohammed conducted his intrigues against the British.

About the middle of July, large bodies of Afridis gathered in the Bazar valley, south-west of Ali Masjid, and it was evident that an attack on this section of the Khyber was contemplated. On the 17th of July, the situation became so threatening that General Dobell, commanding the 2nd Division, closed the Khyber for animal convoys, and issued orders that no mechanical transport should move between Jamrud and Ali Masjid until armoured cars had patrolled the road and reported it to be clear of the enemy. On the following morning, the 18th, the Afridis attacked the Khyber posts from Bagiari to Ali Masjid (see map facing page 43).

Ali Masjid is situated in the narrowest part of the Khyber. The ground is so broken that it is not possible to locate a large body of troops in any one place. The 2/8th Gurkha Rifles less 2 companies, the rest camp and the mule transport were on the small piece of flat ground, half a mile south-east of the fort. The 1st Bn., Royal Sussex Regiment, one company, 1st Bn., South Lancashire Regiment, 2 companies, 2/8th Gurkha Rifles, No. 3 Mountain Artillery Brigade and the 2/33rd Punjabis, less detachments towards Landi Kotal were on the ridge north of Saiyid Ali. To the west of the road were the camps for the camels and the segregation camp. The 2/67th Punjabis were scattered in posts from Bagiari to Ali Masjid (both inclusive) with headquarters at Shagai.

Attack on Barley Hill piquet. At 0630 hours on the 18th of July, bands of Afridis began to fire on all the piquets in the vicinity of Fort Maude and Shagai. At 0645, a body of 300 to 400 tribesmen, many of them in the uniform of the Khyber Rifles, attacked the piquet on Barley Hill, 950 yards south of Fort Maude, which was held by one Indian Officer and 30 men of the 2/67th Punjabis. The enemy made several attempts to rush the piquet under a heavy covering fire, but they were beaten off by the garrison, aided by rifle fire from Fort Maude. At 0800 hours, there was a lull in the firing, so the Officer Commanding Fort Maude, sent forward three parties, amounting in all to one Indian Officer and 35 rifles, to reinforce the piquet, and to replenish their ammunition.

Lieutenant-Colonel T. Luck, commanding the 2/67th Punjabis, had left Shagai early in the morning to inspect his detachment in Ali Masjid Fort. On arriving there, he heard of the attack on Barley Hill, and asked the brigade for artillery support. He then hurriedly returned to Shagai (at 0815 hours), which was 2,000 yards from the piquet on Barley Hill. By this time all piquets from Orange Patch to Bagiari were threatened, and bodies of the enemy were seen descending from the Chora Kandao (pass).

At 0940 hours, orders were issued for 2 guns of No. 4 Mountain Battery, R. G. A., with an escort of 1 company of the 1st Bn., Royal Sussex Regiment, to proceed to Orange Patch ridge, and for 2 guns of No. 3 Mountain Battery, R. G. A., with 100 rifles of the 1st Bn., South Lancashire Regiment, to move to Shagai. Both of these parties passed the starting point, the mill on the main road, at 1030 hours. The section of No. 4 Mountain Battery came into action on Orange Patch ridge at 1110 hours. From their position they were unable to distinguish our troops from the enemy on Barley Hill, as the Khyber Rifle deserters were in khaki and had their bayonets fixed, whilst the tribesmen wore clothes dyed gray with a decoction made from the dwarf palm. This section, therefore, did not fire on Barley Hill, but expended a few rounds on a body of the enemy who were seen advancing from the direction of Chora Kandao.

At 1140 hours the ammunition in the piquet was nearly expended. A party of 17 rifles was left in the piquet, whilst the remainder evacuated the wounded and retired on Fort Maude. The Afridis then rushed the piquet and captured the 17 men in it, who had, by this time, fired off all their ammunition. They stripped their prisoners and took away 30 rifles. At 1145 hours the section of No. 3 Mountain Battery, R. G. A., arrived at Shagai, and opened fire on Barley Hill, which was now in the hands of the enemy. The first round scattered the Afridis whilst the prisoners all escaped in the confusion.

At 1425 hours, a small force consisting of 2 machine guns, 100 men of the 1st Bn., Royal Sussex Regiment, and 100 men of the 2/8th Gurkha Rifles were placed in the empty lorries of the down mechanical transport convoy, and sent to Fort Maude to recapture Barley Hill. This was accomplished without any casualties at 1645 hours.

Our losses in this action were:—

Killed—

Jemadar Mohammed Hassan.
Indian other ranks, 8.

Wounded—

Indian other ranks. 25.
all of the 2/67th Punjabis.

The failure to provide artillery and infantry support to the piquet on Barley Hill was due to a variety of causes. The actual number of Afridis who had gathered to attack our posts was about 6,000. Not one, but every piquet south and west of the road was threatened by them, and less than a tenth of their total strength were actually engaged against Barley Hill. It was expected that their principal effort would be directed on Orange Patch, which is the most important tactical feature in the locality. It was not until too late that it was realized where their main attack was taking place. There was no necessity to have pushed out guns to Orange Patch ridge and to Shagai, for the range from the camp near Saiyid Ali was only 4,500 yards, although it was nearly six miles by road. The artillery scheme, which had been prepared for the defence of the outlying piquets, should have been put into operation at once, but it appears to have been overlooked owing to the anxiety of the local command for the security of Orange Patch. The infantry brigade headquarters in Ali Masjid fort and the artillery brigade headquarters near Saiyid Ali were three quarters of a mile apart, and, although they were connected by telephone, it would have been better to have established a battle headquarters at Saiyid Ali. The smallness of the striking force available was due to the large number of piquets which had to be supplied for the defence of the road and of the numerous camps necessitated by the configuration of the ground. Had it been realized earlier that the main attack was on Barley Hill, and had the artillery plan which had been prepared beforehand been put into operation, the attack on Barley Hill could not have been successful. It is impossible not to admire the courage of the men of the Khyber Rifles who assaulted the piquet, and the skill with which they carried out the operation. Their covering fire was well organized, and their attacks were pressed home with determination. When they had taken the position, they set up a captured helio and called up our stations out of sheer bravado. Their losses were considerable, as 50 men were killed and 60 severly wounded.

At 2000 hours the Afridis again began to harass the piquets, this time extending their efforts as far as Katakushta 1½ miles north of Ali Masjid. Determined attacks were made on No. 4 piquet on Orange Patch ridge, which was held by 30 men of the 1st Bn., Royal Sussex Regiment. The enemy penetrated the barbed wire fence three times, only to be counter-attacked and driven off by bombs and by the bayonet. Three attacks were also made on the Ropeway Construction camp, which was held by 2 platoons of the 2/33rd Punjabis and by No. 26 and No. 27 Railway Companies, 1st Sappers and Miners, but the enemy were driven off without any loss on our side. A less determined attempt was made to take the piquet on hill 2617, half-way between Fort Maude and Bagiari, and this proved equally abortive.

Column sent to the Khyber.

On hearing of the fighting in the Khyber, General Dobell sent forward the following troops from Peshawar to clear up the situation and to open the road:—

To Kacha Garhi—

2 squadrons, 30th Lancers

To Jamrud—

74th Battery, R. F. A., less 1 section.

89th Battery, R. F. A. (only 3 guns owing to shortage in personnel).

No. 222 Company Machine Gun Corps, less 1 section.

1 composite battalion from the 44th Infantry Brigade.

On the 19th of July, a column under Major General S. H. Shepherd, C.B., C.M.G., D.S.O., commanding the 5th Infantry Bde. consisting of—

1 squadron, 30th Lancers,

74th Battery, R. F. A., less 1 section,

No. 222 Company, Machine Gun Corps, less 1 section,

1 Armoured Car Battery,

1/61st Pioneers,

2/61st Pioneers, less 2 companies,

3/39th Garhwal Rifles,

left Jamrud and proceeded up the Khyber. A few tribesmen were seen near the mouth of the pass, but they dispersed. At 0900 hours, the column reached Fort Maude, where they were joined by 2 machine guns, 100 men of the 1st Bn., Royal Sussex Regiment and 100 men of the 2/8th Gurkha Rifles from Ali Masjid. The road had thus been cleared, and our convoys were able to move along it. About 1200 hours, a party of some 700 tribesmen were seen in the low ground south of Barley Hill. Arrangements were made to attack this body, but they withdrew through Shudana to Chora Kandao. The 74th Battery, R. F. A., less 1 section and No. 222 Company, Machine Gun Corps, then moved forward to Ali Masjid, and the remainder of the troops returned to their respective camps.

After this, with the exception of an occasional sniper, there was no enemy action in the Khyber during the campaign. Yar Mohammed still remained to be dealt with, and although the operations against his fort at Chora took place after peace was signed, they can be fittingly included in this book, as they were undertaken as a punishment for his acts of hostility during the campaign. It was decided to destroy this fort, and careful preparations were made to ensure the success of the undertaking. The garrison of Ali Masjid was reinforced by the following units:—

1 section, No. 60 Battery, R. G. A. (6″ howitzers tractor drawn).

No. 11 Field Company, 2nd Sappers & Miners.

1st Bn., South Lancashire Regiment.

2/35th Sikhs.

Destruction of Chora Fort.

A road, 3 miles long, was constructed for the artillery following the alignment of the mule track from the Khyber stream near Ali Masjid to Chora. Many reconnaissances were made, artillery and piquet positions were chosen, and the plan of operations was

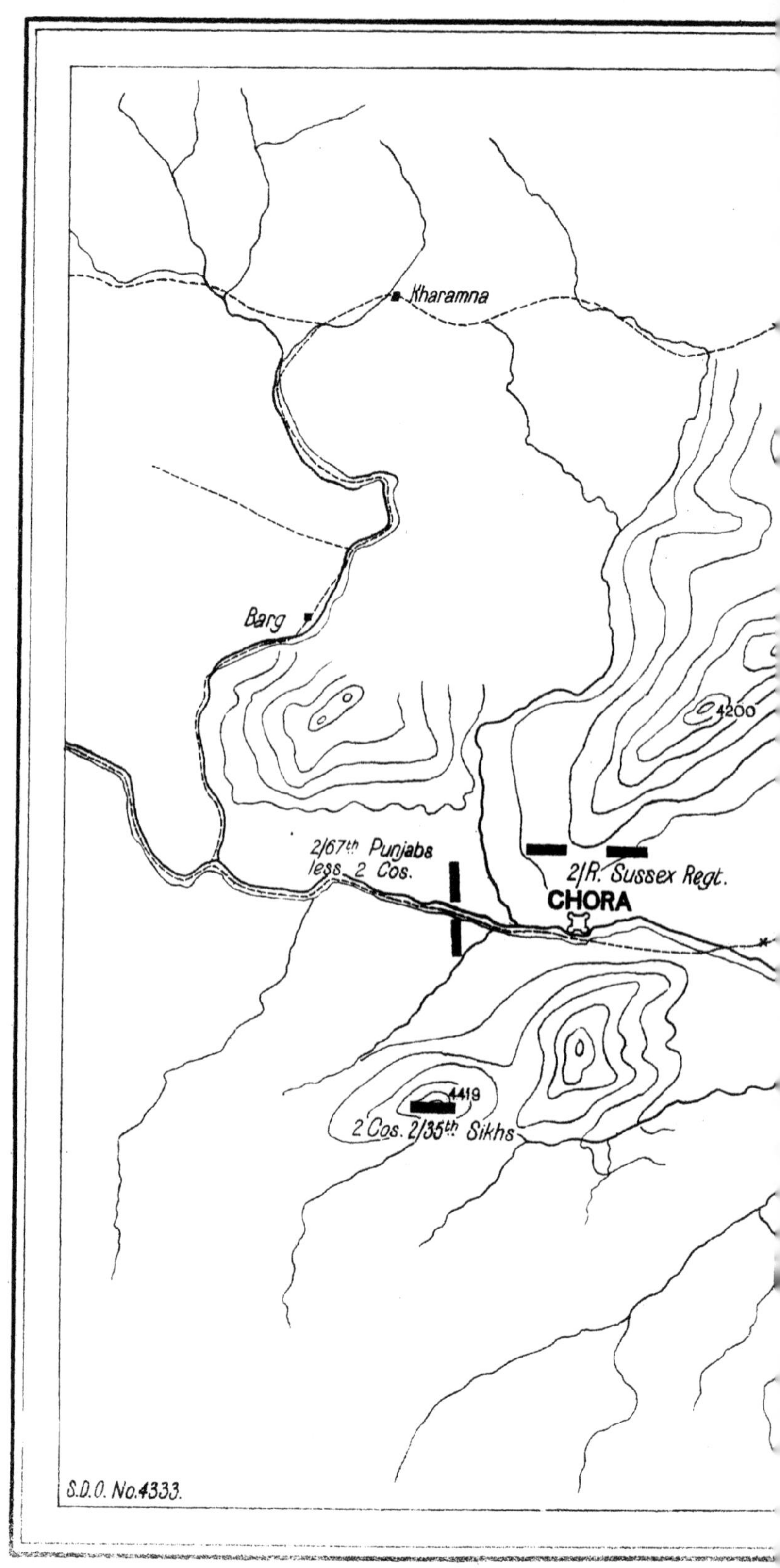

Reg. No. 14 E. D. D. 1926 -1500

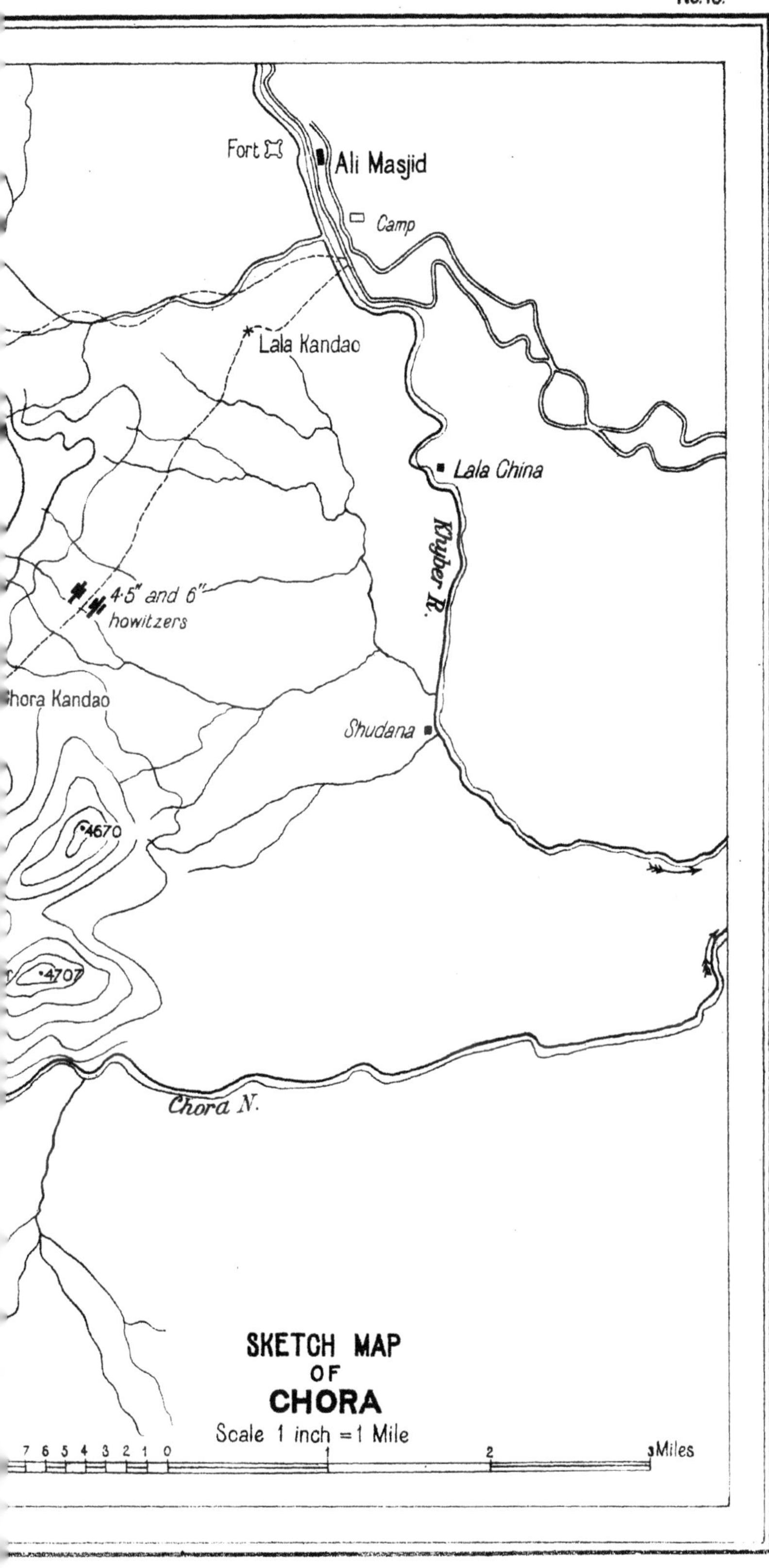

Heliozincographed at the Survey of India Offices, Dehra Dun

To face page 70

thoroughly understood by all commanders. Brigadier-General G. A. H. Beatty, C.M.G., D.S.O., commanding the 6th Infantry Brigade took charge of the operation, which was timed for the 13th of September. The distribution of the troops was as follows:—

Advanced Guard—

Commanding Lieut.-Col. W. K. Bourne, 2/35th Sikhs.

Troops—No. 4 Mountain Bty., R. G. A., less 1 section (2·75″ guns).

No. 222 Coy., Machine Gun Corps, less 3 sections.

2/35th Sikhs.

Main Body—

Headquarters, 6th Infantry Brigade.

1st Bn., Royal Sussex Regiment, less 2 companies.

1 section, No. 4 Mountain Battery, R. G. A. (3·7″ howitzers).

1 section No. 222 Co., Machine Gun Corps.

2/67th Punjabis

60 water mules.

No. 11 Field Co., 2nd Sappers & Miners.

Tehri-Garhwal Sappers.

74th Battery, R. F. A., less 1 section, with its escort, 1 platoon, 2/33rd Punjabis.

200 men of the Labour Corps.

No. 13, Combined Field Ambulance.

Brigade Ammunition Column.

Rear guard—

Commanding, Lieut.-Col. Willoughby-Osborne, 1st South Lancs. Regiment.

1st Bn., South Lancashire Regiment, less 2 companies.

70 water camels.

Right & Left Flank guards—

2/33rd Punjabis, less 2 platoons.

The two 6″ howitzers with their escort of 1 platoon of the 2/33rd Punjabis followed the rear-guard.

The troops fell in at midnight on the 12/13th of September and, at 0200 hours, the head of the main body passed through our outposts at Lala Kandao, 1¼ miles south-west of Ali Masjid fort. At 0345 hours, the advanced guard reached the point 1 mile east of the Chora Kandao where the 4·5″ and 6″ howitzers were to come into action. Meanwhile the 2/33rd Punjabis less 2 companies under Lieutenant-Colonel A. L. Barrett had advanced up the Alarchi Kandao, and had seized the high hills known as points 4687, 4750 and 4200, between the Alarchi and Chora Kandaos (passes). Major S. Williams, with 2 companies, less 2 platoons of the 2/33rd Punjabis, had also moved down the Khyber Nala to Shudana, and from there had occupied hills 4670 and 4707 (Zera Sar) south of the Chora Kandao. One of the 4·5″ howitzers broke down on the road, but the remaining three took up a position 1 mile north-east of the pass, whilst the two 6″ howitzers came into action on the road, 1 mile from the pass. With each of these artillery detachments was an escort of 1 platoon of the 2/33rd Punjabis.

At 0420 hours, the advanced guard came into contact with 30 to 40 tribesmen on the Chora Kandao. These gave little trouble, and the march was resumed at 0510 hours. Descending from the pass, it was found that the enemy were occupying the small village of Sara Garhi, 1½ miles east of Chora, where the track from Ali Masjid meets the stream and takes a turn to the west. At 0630 hours, the 3·7″ howitzer section of No. 4 Mountain Battery, R. G. A., came into action on the Chora Kandao, and fired on Sara Garhi and on Chora fort. The R. A. F. also bombed Chora, but one machine was shot down, and the pilot and observer were captured. At 0645 the R. A. F. began to register the 6″ howitzers, but their wireless was out of order, and they withdrew to refit.

At 0720 hours, Sara Garhi was occupied, and at 0840 hours the fort was bombarded for 20 minutes by all the howitzers. The shooting was very effective, and the 6″ howitzers alone secured 11 direct hits, which did much damage.

For the protection of the troops who were to carry on the demolition, detachments were placed on all four sides of Chora. No. 4 Mountain Battery, less 1 section, No. 222 Company Machine Gun Corps less 3 sections, and the 2/35th Sikhs less 2 companies took up a position near Sara Garhi. Two Companies of the 2/35th Sikhs crossed the Nala and occupied Hill 4419 to the south. The 1st Bn., Royal Sussex Regiment, less 2 companies and one section of No. 4 Mountain Battery, R. G. A., extended between Chora and Hill 4200 to protect the fort from the north, whilst the 2/67th Punjabis, less 2 companies moved up the nala to deal with any enemy advancing from the west. The 1st Bn., South Lancashire Regiment, less 2 companies, and 2 companies of the 2/67th Punjabis formed the general reserve near Sara Garhi.

At 0945 hours, Chora was occupied, and, at 1000 hours, No. 11 Company, 2nd Sappers & Miners and the Tehri Sappers started to prepare the fort for demolition under the direction of Major C. J. S. King, R.E. At 1400 hours everything was prepared and the charges were exploded. Owing to defective fuzes, 12 of these failed to go off. Work was again commenced and at 1530 hours three more explosions took place and Chora fort was levelled to the ground.

The withdrawal then began, and was carried out in successive lines.

1st Line.—Sara Garhi.

1st Bn., Royal Sussex Regiment, less 2 companies.

2 companies, 2/35th Sikhs.

1 section, No. 222 Company, Machine Gun Corps.

2nd Line.—Half-way between Sara Garhi and Chora Kandao.

1 section, No. 4 Mountain Battery, R. G. A.

1 section, No. 222 Company, Machine Gun Corps.

1st Bn., South Lancashire Regiment, less 2 companies.

3rd Line.—Chora Kandao.

2/67th Punjabis, less 2 companies.

1 section, No. 222 Company, Machine Gun Corps.

The remainder of the troops moved straight back to Ali Masjid. At 1815 hours all troops were beyond the Chora Kandao, and by 2200 hours the last man had passed through the outposts at Lala Kandao. But for the foresight of the commander, the troops might have suffered from thirst. To prevent this, two canvas tanks, each with a capacity of 2,300 gallons, were placed near the 6″ howitzers, and these were kept filled by the convoy of 70 camels carrying small galvanized iron tanks. Arrangements were also made for drawing and chlorinating water at Chora.

Our casualties from enemy action during the day were 1 Indian other rank killed and 5 wounded. In addition to this, 5 Indian other ranks and 2 followers were killed whilst examining an aeroplane bomb near the wrecked machine.

PESHAWAR.

Whilst the Afridis only occasionally attacked our line of communication through the Khyber, gangs of this tribe raided the villages in the Peshawar plain almost daily. Bands of them even penetrated Peshawar itself, and there were few nights when shots were not fired either in the city or in cantonments.

Early in June, the village of Badhber, on the Kohat road, 6 miles south of Peshawar, began to harbour raiders and also to join them in robbing the neighbouring villages. On the night of the 6/7th of June, Brigadier-General L. W. Y. Campbell, commanding the Peshawar Area, took out a column consisting of:—

30 Lancers,

1 section, 90th Battery, R. F. A.,

1 Armoured Car Battery,

and surrounded Badhber in the dark. At dawn the civil authorities entered the village, arrested several bad characters, and seized a quantity of arms of all descriptions. After this the inhabitants of Badhber ceased to give trouble.

During the next few days, there were a few minor actions on the Bara road. On the 20th of May, a patrol of the 17th Cavalry arrested 5 armed Mohmand raiders on the Michni road. The squadron to which the patrol belonged was raised from the local Khalil Pathans, and it was due to their intimate knowledge of the people of the district that these men were arrested.

The Afridi raiders had made their headquarters on the Besai ridge. This feature runs out like a finger into the plain from near the junction of the Bazar and Khyber Nalas, 3 miles south-west of Jamrud, to Narai Khwar Police Station, 5 miles south-east of Jamrud (see map facing this page). To the north is a barren stretch of level ground reaching to the Peshawar-Jamrud road, whilst to the south is the Kajuri plain, the winter headquarters of the Sipah Afridis. To the east are the highly cultivated lands, irrigated by the waters of the Bara river, which are held by the Kuz, or Bara, Mohmands. These latter should not be confused with their kinsmen north of the Kabul river, from whom they separated 150 years ago.

Drive across Kajuri plain.

It was decided to seize the Besai ridge, and to round up any gangs found in the Kajuri plain. Infantry were to be employed to hold the ridge and the line of the Narai Khwar and the Bara river, whilst cavalry were to form a line from just south of Jamrud to the Bara river. The mounted troops were then to move east and to drive any enemy found on the plain on to the infantry cordon. Three columns and a reserve were collected for this purpose on the night of the 20/21st of June to converge on the area from different directions—

Northern Column (Jamrud)—

Commanding—Lt.-Colonel C. M. Hawes, D.S.O., M.V.O.

Troops—

1 squadron, 12th Cavalry.

1 squadron, 17th Cavalry.

23rd Cavalry, F. F.

1 armoured car battery.

3/39th Garhwal Rifles.

Southern Column (Ilm Gudr)—

Commanding—Lt.-Colonel W. Gledstanes.

Troops—

30th Lancers.

1st Battalion, South Lancashire Regiment.

Infantry Column (Kacha Garhi)—

Commanding—Lt.-Colonel W. K. Bourne.

Troops—

1 armoured car battery.

2/35th Sikhs.

3/5th Gurkha Rifles.

Bearer sub-division No. 12, C. F. A.

Reserve (Bara)—

74th Battery, R. F. A., less 1 section.

1 section, 90th Battery, R. F. A.

1 armoured car battery.

2/4th Border Regiment, less 2 companies.

No. 17

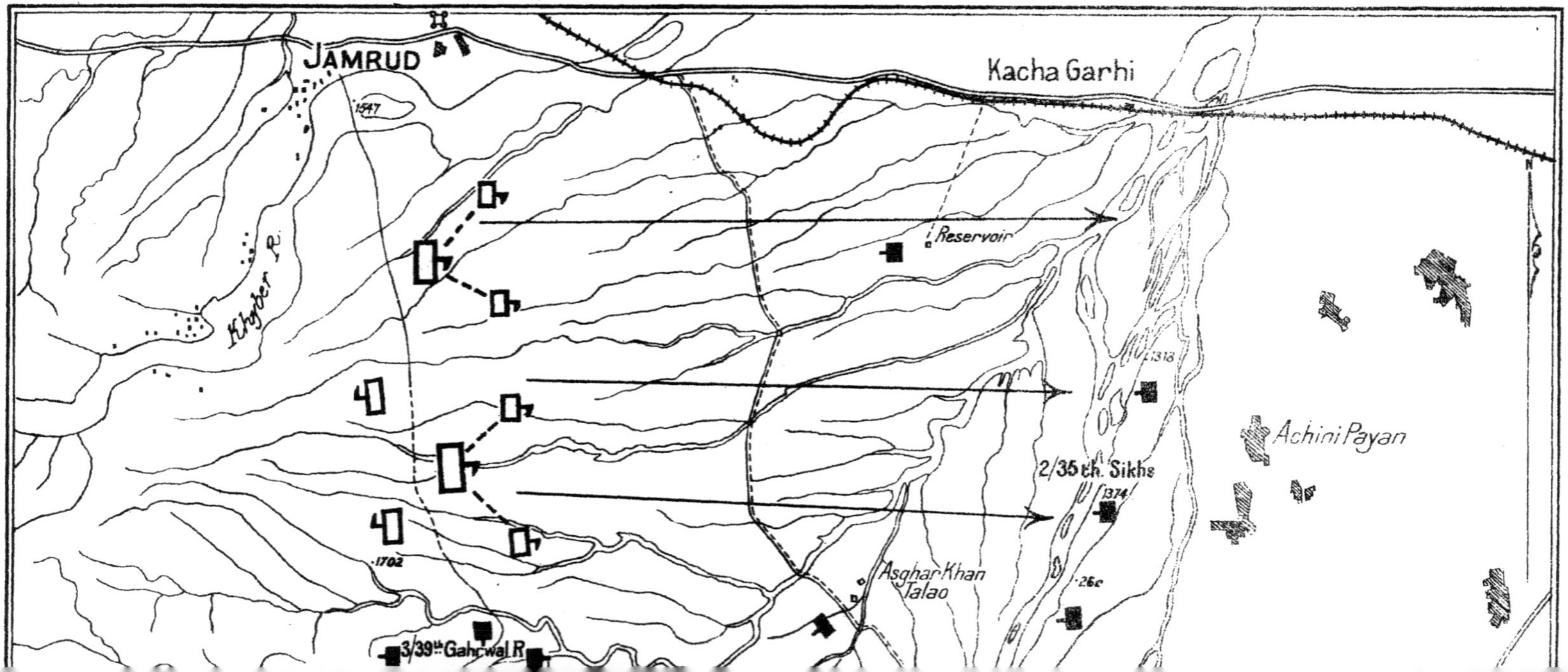

JAMRUD
Kacha Garhi
1547
Reservoir
Khyber R.
1318
Achini Payan
2/35th. Sikhs
1374
1702
Asghar Khan Talao
26c
3/39th Gahrwal R.

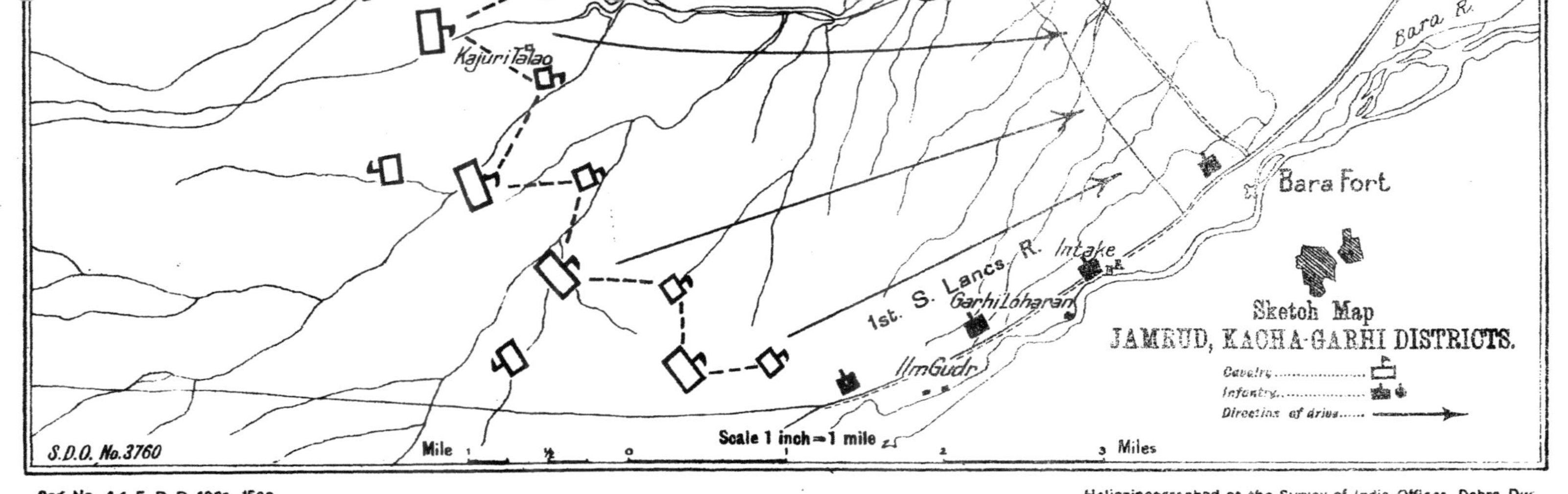

Reg. No. 14 E. D. D. 1926–1500

Heliozincographed at the Survey of India Offices, Dehra Dun.

To face page 83

At 0400 hours on the 21st of May, the Northern Column reached the mouth of the Samghakhai defile. The infantry seized the pass and the heights east and west of it. A few shots were fired at them from long range, but no enemy were actually seen. The cavalry passed through the defile at 0600 hours, and joined hands with the cavalry of the Southern Column at Kajuri Talao, where the latter had arrived at 0430 hours.

The Southern Column passed Bara Fort at 0230 hours, and moved on to Ilm Gudr. The South Lancashires piquetted the line of the Bara river from the waterworks intake to beyond Ilm Gudr, whilst the 30th Lancers moved north to link up with the Northern Column.

The Infantry Column left Kacha Garhi about midnight, and advanced down the Narai Khwar, which they secured by placing piquets along it. The 3/5th Gurkha Rifles then climbed the steep sides of Besai Hill and posted piquets on this spur. At 0650 hours all troops were in position, and the signal for the drive to commence was given by firing two white and one red Very light from Besai. The cavalry then advanced towards the east. A body of 200 to 300 armed men were seen south of our piquets on the Bara river, outside the area of the drive. The armoured car battery from the reserve at Bara and a squadron of the 30th Lancers were detached to engage this party. The armoured cars advanced and opened machine gun fire at a range of 1,500 yards. The enemy then disappeared into the surrounding nalas before the cavalry could come up, and they were not seen again.

At 0930 hours, the cavalry reached the line of the Bara river and the Narai Khwar. The Northern Column took no prisoners, but the Southern Column captured 30 men, who claimed to be sepoys of the South Waziristan Militia returning from leave.

The results were disappointing. Had the area south of Ilm Gudr been included in the drive, as was originally intended, the country might have been cleared of the large gang fired on by the armoured cars. This portion had been excluded at the instance of the Chief Commissioner with unsatisfactory results. The raiding went on unchecked. Ilm Gudr was twice surrounded, on the 26th of June and the 13th of July, but no raiders were found.

On the 19th of July, the day after the attack on Barley Hill, two columns were sent out to discover whether there were any Afridi gangs on the Kajuri plain. The first went from Kacha Garhi to the Samghakhai pass, but failed to find any enemy. The second, which was composed of 2 squadrons of the 23rd Cavalry F. F. and No. 15 Motor Machine Gun Battery, moved from Bara due west across the Kajuri plain. They found a body of 500 tribesmen on Karawal Hill, $7\frac{1}{2}$ miles west of Bara fort. On the 20th and 21st, this party was still there, so it was decided to attack the hill on the 22nd of July.

Ation o Karawal.

The Kajuri plain is shaped like a horse's hoof, the frog being Karawal Hill, which divides the western portion. On the south-eastern spur, and 1,200 yards from the summit, is a small tower. On the 22nd the hill was held by about 200 Afridis. To attack this position, two columns were formed, one at Bara and one at Kacha Garhi. Their composition was:—

Bara Column—

Commanding, Major C. S. Cameron, 23rd Cavalry, F. F.

23rd Cavalry, F. F.

2 squadrons, 30th Lancers.

1 section, 89th Battery, R. F. A.

2 armoured motor batteries.

4 motor ambulances.

Kacha Garhi Column—

Commanding, Lt.-Colonel W. K. Bourne, 2/35th Sikhs.

1 squadron, 30th Lancers.

1 section, 90th Battery, R. F. A.

1 armoured motor battery.

3/5th Gurkha Rifles.

2 companies, 2/35th Sikhs.

4 motor ambulances.

Brigadier-General L. W. Y. Campbell was in command of the operation, with headquarters at Bara.

At 0200 hours, the Kacha Garhi column moved out, and arrived at the Samghakhai pass at 0555 hours. This was found to be occupied by about 100 tribesmen. The 3/5th Gurkha Rifles advanced under the fire of the section of the 90th Battery, R. F. A., and captured the defile with little loss. The enemy retired towards the west and disappeared. The squadron of the 30th Lancers then crossed over to the Kajuri Plain, and linked up with the cavalry of the Bara Column, which was advancing from the east. The whole of the cavalry then attacked Karawal Hill, supported by the fire of the section of the 89th Battery, R. F. A. The three squadrons of the 30th Lancers advanced from the north-east, the headquarters and one squadron of the 23rd Cavalry, F. F., from the east, whilst three squadrons of the 23rd Cavalry, F. F., were ordered to move by Ashgar Talao, and then to wheel and to attack from the south west. The armoured cars proceeded to Mukha, 3 miles west (and in rear) of Karawal Hill. These three squadrons of the 23rd Cavalry, F. F., kept their direction as far as Ashgar Talao, but instead of wheeling and coming up behind the hill, they got their left shoulders too far forward and came up against the tower on the south eastern spur. They were withdrawn, and another attempt was made to get round the enemy flank, but this movement was again not wide enough. Meanwhile the action of the 30th Lancers to the north drove the enemy to the south-west, where they came under the fire of the machine guns of the armoured cars. The 23rd Cavalry, F. F., then joined hands with the 30th Lancers, and the hill was swept from west to east without finding any trace of the enemy. About 1630 the columns withdrew to Kacha Garhi and to Peshawar.

SKETCH MAP OF

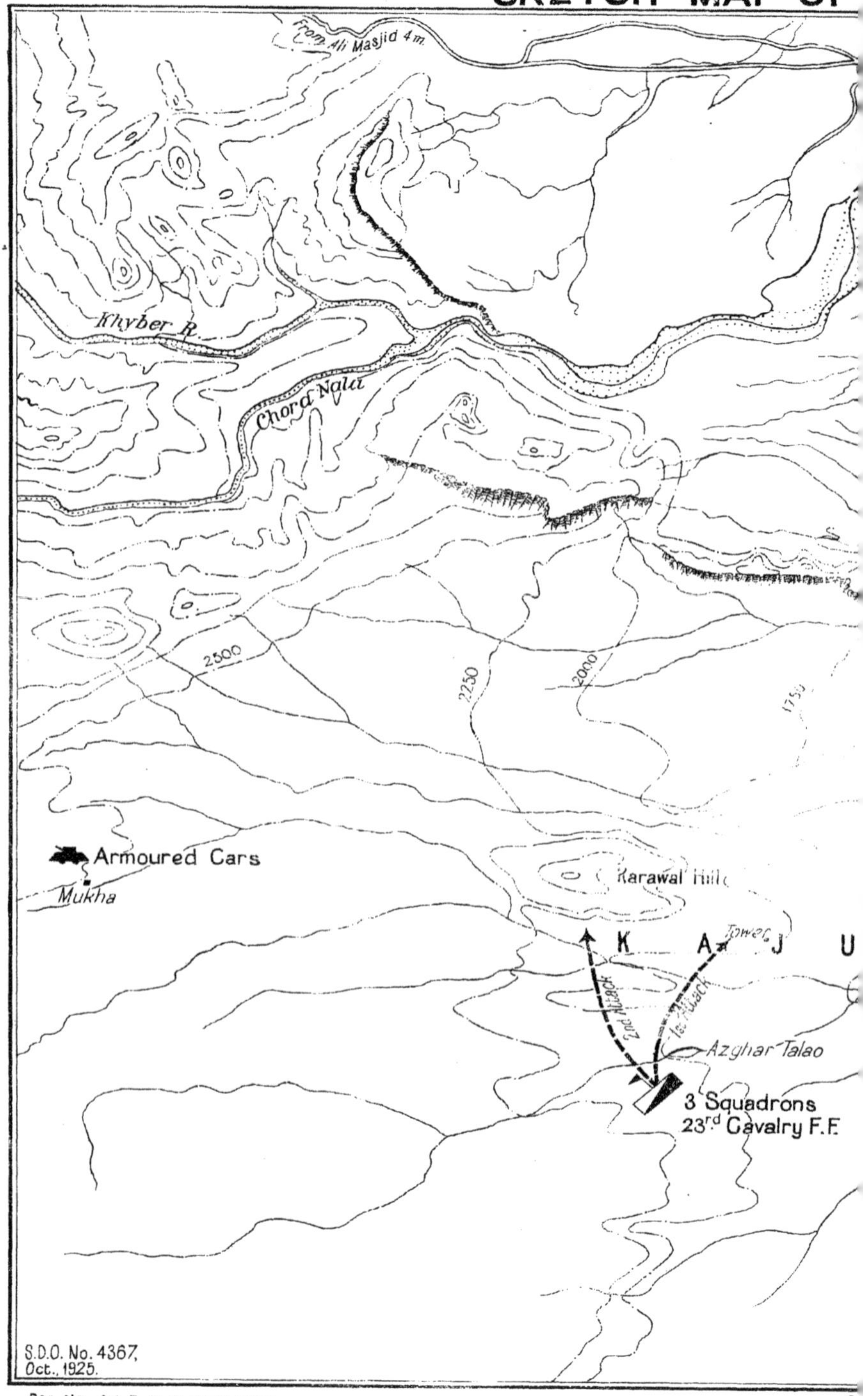

Reg. No. 14 E. D. D. 1926 -1500

AL 22nd JULY 1919

No.18

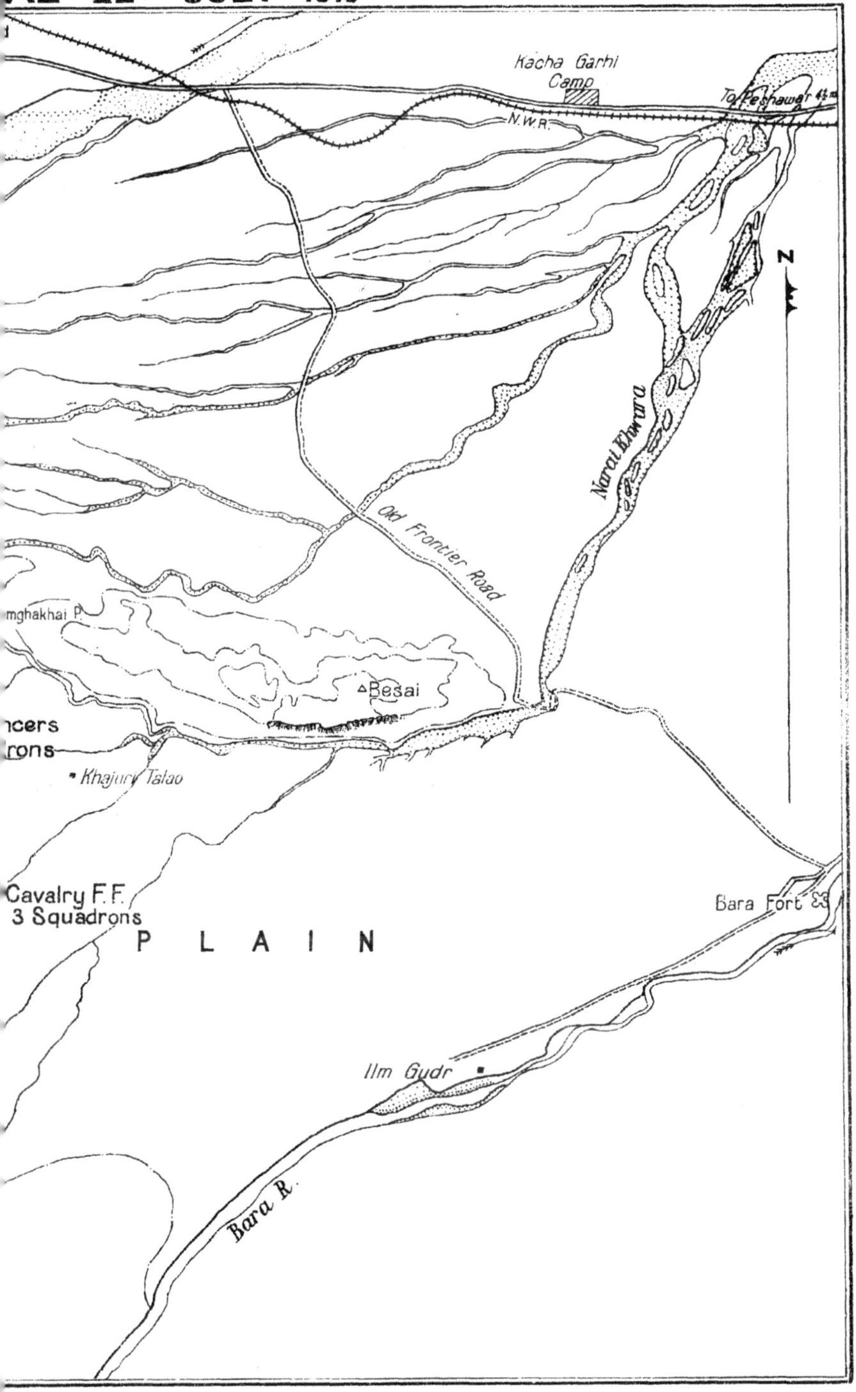

Kacha Garhi Camp

To Peshawar 4½ m

N.W.R.

N

Narai Khwara

Old Frontier Road

mghakhai P.

Besai

ncers
rons

Khajuri Talao

Cavalry F.F.
3 Squadrons

P L A I N

Bara Fort

Ilm Gudr

Bara R.

e.

2 3 Miles

Heliozincographed at the Survey of India Offices, Dehra Dun

To face page. 85

Our casualties during the day were:—

Wounded—

1 Indian other rank.

1 follower.

Died of heatstroke—

Indian other ranks 3,

all of the 3/5th Gurkha Rifles.

After this the raiding gradually died down. This was largely due to a fall of rain in the Tirah, which made the Afridis anxious to plough their lands to get them ready for sowing the spring crops. The return to normal conditions was gradual, but after the signing of peace on the 8th of August, the civil authorities were able to deal with the situation, and to resume political control over the Afridis.

No.19.

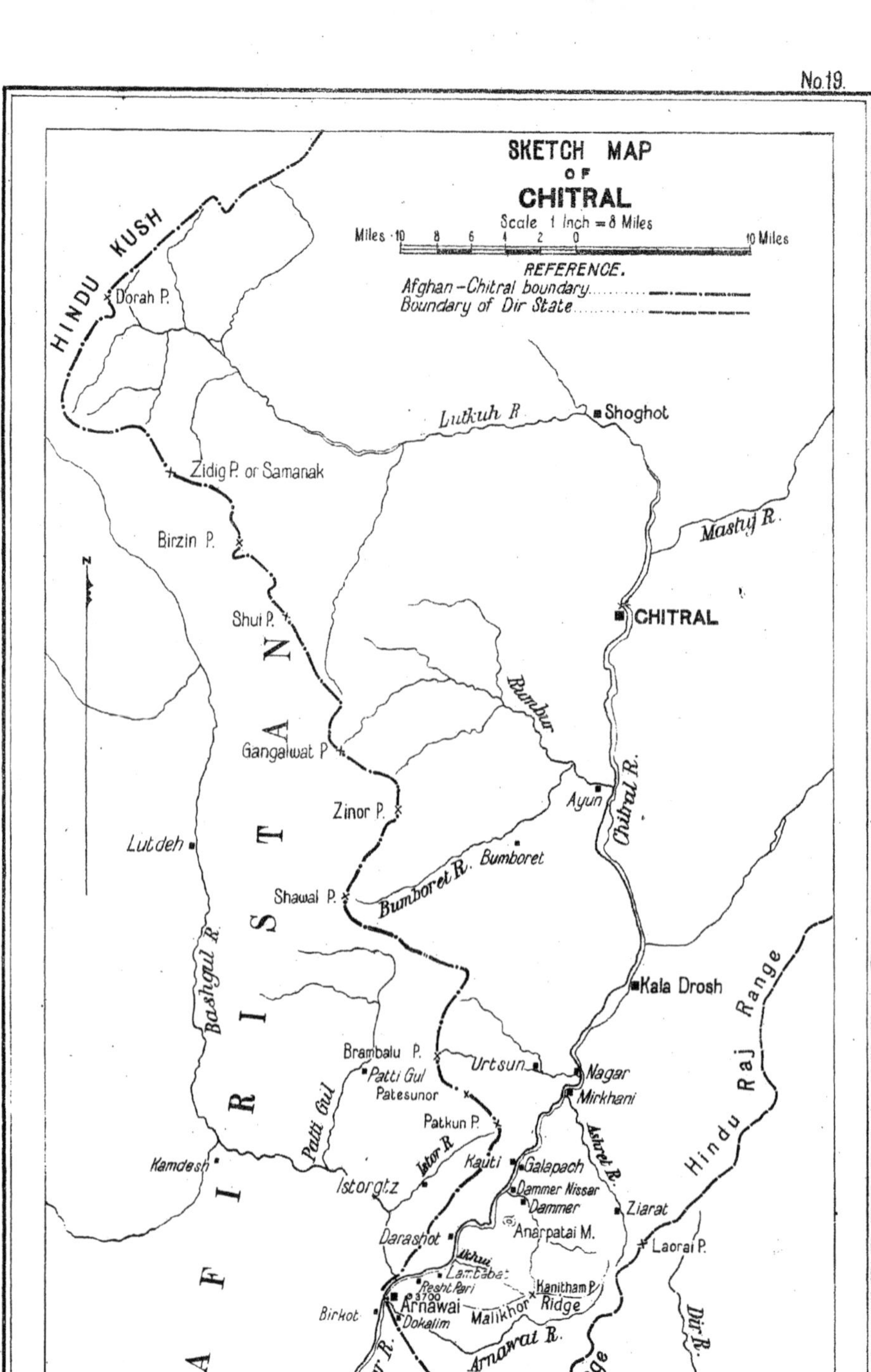

Reg No. 14 E. D D. 1926 -1500

Heliozincographed at the Survey of India Offices, Dehra Dun.

To face page 87

CHAPTER VIII.

NORTHERN FRONT—EVENTS IN CHITRAL.

Chitral is so shut off from India that operations there bear little relation to the remainder of the campaign. It is a bleak, highland country formed by the ridges and spurs of the Eastern Hindu Kush. Its rivers and streams carry the waters from the glaciers of the Central Asian mountain system into the Chitral River. This is known as the Kunar in its lower reaches after its entry into Afghanistan near Arnawai, and joins the Kabul River near Jalalabad.

Inhabitants.

Its inhabitants are a mixed race, probably of pre-Aryan stock, intermingled with later invasions from the west, north and east. Although there are many tongues and dialects spoken within the narrow limits of Chitral, the prevailing language is Khowar, which is made up of words from various sources, as far divergent as Sanskrit and Turki. In religion the Chitralis are Mohammedans, but they are not fanatical. The people in the lowlands are orthodox, or Sunni, Mohammedans, whilst those of the highlands mostly belong to a sect of the Shiahs. Amongst themselves, this sect is known as Ismaili, but the Sunnis call them Maulais. This latter word is a corruption of the Arabic "Mulahid-ul-Millat" (extinguishers of the lamp, *i.e.*, of faith), a term applied to them for the ruthlessness with which they waged war on the rest of the Mohammedan world, in revenge for the cruel persecution they experienced for their heterodoxy. In English literature, Sir Walter Scott has given a graphic account of their early history in "**The Talisman**", where he described them as the "Assassins" and their chief as "The Old Man of the Mountains". The present head of the sect is His Highness the Aga Khan, and every year these highlanders faithfully send their tithes (nazarana) to their spiritual leader in Poona. The inhabitants are of fine physique, hardy cragmen, good shots, and fair riders. They are fond of polo, which they play whenever they have the opportunity. Although they have, in the past, not had the reputation of being good fighting material, under competent leaders they have been capable of dealing with invading hordes of Pathans.

Religion.

Characteristics.

Topographical.

Chitral is bordered on the southwest, west and north by Afghan provinces. To the east lies the Kashmir province of Gilgit, whilst to the south is the Yusafzai state of Dir. To the west is the main range of the Hindu Kush: to the north are the Pamirs: to the east, separating Chitral from Gilgit is the Shandur Range. To the south-east, between Chitral and Dir, is the Hindu Raj Range over which the road to India crosses the Laorai pass, 10,250 feet above the level of the sea. This pass is liable to be blocked with snow during the winter and early spring, whilst the passage of troops over this obstacle is limited to the summer and early autumn. Only on the south-west, along the valley of the Kunar in Afghanistan, is there a comparatively easy route into the country, and even here the narrowness of the valley of the Chitral River, and the steepness of the mountains which overshadow it, form a serious obstacle to military operations. It might be said that geographically Chitral should form part of Afghanistan, but ethnographically and historically the two peoples are bitterly opposed to each other.

The Afghan provinces which border on Chitral are Wakhan, Badakhshan and Jalalabad. Wakhan is on the high Pamirs, and is the basin of the head waters of the Ab-i-Panja, which later becomes the Oxus River. It is a narrow strip of territory 180 miles long, which varies in breadth from 6 to 36 miles. It is a bleak and inhospitable country, which barely supports its small, nomadic population. Badakhshan comprises the main range of the Hindu Kush. South-east of Badakhshan is the portion of the Jalalabad province known as Kafiristan from its inhabitants, the Kafirs. The origin of this people is obscure, but they have no affinity with the inhabitants of the remainder of Afghanistan, and probably little with the Chitralis. They were subdued and converted to Mohammedanism by Amir Abdur Rahman in 1896.

Previous dealings with Chitral.

Our first connection with Chitral dates back to 1885, when Colonel (afterwards Sir William) Lockhart was sent by the Government of India to examine the passes over the Hindu Kush. He entered into negotiations with the Mehtar (the hereditary title of the ruler of Chitral), to whom he presented some rifles. He was followed in 1888 and 1889 by Colonel A. Durand, who made an agreement with the Mehtar, Aman-ul-Mulk, by which the latter should receive an annual subsidy of Rs. 6,000 (which was increased to Rs. 12,000 in 1891) together with a further present of rifles.

In 1892, Aman-ul-Mulk died, to the great relief of the Chitralis, over whom he had tyrannized to an unheard of extent. This event was followed by a period of anarchy. His son, Afzul-ul-Mulk, first occupied the throne, but his uncle Sher Afzul, an Afghan nominee, took Chitral by storm and put him to death. Sher Afzul was, in turn, compelled to fly to Kabul by Nizam-ul-Mulk, another son of Aman-ul-Mulk, who proclaimed himself Mehtar. Nizam-ul-Mulk asked that a British officer should be sent to Chitral, and, at the same time, he offered to place the control of his foreign affairs in the hands of the Government of India. Surgeon-Major Robertson was appointed as British Representative, and proceeded to Chitral from Gilgit with an escort of 50 men of the 15th Sikhs under Lieutenant J. L. R. Gordon (who commanded the 57th Infantry Brigade in 1919). Other officers accompanying the party included Captain (now Sir Francis) Younghusband and Lieutenant (now Brigadier-General) the Honourable C. G. Bruce of Everest fame.

On the 1st of January, 1895, Nizam-ul-Mulk was murdered by one of his brothers, Amir-ul-Mulk, who in his turn proclaimed himself Mehtar. The new ruler was known to be both weak and unfriendly, so the British garrison was increased to 99 men of the 14th Sikhs and 320 men of the Kashmir Imperial Service Troops. Sher Afzal now again appeared from Afghanistan. Surgeon-Major Robertson was faced with an active enemy without in the person of Sher Afzal and a treacherous friend within in the shape of the Mehtar, Amir-ul-Mulk. He placed the latter in confinement and fought Sher Afzal, at the same time proclaiming a boy of 12 years old, Shuja-ul-Mulk, another son of Aman-ul-Mulk, as Mehtar.

The siege of Chitral.

The long siege of Chitral, its defence by Captain (later Sir Charles) Townshend, its relief by Colonel Kelly, and the operations by Sir Robert Low in the Swat and Panjkora valleys have been fully described in the works of Surgeon-Major Robertson, and of Sir Francis and Sir George Younghusband, and will not be referred to here. After the relief, two battalions of Indian infantry, a section of mountain artillery and a section of Sappers and Miners were stationed in Chitral. This garrison was reduced by one battalion of infantry in 1899. One company of infantry was in the capital, but the remainder of the troops were located at Kala Drosh, 26¼ miles south of Chitral.

Armed forces in Chitral.

On the outbreak of hostilities with Afghanistan, Shuja-ul-Mulk was still Mehtar. The armed forces in Chitral consisted of:—

1/11th Rajputs (450 rifles).

One section, No. 23 Mountain Battery.

One section, 2nd Sappers and Miners.

Chitral Scouts, 1,000 rifles.

Mehtar's Bodyguard—about 2,000 men of whom 150 were armed with Martini Henry Rifles and the remainder with muzzle loaders and matchlocks.

One Russian machine gun brought over the Pamirs by a refugee, Colonel Fenin.

Afghan forces.

The Afghans had 3 battalions of infantry, 4 machine guns and 8 mountain guns at Birkot and Asmar in the Upper Kunar and 3 battalions of infantry and 4 guns at Sarkanri and Chigha Sarai in the Lower Kunar. Five more battalions of infantry were reported to be on their way to the Kunar from Kabul and Jalalabad.

Preliminary measures.

On the 5th of May, Major Reilly, the Assistant Political Agent, who had become suspicious of this movement of Afghan troops, ordered the mobilization of 3 companies of the Chitral Scouts on his own responsibility. On the 8th of May, a highly inflammatory proclamation (firman) was received from the Amir, in which he invoked the assistance of the Mehtar against the British. Major Reilly then mobilized the remainder of the Chitral Scouts in anticipation of sanction. Lieutenant-Colonel F. C. S. Sambourne-Palmer, 1/11th Rajputs, who commanded the British garrison, began to place Kala Drosh in a state of defence on the 9th of May. A company of Scouts were sent to Galapach on the left bank of the Chitral river, 6 miles downstream from Mirkhani, to watch the track along the Chitral River, whilst patrols were stationed on the passes leading from Kafiristan.

Afghans invade Chitral.

On the night of the 13/14th of May, Major Reilly learnt that a body of 300 Afghan irregulars had crossed the Chitral border on the 12th of May and seized the small post of Dokalim. On the 13th they had advanced towards Dammar Nissar on the left bank of the Chitral river, 8 miles south south-west of Mirkhani. At the same time a beacon fire was lighted on the Paitasun or Pakkun pass, 5 miles south-west of Mirkhani, which was a signal that the Afghans were advancing from the west. Major Reilly left Drosh with 2 companies of Scouts, and 120 of the Mehtar's bodyguard for Mirkhani. To guard his rear Major Reilly left 30 men at Nagar, 2 miles north of Mirkhani, with orders to break the temporary bridge over the Chitral River if

Major Reilly attacks Afghans.

the enemy attacked from the direction of the Pakkun Pass. It was afterwards found that this precaution was unnecessary as there were no Afghans on the Pakkun.

On arriving at Mirkhani, Major Reilly learnt that the Afghans had occupied Dammar Nissar and Kauti on the right bank of the river opposite Galapach, whilst the company of Scouts at the latter place were retiring on Mirkhani. He, therefore, sent one company of Scouts and 50 of the Mehtar's bodyguard across the river, and advanced down the left bank with the remainder of his force. He picked up the company which was retiring and re-occupied Galapach. From there he opened fire on the Afghans at Kauti. The force on the right bank then came up and the Afghans retired, leaving their standard behind them. Both columns then advanced and an attack was made on the enemy at Dammar Nissar, who fled towards Arnawai and Birkot. The Afghans lost 30 killed and 40 wounded in these two actions.

Major Reilly and the Scouts, who had suffered no casualties, then retired to a strong defensive position astride the river near the villages of Kauti and Galapach, and the Afghans retired on Arnawai.

British advance on Arnawai.

On the 19th of May the defences of Kala Drosh were completed. The passes over the Hindu Kush leading into Badakhshan were covered with snow, so there was little chance of an Afghan invasion from the west. The Kafirs from the south-west began to join our forces. Colonel Sambourne-Palmer, therefore, determined to advance on Arnawai (also called Arandu), and to attack the Afghans with as large a force as he could muster. After their defeat at Galapach, the enemy had taken up a position astride the Chitral River near Arnawai with advanced detachments at Darashot and at Istorgtz on the Istor stream, a tributary of the Bashgul river. Their right rested on hill 3,700, 1 mile east of Arnawai, whilst their left was extended along the Bashgul. They now numbered 600 rifles and 4 guns.

The force advanced in four columns. The right column, which was commanded by Nasr-ul-Mulk, the eldest son of the Mehtar was a mixed force of one company of Scouts, 1,000 men of the Mehtar's bodyguard and a few Kafirs. It was ordered to enter the Istor valley by the Patesun pass, and to advance down the Istor to its junction with the Bashgul. After leaving 50 men to guard the bridge over the latter river, they were to push on south and to occupy the heights west of the Afghan cantonment of Birkot. A body of 300 Chitrali tribesmen armed with muzzle loading rifles were to move down the ridge which forms the watershed between the Istor and the Chitral river and to maintain communication between Nasr-ul-Mulk's force and the right bank column. This latter, which consisted of 2 companies of the Chitral Scouts under Lieutenant Bowers, 1/11th Rajputs, was to advance down the right bank of the Chitral River, and to storm the bridge over the Bashgul near its junction with the Chitral. The main column, known as the Mobile Column, under the direct command of Lieutenant-Colonel Sambourne-Palmer, was to advance along the left bank of the river and to capture Arnawai. It consisted of:—

2 companies, Chitral Scouts under Major Reilly.
1/11th Rajputs, less 1 company.
1 section, No. 23 Mountain Battery.
Detachment, 2nd Sappers and Miners.

The left column, which was composed of 3 companies of the Chitral Scouts under Captain Crimmin, was to advance from Dammar Nissar, through Dammar, to the Kanithan Pass. From there, it was to move down the Malikhor ridge, north of the Arnawai valley and attack the Afghan right flank.

All four columns were to leave Mirkhani on the 21st of May and to arrive before their final objectives on the 23rd of May.

The right column under Nasr-ul-Mulk met a small enemy party at the bridge at Istrogtz, whom they attacked. The bridge was carried by storm, and the party advanced down the Istor stream. On the 22nd Nasr-ul-Mulk crossed the Bashgul and took up a position on the heights west of Birkot, having outflanked the Afghans. A Chitrali went forward during the night of the 22nd-23rd and cut the bridge over the Chitral (or rather Kunar) River, which connected Birkot with Arnawai. **Operations of the right column.**

The right bank column and the Mobile column advanced down the Chitral River and camped near Dammar Nissar on the night of the 21st of May. A temporary bridge was thrown over the river here and Lieutenant Bowers and his force crossed to the right bank. **The Mobile column.**

On the 22nd, the Mobile column moved to Angarpatai Pari, a distance of 2 miles. Here the road, which runs along the face of a precipice, was found to be broken, and the column camped whilst the Chitralis repaired the breach. The two companies of Scouts under Major Reilly pushed forward to Lambabat, 4 miles north-east of Arnawai.

On the morning of the 23rd of May, the Mobile Column left camp at 0300 hours, and, at 0500 hours, reached the Arkhrui torrent, 1 mile north-east of Lambabat to find the bridge over the stream broken. Major Reilly with his Scouts pushed forward to Resht Pari, 1 mile north-east of the junction of the Chitral River and the Bashgul, where they came in contact with the enemy. At 0600 hours, Captain Crimmin with the left column, advancing along the Malikhor Ridge, came into position on the left of Major Reilly's party. The enemy resistance now stiffened. At 0740 hours the guns came into action 500 yards south of Lambabat, and one company and the regimental scouts of the 1/11th Rajputs were directed to attack the Dokalim ridge on the right of Major Reilly. The whole line now advanced and the Afghans began to retire. A nest of 25 snipers, however, held their ground in a nala under some huge boulders screened by brushwood. They commanded the track by which the 1/11th Rajputs were advancing at a range of 50 yards, and caused most of the casualties incurred by that unit. Leaving the regimental scouts and one platoon under Jemadar Ram Singh to deal with these men, the company pressed on. Ram Singh led two bayonet charges against these snipers, and accounted for two with his revolver. Eventually, they were all bombed out and killed. At 1005 hours the forward line was reinforced by two platoons, followed at 1115 hours by three more platoons. The enemy began to evacuate Arnawai, which they set on fire. At 1410 hours Dokalim ridge was occupied, and by 1630 hours all opposition ceased and the enemy were in full flight southwards towards Asmar.

Right bank column.

Whilst the main force was engaging the enemy on the left bank, Lieutenant Bowers and the two companies of the Chitral Scouts on the right bank of the river advanced and stormed the bridge over the Bashgul. From there they moved forward on Birkot, together with the right column under Nasr-ul-Mulk. Birkot was captured and looted, the bodyguard and the Kafirs getting away with most of the booty.

The troops on the left bank were now withdrawn to a camp on the plateau north-east of Arnawai, whilst those on the right bank remained in the vicinity of Birkot. Whilst this movement was in progress, a band of desperate men, who had hidden themselves in the standing corn near the Arnawai stream, opened fire on the headquarter party, and wounded Lieutenant-Colonel Sambourne Palmer and Major Reilly's two orderlies. They were all bayoneted by men of the 1/11th Rajputs.

Our casualties during these three days amounted to:—

	Killed.	Wounded.
Chitral Scouts	8	23
Mehtar's bodyguards	5	13
1-11th Rajputs	3	12
Total	16	48

The number of casualties among the Kafir tribesmen was never ascertained. The Afghans were believed to have lost 250 men. Four guns, two of which were breechloaders, and a large quantity of ammunition and stores were captured, together with 55 prisoners.

Having defeated the enemy, a further advance was neither practical nor desirable. It was known that the Afghans collecting at Asmar were superior in numbers to our forces, the local inhabitants along the Kunar were hostile, the attitude of the Dirwals was doubtful and the communications with Chitral were bad. The snow on the passes to the west over the Hindu Kush was melting, and the Afghan forces in Badakhshan would soon be moving towards the frontier. The next few days, therefore, were spent in collecting supplies. The Afghan villages in the neighbourhood were looted and burnt, whilst the Kafir tribesmen harried the inhabitants by carrying off their cattle and goats.

Our forces retire on Drosh.

On the 1st of June, reliable information was received that the enemy had concentrated three battalions of infantry and a regiment of cavalry near Sao, 12½ miles south of Arnawai. A body of 6,000 Salarzais was said to be gathering on the Uchir Range, ready to threaten our left flank, or to loot the Afghans at Asmar as opportunity offered. It was decided to evacuate Arnawai, and to retire on Kala Drosh. Accordingly after dark on the 1st of June, the troops on the right bank left their camp fires burning and retired behind the Bashgul. On the 2nd of June, the whole force started to retire in the same four columns, each following the route by which the advance was made. On the 4th of June, Mirkhani was reached without incident. Here a body of 400 Scouts and 400 of the bodyguard and 2 Lewis guns remained, whilst the rest of the force returned to Kala Drosh on the 5th of June. Defensive positions were prepared at Mirkhani, and near Galatak, half way between Mirkhani and Kala Drosh.

Although the armistice was signed on the 3rd of June, the Afghan commanders on the Chitral front were not prepared to adhere to its terms. In Badakhshan, a force of 5 or 6 battalions was concentrated at Faizabad with advanced detachments in Wakhan threatening the Baroghil and Manjan passes. At Asmar, Wakhil Khan was preparing to advance into Chitral with 7 battalions of infantry and a body of Mohmands and Bajauris. To the south-east, a notorious firebrand, known as the Sandakai Mullah, was endeavouring to incite the Yusafzais of the Swat valley to attack Chakdara, the British post on the Swat, where the road to Chitral crosses that river.

If these attacks had materialized, the only way of reinforcing Chitral would have been from Gilgit, on the route by which Colonel Kelly advanced in 1895. At Bunji, 34½ miles south-east of Gilgit there were two battalions of infantry and one battery of the Kashmir Imperial Service troops. The troops of the 16th Division which should have been in Nowshera ready to meet the menace in the Swat valley, were at that time employed in the Kohat-Kurram area, and no others were available. The Sandakai Mullah, however, was unsuccessful in his efforts, and the Afghans in Badakhshan, although they advanced to the foot of the Dorah pass, did not actually cross the frontier.

Arnawai and Dokalim again occupied by the Afghans.

Chitralis raid Kamdesh.

Abdul Wakil moved north from Asmar, and reached Birkot on the 23rd of June. The armistice was soon broken. Afghan irregulars occupied Arnawai and Dokalim, and, on the 23rd of June, the Mehtar's bodyguard made an unauthorized raid on Kamdesh, where the Bashgul takes a turn to the east to join the Chitral river. On the 24th of June, Abdul Wakil sent one battalion to occupy Dokalim near Arnawai in Chitral territory, and he himself with 3 battalions of infantry and 1,500 tribesmen advanced up the Bashgul to punish the Kafirs for the assistance which they had given to the British. The Chitralis of the bodyguard retired from Kamdesh to Pattigul, where they were joined by a company of Scouts. Abdul Wakil advanced to Lutdeh in Kafiristan on the 29th of June. He carried out punitive measures against the offending Kafirs and arrested their leading men. He was now in a position from where he could threaten Chitral from the west, and also where he could combine with any Afghan force advancing from Badakhshan.

Abdul Wakil moves up the Bashgul river.

To meet these movements, a striking force, composed of two companies of Scouts and two weak companies of the Mehtar's bodyguard was concentrated at Ayun, half way between Chitral and Kala Drosh, where the Bumboret and Rumbur streams join the Chitral river. On the 1st of June, the force at Pattigul was withdrawn to Utsun, 2½ miles north-west of Mirkhani. Two companies of Chitral Scouts was sent to Shogkot in the Lutkuh valley to watch for any movement over the Dorah pass from Badakhshan. To the north, 3 companies of Gilgit Scouts watched the passes over the Pamirs.

Lutkuh threatened.

During the first half of July, Abdul Wakil continued his aggressive movements in the Upper Bashgul. On the 16th of July, a small party of Afghans crossed the Zidig (or Samanak) pass and threatened the Lutkuh valley. This river unites with the Mastuj five miles north of Chitral town and the combined waters form the Chitral River. Nothing came of this movement as the Afghans retired soon afterwards to Kafiristan.

On the 17th of July, a force of 400 tribesmen and 400 Afghan regulars invaded the Bumboret valley and advanced to within a mile of Bumboret village, 10 miles north-west of Kala Drosh. Here they were attacked by a company of Chitral Scouts from Ayun, and were driven back with a loss of 10 killed. They retired to the Bashgul valley after driving off about 900 head of cattle and burning the huts along the Bumboret. During the 18th and 19th of July, the Afghans occupied the whole of the passes leading from the Bashgul into Chitral from the Brambalu, 12 miles west south-west of Kala Drosh, to the Zidig, 26 miles west north-west of Chitral.

Abdul Wakil now changed his tactics, probably owing to pressure brought on him from Kabul. Whilst still holding the passes and encouraging the tribesmen to carry out raids, he prevented the regulars under his command from crossing the Chitral border. His intrigues with the tribesmen in Bajaur were so far successful that a body of 600 men under Mullah Shah Badshah collected on the Loarai pass on the 21st of July, and threatened the Chitrali post of Ziarat. On the 24th of July, Lieutenant Bowers with two companies of Chitral Scouts advanced from Mirkhani up the high ridge to the west of the Ashret stream and attacked the Mullah and his following. After a smart action he drove off the raiders, who lost 15 men killed and over 40 wounded, whilst his own casualties were only three men wounded. The tribesmen took refuge in Dir, and dispersed in a couple of days.

Tribesmen threaten Ziarat.

Defeated by Lieutenant Bowers.

Afghans advance from Badakshan.

On the 28th of July, an Afghan force of 100 cavalry, 800 infantry, 6 guns and 2 machine guns from Badakhshan under Colonel Abdul Aziz arrived at Topkhana, 10 miles west of the Dorah pass. On the 31st of July this detachment began to retire northwards and marched off to its own cantonments.

Peace signed.

The signing of peace on the 8th of August put an end to hostilities in Chitral. Arnawai and Dokalim, however, were not handed over to the Mehtar till the 17th of January, 1922.

In some respects the operations in Chitral resemble those in the Upper Kurram. In both cases we have the local inhabitants, and locally raised forces fighting the invaders with the aid of regulars, and giving a good account of themselves. In the case of Chitral, our forces were completely isolated and could expect no reinforcements. The pressure from the Kunar valley would have been released when the British had taken Jalalabad, but an attack from Badakhshan might have taken place. It is probable, however, that the difficulty of supplying troops in the inhospitable Hindu Kush would have made an invasion from this direction a feeble affair which could be dealt with by the troops on the spot. As it was, it was proved that the Chitrali, when led by British officers and backed by regular troops, was more than a match for the Afghan.

CHAPTER IX.

SOUTHERN FRONT, EXCLUDING ZHOB.

The problems which faced General Wapshare in Baluchistan, differed materially from those in the Northern and Central areas. There were no independent tribes, whose borders Government servants were forbidden to cross. The whole country was administered right up to the Durand Line from the Gomal in the north to the borders of Persia in the west. The troops, instead of being stationed in unhealthy stations in the plains, were located in the comparatively cool and bracing uplands, where strategically they were well placed to resist invasion or to initiate an advance into Afghanistan.

The only communication between Quetta and the rest of India is by a broad gauge railway line, as there are no metalled roads in Sind. At Ruk, the line to Quetta takes off from the Indus River lines and runs across the Sind desert to Sibi. In summer the heat on the latter section is almost unbearable, and inflicts great hardship on troops travelling across this waterless waste. From Sibi there are two lines. The main line follows the Bolan pass, and goes through Quetta to New Chaman, 1½ miles from the Afghan border. The steep gradients between Sibi and Quetta, which in some cases are as heavy as 1 in 24, necessitate the use of half trains with two and three engines of special design, and the carrying capacity of the railway is thus greatly reduced.

Between Quetta and Chaman is the Shelabagh tunnel under the Khojak pass. It is 2½ miles in length, and trains can only pass through it at intervals of 2 hours owing to the dangers of asphyxiation from the fumes generated by the engines.

A loop line runs from Sibi through Harnai, which crosses the watershed of the Zhob at Chappar and joins the main line at Bostan, 20 miles north of Quetta. At Khanai, 24 miles from Bostan, a 2′ 6″ railway takes off from the loop line and runs in a north-easterly direction to Hindubagh in the Upper Zhob.

At Spezand, 15 miles south of Quetta, the Duzdap branch leaves the main line and runs through Nushki and along the southern boundary of Afghanistan to Duzdap in Persian Sistan.

Geographically the southern front fell into three areas during hostilities against Afghanistan, *i.e.*, the Zhob, the Chaman front, and the lines of communication with Meshed in north-east Persia, which ran along the southern and western frontiers of Afghanistan. The operations in the Zhob will be described in the next chapter, whilst the lines of communication to Meshed do not come within the scope of this work.

On the 6th of May, the distribution of the troops in Baluchistan was as follows:—

Table showing the distribution of troops in Baluchistan on the 6th of May, 1919:—

Formation.	Unit.	Station.
12th Mounted Brigade . .	Headquarters	Shaikh Manda.
	40th Cavalry	Baleli.
	41st Cavalry, less 2 squadrons .	Do.
	42nd Cavalry	Do.
	22nd Squadron, Machine Gun Corps	Do.
	No. 7 Field Troop, Sappers and Miners.	Quetta.
4th Division . . .	Headquarters	Do.
	25th Cavalry, F. F. . . .	Do.
	102nd Battery, R. F. A. .	Do.
	No. 4 Mountain Artillery Brigade	Do.
	No. 1 Mountain Battery, R. G. A.	Do.
	No. 9 Mountain Battery, R. G. A.	Do.
	No. 73 Field Company, 3rd Sappers and Miners, less 2 sections.	Do.
	No. 33 Divisional Signal Company	Do.
	No. 270 Company, Machine Gun Corps.	Do.
	10th Infantry Brigade . .	Do.
	2nd Battalion, King's (Liverpool) Regiment.	Do.
	2/56th Rifles, F. F. . . .	Do.
	1/5th Light Infantry . .	Harnai.
	11th Infantry Brigade . .	Quetta.
	1/22nd Punjabis . . .	Do.
	1/4th Gurkha Rifles . . .	Do.
	2/10th Gurkha Rifles . . .	Chaman.
	57th Infantry Brigade . .	Quetta.
	1/4th Royal West Kent Regt. .	Do.
	2/119th Infantry . . .	Peshin.
	1/129th Baluchis . . .	Quetta.
	3/7th Gurkha Rifles . . .	Do.
Internal Security . . .	No. 38 Mountain Battery . .	Do.
Ditto . . .	No. 19 Motor Machine Gun Battery.	Do.
Ditto . . .	3rd Skinner's Horse . . .	Loralai.
Ditto . . .	2/11th Rajputs . . .	Loralai and outposts.
Ditto . . .	3/1st Gurkha Rifles . . .	Fort Sandeman and outposts.

In addition to the above, the following troops were employed on the lines of communication between Spezand and Meshed:—

2 squadrons, 41st Cavalry.

1/98th Infantry (6 companies).

120th Infantry (2 companies).

107th Pioneers.

No. 71 Field Company, 3rd Sappers and Miners.

2 sections, No. 73 Field Company, 3rd Sappers and Miners, whilst the 28th Light Cavalry and the 1/19th Punjabis were in Meshed.

On the 7th of May, the whole of these troops became the Baluchistan Force. As no staff for this new formation was appointed, the 4th Division continued to function in a dual capacity for three weeks, when arrangements were made to provide the 4th Division with a staff separate from that of the Baluchistan Force. Reinforcements were sent to Quetta as is shown in the table below:—

Table showing the arrival of reinforcements in Quetta:—

Date of arrival in Quetta.	Unit.	From	REMARKS.
14th May .	101st Battery, R. F. A. .	Hyderabad.	
	2/23rd Sikh Pioneers .	Ambala.	
16th May .	1107th Battery, R. F. A.	Hyderabad.	
17th May .	1st Battalion, Duke of Wellington's Regiment.	Lahore . .	11th Infantry Bde.
19th May .	No 24 Field Co., 3rd S. and M.	Kirkee.	
	2/15th Sikhs . .	Ferozepore .	Internal Security.
20th May .	No. 17 Field Coy., 3rd S. and M. (less 2 sections).		
	H. Q. XXIst Bde., R. F. A.	Hyderabad.	
	No. 4 D. A. C. .	Do.	
	2/129th Baluchis . .	Karachi . .	10th Infantry Bde.
21st May .	No. 281 Co., Machine Gun Corps.	Mhow.	
22nd May .	No 6 Cavalry Brigade Signal Troop.	Poona . .	12th Mounted Bde
	No. 17 Special Battalion	Deolali . .	Internal Security.
23/24th May .	No. 3 L. of C. Signal Section.	Poona.	
28th May . .	1st Patiala Lancers .	Patiala . .	Ditto.
30th May . .	13th Lancers . .	Meerut . .	Ditto.
7th June . .	3/124th Baluchistan Infantry.	Karachi . .	Ditto.

The Afghan troops in south-east Afghanistan were:—

Kandahar.—

5 battalions infantry.

1 regiment cavalry.

25 guns.

Kalat-i-Ghilzai.—

2 battalions infantry.

6 guns.

Mukur.—

1 battalion infantry.

2 machine guns.

In addition to these, it was known that reinforcements amounting to 1,500 men were on their way from Kabul under the Prime Minister (Sadr-i-Azam), Abdul Qudus.

If the Afghans decided to take the offensive, it was probable that they would invade Baluchistan through Chaman and the Khojak pass. There are many tracks to the north of this route, but none of them are capable of carrying large bodies of troops, whilst to the south, the waterless deserts of Registan present a formidable obstacle to any force marching on Nushki from the direction of Kandahar. Nine miles east of Chaman is the Khwaja Amran range, which affords a fine defensive position against an attack from the west. It can be turned from the north, however, through the valley of the Kadanai. General Wapshare decided to reinforce New Chaman, and to concentrate as large a force as possible at Kila Abdulla, 9 miles east of the Khwaja Amran. Work was commenced on a pipe line to bring water to the camps at Kila Abdulla from the headworks 7 miles north of the railway station. The 102nd Battery, R. F. A., and the 1/22nd Punjabis and the 1/4th Gurkha Rifles of the 11th Infantry Brigade were pushed forward to New Chaman, whilst the 57th Infantry Brigade, less the 2/119th Infantry at Peshin, were concentrated at Kila Abdulla by the 18th of May.

Although the two available aeroplanes were wrecked at Quetta on the 12th of May, and the enemy forces could not be kept under observation from the air, it was ascertained from other sources that Abdul Qudus could not arrive in Kandahar till the 16th at the earliest, and that no movement of troops from the latter place towards the east had taken place up to the 15th of May. Attempts were being made to raise the Pathans in Baluchistan, the Marri and Bugti tribes of the Baluchis east of Quetta, and the Brahuis of Jhalawan south of Kalat, but these efforts had not been very successful. The Achakzai Pathans, who live north of Chaman, partly in our territory and partly in Afghanistan, were showing symptoms of unrest, but the other tribes were quiet for the moment. Lack of transport prevented any extensive invasion of Afghanistan, but it was considered that a moral effect could be obtained by the reduction of Spin Baldak, which lies 6 miles north-west of New Chaman, and was reputed to be the second strongest fort in Afghanistan.

General Wapshare decided to capture this place by a surprise attack, and to effect this he concentrated the following force at New Chaman by the 26th of May:—

Cavalry.—

25th Cavalry, F. F. less 1 squadron.

42nd Cavalry.

No. 22 Squadron, Machine Gun Corps.

Artillery.—

XXIst Brigade, R. F. A. less 1 battery.

102nd Battery, R. F. A. (18 pounders).

1107th Battery, R. F. A. (two 4·5″ howitzers and four 5″ howitzers).

Engineers.—

No. 24 Field Co., 3rd Sappers and Miners.

No. 73 Field Company, 3rd Sappers and Miners (less 2 sections).

1 company, 2/23rd Sikh Pioneers.

Machine Guns.—

No. 270 Company, Machine Gun Corps.

Infantry.—

11th Infantry Brigade.

1st Battalion, Duke of Wellington's Regiment.

1/22nd Punjabis.

1/4th Gurkha Rifles.

2/10th Gurkha Rifles.

57th Infantry Brigade.

1/4th Royal West Kent Regiment.

1/129th Baluchis.

Medical.—

No. 15 Combined Field Ambulance.

No. 51 Combined Field Ambulance.

Veterinary.—

No. 15 Mobile Veterinary Section.

To the west of the Khwaja Amran range, the country is open and slopes gently downwards to Kandahar and the basin of the Helmund. This plain presents no difficulties to the movements of all arms, but it is broken by a number of isolated hills which rise from it. On the easternmost of these outcrops of rock, Spin Baldak is situated (see map facing page 99). This ridge, which rises 200 feet above the plain, is 600 yards long and runs from north-east to south-west. There are three knolls, which are known for reference as "A" "B", and "C". "A", which is on the north-east of the ridge is the highest, and "C" on the south-west, is the lowest. From "C" the ground slopes gently to the plain, where the fort was situated at the base of the hill. It was a square work, with an inner and an outer wall, and it was surrounded by a moat, 25 feet deep and 25 feet broad, which was usually dry. The faces of the outer wall were 250 yards long, and from 25 to 30 feet high. At each corner and in the centre of each face were bastions, and the walls were pierced by two tiers of loopholes. Between the outer and the inner walls, was a clear space of 20 yards. The inner walls were strongly buttressed with rammed earth on the outside, whilst on the inner side were domed casemates in which the garrison were housed. Between the fort and the top of hill "C" were three towers. Each of these had 3 tiers of loopholes, and was encircled by a loopholed wall with a radius of 20 to 30 yards. Double walls connected the towers with the fort and with each other, thus providing a covered way for the garrison. Gun platforms had been prepared on Hill "A" and Hill "B", and trenches had been dug and breastworks erected for the defence of these features.

To the west of the ridge were two walled enclosures. The first was a garden 200 yards west of the fort, whilst 100 yards north of the garden was a square staging post (sarai) with bastions at each corner. South of the fort was another walled garden, 200 yards square.

It was decided to employ two columns of cavalry to form a cordon to the north, west and south in order to prevent the garrison from escaping, whilst two infantry columns, covered by the fire of the artillery, were to storm the ridge and the fort. The right cavalry column which consisted of the 42nd Cavalry, and half a section (2 guns) of No. 22 Squadron, Machine Gun Corps, under the command of Lieutenant-Colonel Taylor, was to proceed to the north-east of Spin Baldak, and to deal with any of the garrison who attempted to escape "east of a north and south line through the east edge of Spin Baldak ridge".

The left cavalry column, which was made up of the 25th Cavalry less 1 squadron and No. 22 Squadron, Machine Gun Corps, less 1½ sections (6 guns) was to get into position west of Spin Baldak, and to prevent the Afghans from escaping "west of a north and south line through the east edge of Spin Baldak ridge". Both columns were instructed not to carry on the pursuit farther than 4 miles, and they were warned against becoming involved in village fighting.

The right infantry attack under Brigadier General J. L. R. Gordon, C.B., commanding the 57th Infantry Brigade, was composed of:—

1/4th Royal West Kent Regiment.

1/129th Baluchis.

1 section, No. 270 Co., Machine Gun Corps.

No. 73 Field Co., 3rd Sappers and Miners (less 2 sections).

It was ordered to advance up the ridge from the north-east, and to capture the knolls and the towers. When this was accomplished, fresh orders would be issued for the assault on the northern face of the fort.

The left infantry attack under Major-General T. H. Hardy, C.B., commanding the 11th Infantry Brigade, consisted of:—

1/22nd Punjabis.

1/4th Gurkha Rifles.

1 section, No. 270 Co., Machine Gun Corps.

No. 24 Field Co., 3rd Sappers and Miners, less 2 sections.

It was to advance astride the Chaman-Spin Baldak-Kandahar road, and, after giving the garrison the opportunity to surrender, to capture the gardens and buildings south and west of the fort. Orders would then be issued for the assault of the fort from these faces.

The General Reserve under Lieutenant-Colonel E. H. Boutflower, 1st Duke of Wellington's Regiment, consisted of:—

1 troop, 42nd Cavalry.

2 sections, No. 24 Field Company, 3rd S. and M.

No. 270 Co., Machine Gun Corps, less 2 sections.

1 Co., 2/23rd Sikh Pioneers.

1st Battalion, Duke of Wellington's Regiment.

2/10th Gurkha Rifles less 1½ companies.

There were two batteries of artillery, the 102nd armed with six 18-prs. and the 1107th armed with two 4·5″ and four 5″ howitzers. The 18-prs. were ordered to come into action 3,000 yards from the ridge, and to register for a creeping barrage. Zero was fixed at 0800 hours, and at 0830 hours they were to put down a creeping enfilade barrage commencing from a line 100 yards north east of Hill "A". After 10 minutes they were to lift 100 yards to the south-west, and then to continue lifting 100 yards at a time at intervals of 5 minutes. At 0915 hours they would be firing on the fort itself. The 4·5″ howitzers were ordered to fire on the towers, keeping pace with the barrage of the 18-prs., whilst the 5″ howitzers were to fire on the fort itself.

The utmost secrecy was maintained with regard to the attack, so as to prevent the garrison from evacuating the fort and decamping. If they should manage to escape, there were no means of delivering a blow at the Afghans with the transport then available. Light ladders were constructed for scaling the walls, and rafts were made up to cross the moat with if the latter was found to be full of water.

At 0430 the two cavalry columns left camp and took up the position assigned to them without opposition. They were followed by the infantry columns, the general reserve and the artillery. The left attack reached the position of deployment, 2,000 yards from the fort, at 0630 hours. Major General Hardy then sent forward a flag of truce to demand the surrender of the garrison. The Afghans, who do not subscribe to the Geneva Convention, mistook the meaning of the white flag, and opened fire on the parliamentaire. Their method of demanding a temporary cessation of hostilities is to send forward a priest with a copy of the Koran, and it would have been better to have followed their procedure on this occasion. By 0730 hours, the right column was in its position of deployment, 2,000 yards north-east of Hill "A" and ready to commence the attack.

At 0800 hours the guns opened fire and the infantry started to advance. To take the right column first. The 1/4th Royal West Kent Regiment led the attack on a frontage of one company, followed by the 1/129th Baluchis. The progress was slow, as the line of advance lay over sandhills which made the going heavy, so General Gordon asked that Zero should be postponed for half an hour in order to allow his brigade to keep time with the artillery time table. It was, however, too late, and the artillery barrage passed over Hill "A" when the West Kents were 1,000 yards from it and had to be repeated. There was little opposition to this advance, and the leading company reached an underfeature, 150 yards from Hill "A" at 0915 hours. Here they were held up for two hours by a few men who manned the breastworks.

On the left, 3 companies of the 1/4th Gurkha Rifles advanced on the right of the road and attacked the garden south of the fort, whilst the 1/22nd Punjabis on the left of the road moved against the southern wall of the garden further west. The 1/4th Gurkha Rifles succeeded in taking their objective by 0845 hours with a loss of 1 man wounded. The 1/22nd Punjabis found themselves confronted by a wall 15 feet high and from 2 to 3 feet thick. They began to make a breach with entrenching tools and with their bayonets, and sent back to the reserve for scaling ladders. Whilst engaged on this work, an aeroplane bomb intended for the fort fell on "A" Company. One British Officer, one Indian Officer and 3 men were killed, whilst two British officers and 8 men were wounded by the explosion. By 0930 hours, three holes had been made sufficiently large to admit men in single file. The garden was rushed but it was found to be unoccupied. The eastern wall was then breached in preparation for an attack on the fort itself, whilst two platoons with a Lewis gun skirted the western face of the garden and occupied the sarai to the north unopposed. The fort was now under rifle and Lewis gun fire at a range of 200 yards from both the gardens and from the sarai. This and the artillery bombardment combined proved too much for some of the garrison. At 0950 hours a party of 200 men attempted to escape from the fort towards the north. They suffered many casualties from the fire of the detachment of the 1/22nd Punjabis in the sarai, and from No. 22 Squadron, Machine Gun Corps, who galloped after them, came into action and opened fire. Had the cavalry acted promptly and attacked them mounted, not a man would have escaped. Each cavalry commander, however, thought that the other was responsible for the terrain traversed by the fugitives, and, though some dismounted men opened fire, a large number of this party got clear away. Such a mistake could not have occurred if a "locking point" had been selected and definitely allotted to one or other of the cavalry columns. A suitable spot would have been where the Spin Baldak-Saiadan-Kandahar road crosses the bed of the Kadanai stream.

By 1300 hours, the artillery had breached the tower on Hill "C" and the southern wall of the fort. The western wall and the main or western gate were still intact, so General Hardy asked for a howitzer to batter the gate in. A 5" howitzer was brought forward and opened fire at a range of 200 yards. Three rounds were expended but failed to blow in the gate.

Meanwhile, at 1005 hours, as the 1/4th Royal West Kents had failed to make any progress, General Wapshare ordered the 1st Battalion, Duke of Wellington's Regiment, and one section, No. 270 Company, Machine Gun Corps, to make a frontal attack on the ridge from the south. This battalion reached the gardens at the foot of the hill, 500 yards east of the south-east bastion of the fort at 1115 hours. Two minutes previous to this the West Kents had taken Hill "A". At 1140 hours the 102nd Battery, R. F. A., opened fire on the towers and kept it up for ten minutes. The Duke of Wellington's advanced up the slope and took Hill "C" without any difficulty. A few desperate men hung on to Hill "B", and the West Kents were again held up. The Duke of Wellington's Regiment, accordingly, sent 1 company to their right to deal with the Afghans on Hill "B", and at the same time, a party of the 1/129th Baluchis, who had come up on the right of the West Kents attacked them from the north-east. They refused to surrender and were killed to a man.

As soon as the 1/4th Gurkha Rifles and the 1/22nd Punjabis saw that Hill "C" had been captured, they rushed at the fort. The 1/4th Gurkha Rifles penetrated the southern face through a breach made by the artillery, and through a drainage hole in the south-west corner of the wall. Once inside they opened the gate for the 1/22nd Punjabis, who were climbing the wall with the aid of the scaling ladders. Both battalions then entered the enclosure. Parties of Afghans who had taken refuge in dark rooms refused to surrender and opened fire on the attackers. These were bombed, and most of them killed. By 1345 the fort was completely in our possession, and 169 prisoners had been collected and despatched to Chaman.

Our casualties during the day were:—

Killed or died of wounds.—

Lieutenant C. A. M. Holden, 1/22nd Punjabis.

Lieutenant A. L. Ambrose, 1/22nd Punjabis.

Subedar Sohel Singh, 1/22nd Punjabis.

British other ranks 5.

Indian other ranks 10.

Wounded.—

Captain W. H. Styles, 1/4th Royal West Kent Regiment.

Lieutenant Morrison, 1/22nd Punjabis (subsequently died of wounds).

Lieutenant W. H. Bunning, 1/4th Gurkha Rifles.

British other ranks 10.

Indian other ranks 27.

Of the 600 men who formed the garrison of Spin Baldak, 169 were taken prisoners as already mentioned, and 17 more men were subsequently found hidden in the fort. Our troops buried 170 enemy dead and more were killed and wounded but not found at the time.

The attack had come as a complete surprise. When once the cavalry had surrounded the fort, its reduction was only a matter of time. The fortifications were shell traps, but the ignorance of the

Afghans made them trust their stone walls. It is impossible not to admire the courage with which they fought to the end without a thought of surrender, but they would have been better advised to cut their way through the thin cavalry screen, and to have escaped in the direction of Kandahar.

Instead of fixing zero hour on the previous evening, it would have been better to have communicated it on the ground when the advance of the troops could be observed. This latter method was employed at Bagh, the zero hour being fixed after all detachments had reported that they were ready. Had similar methods been employed at Spin Baldak, there would have been no necessity to have repeated the artillery barrage.

The captured position was consolidated and held by a mixed force under Brigadier General J. L. R. Gordon, C.B., which consisted of:—

Headquarters, 57th Infantry Brigade.

1/4th Royal West Kent Regiment.

1/129th Baluchis.

1 squadron, 25th Cavalry, F. F.

No. 73 Field Company, 3rd Sappers and Miners, less 2 sections.

No. 24 Field Company, 3rd Sappers and Miners.

1 company, 2/23rd Sikh Pioneers.

1 section, No. 270 Company, Machine Gun Corps.

2 howitzers (5″), 1107th Battery, R. F. A.

The remainder of the troops marched back to Chaman at 1500 hours.

The ridge was held by the 1/129th Baluchis, and the fort and sarai by the 1/4th Royal West Kent Regiment. The squadron of cavalry was accommodated in the sarai, whilst the sappers, pioneers and artillery were located in the fort. It was originally intended to demolish the fort and the towers on the ridge, but it was finally decided to keep them intact to facilitate a forward move into Afghanistan.

The first difficulty was the water supply. This was obtained from two tanks, which were filled by an open channel, which took off from the Kadanai at Murgha Chaman, just before the latter stream goes to ground. The flow was uncertain, as the water was used for irrigation, and could be turned off into the fields. The channel itself was so filthy that the troops could not possibly drink from the tanks. A camel train was organized, which carried 200 kegs, each with a capacity of 14 gallons, from Chaman to Spin Baldak. This water convoy performed the journey daily until the channel had been cleaned out, and even then it was found necessary to employ it every other day, as, owing to the percolation in the sandy soil, to diversions for cultivation and to enemy action, the water flowing into the tanks was never sufficient for the needs of the garrison. Finally a pipe line was laid down, which was completed on the 10th of July, and water was brought by it from New Chaman to Spin Baldak.

Cavalry reconnaissances were carried out daily, and the country to the north and west as far as Murgha Chaman, Saiadan and Mel Karez was kept under observation. On the 31st of May, Major-General N. G. Woodyatt, C.B., assumed command of the 4th Division, whilst Abdul Qudus arrived at Kandahar with Afghan reinforcements on the same day, and took over the troops in south-west Afghanistan. On the 1st of June, our aeroplanes located a force of several hundred Afghans at Dabrai, 19½ miles north-west of New Chaman. General Woodyatt proposed to surprise this concentration at dawn on the 3rd of June, but the plan was not approved. On the 2nd of June, Abdul Qudus arrived with reinforcements from Kandahar, and made his headquarters at Mel Karez, 32½ miles north-west of New Chaman. The total number of Afghan troops in this area then amounted to:—

1 regiment of cavalry,

5 battalions of infantry,

10 guns,

9,000 tribesmen,

and they were spread out over a front of 32 miles from Aga Jan, 3 miles north of Murgha Chaman, through Dabrai, to Mel Karez, where their right flank was covered by the Dori River and by the deserts to the south.

On the 3rd of June, news was received of the signing of the armistice, and after this date no offensive action was taken by our troops against the Afghans.

Soon after the fall of Spin Baldak, work was commenced on a defensive scheme for the protection of New Chaman. This consisted of an inner and an outer line of defences. The outer line, which was manned by infantry and machine guns, ran from the two small forts at Bogra, 8 miles east of New Chaman, to Boundary pillar No. 85, and thence followed the line of the frontier to Boundary pillar No. 89 (see map facing this page). This line, which was about 8 miles long, was divided into 9 sections, each designed to hold one company of infantry and one machine gun. In each section there were two lunettes in the front line, about 1,000 yards apart and 1,000 yards from the next lunette in the adjacent sections. These were each designed for a garrison of one platoon. Supporting each pair of lunettes, and from 600 to 700 yards in rear of them, was a work with a closed gorge holding two platoons and a machine gun. These works were all completed by the 18th of June. In normal times, sections 1 to 8 were held by two platoons each, whilst No. 9, the left section was not, as a rule, occupied.

The inner line consisted of a series of short fire trenches, surrounded by barbed wire, which formed a perimeter round the two forts, the railway station, the sidings, the mobilization godown and the bazar. In addition to this certain piquet positions were held at night. The normal garrison of these inner defences was two companies of infantry and 9 Lewis guns. Towards the middle of July, the increase in the number of troops in the garrison made it necessary to form a new camp east of the reservoir, which was also wired in and defended in the same manner.

The conditions under the armistice were probably more unsatisfactory at Chaman than on any of the other fronts. Not only did the Afghans refuse to retire 20 miles from our troops, but they occupied Murgha Chaman, and thus gained possession of the water supply of Spin Baldak. Afghan regulars and tribesmen fired on the parties working on the outer line of defences and interfered with our cavalry reconnaissances. It was with the greatest difficulty that hostilities were avoided. An example of this occurred on the 12th of June when 3 squadrons of the 25th Cavalry, F. F. and 3 squadrons of the 42nd Cavalry proceeded to Murgha Chaman to find out why the Spin Baldak water supply had been cut off. On approaching Murgha Chaman it was found that the group of villages there was occupied by some 3,000 Afghan regulars and tribesmen. As our troops had orders to avoid hostilities, the advanced guard retired. The Afghans then left the villages and deployed to attack our troops. Our whole column then retired to some rising ground, about 2 miles south of the villages. Here negotiations were opened with the Afghan commander, who was informed that the cavalry had not come out with the intention of fighting, but to get the water turned into the channel. The Afghan regulars halted about 3,000 yards from our troops, but the tribesmen continued to advance on both flanks, and opened fire on the column. An Afghan officer came out to parley, and gave his word that the water should be turned on provided our troops did not attack. He personally ordered the tribesmen on our flanks to retire, but the latter took no notice of him, and continued to fire intermittently on our troops. By 1500 hours there was no sign of water in the channel, and a further stay would have led to fighting, so the column retired to Chaman. This undignified action did us much harm, as it showed the Afghans to what lengths we were prepared to go to avoid a renewal of hostilities. Moreover the water supply of Spin Baldak was dependent on the good offices of Abdul Qudus until the pipe line was completed a month later.

Although an attack by Afghan regulars was considered unlikely, it was thought that tribesmen might penetrate the Toba plateau, and threaten our lines of communication. Owing to the scarcity of supplies, however, this route could only be traversed by small parties. It was decided that, if any such incursions should be made, the raiders should be dealt with by Internal Security troops. The 12th Mounted Brigade were employed on the defence of the railway at this time, and were distributed between Kila Abdulla and Shelabagh. To provide for the security of the Kila Abdulla, Barshor and Peshin valleys, the 2/119th Infantry and the 13th Lancers were moved to Peshin, whilst the detachment of the 2/119th Infantry at Hindubagh was also ordered to Peshin on relief by a company of the 3/124th Baluchistan Infantry from Quetta. The tribesmen, however, made no attempt to invade the Toba plateau but gathered at Loeband, as will be explained in the next chapter, so that the 2/119th Infantry less 2 companies were despatched to Hindubagh, whilst the company of the 3/124th Baluchistan Infantry was diverted to Peshin.

During the latter half of June, the Afghans in the vicinity of Aga Jan and Murgha Chaman were reinforced. The following additional British troops also arrived in Baluchistan:—

Date.	Unit.	From
19th June . .	No. 11 Armoured Car Battery . . .	Hyderabad.
22nd June . .	2/3rd Gaur Brahmans	Ahmedabad.
23rd June . .	No. 17 Fd. Coy., 3rd S. and M., less 2 sections	Kirkee.
25th June . .	Kapurthala Infantry	Kapurthala.
	Nabha Infantry	Nabha.
	Jind Infantry	Jind.
	Alwar Lancers	Alwar.
27th June . .	102nd Grenadiers	Mhow.
	1104th Battery, R. F. A.	Meerut.
30th June . .	16th Rajputs	Arangaon.
1st July . .	38th Divisional Signal Co. . . .	Poona.
4th July . .	Nawanagar Lancers (1 squadron) . .	Karachi.
	No. 68 Burma Company, 3rd S. and M. .	Mandalay.

Of these the Kapurthala and Nabha Infantry were despatched to Sistan and Duzdap for the protection of the East Persian line.

In the middle of July, there seemed to be every possibility that hostilities would be resumed, as the Afghan peace delegates failed to arrive at Dakka. Preparations were, therefore, made to attack the Afghan concentration near Murgha Chaman. The duties of railway security were taken over by the 2/3rd Gaur Brahmans, one company of the 107th Pioneers, and one company of the 3/124th Baluchistan Infantry. The 12th Mounted Brigade less the 40th Cavalry and two sections of No. 22 Squadron, Machine Gun Corps, together with the 1104th Battery, R. F. A. and the 2/56th Rifles, F. F. were sent forward to New Chaman. The 102nd Grenadiers were moved to Peshin and the Jind Infantry to Hindubagh, whilst the 2/119th Infantry and the 3/124th Baluchistan Infantry were concentrated at Kila Abdulla to form a reserve which could be employed either on the Toba plateau or on the Chaman front. The 16th Rajputs, 2 squadrons of the Alwar Lancers and the one squadron of the Nawanagar Lancers were ordered to Loralai to relieve the 3rd Skinner's Horse, the 1/5th Light Infantry and No. 281 Company, Machine Gun Corps, which were to return to Quetta.

At this time the enemy forces on the Chaman front were:—

At Murgha Chaman, Tsagai Springs and Sheroba.—

3 regiments of cavalry.

7 battalions of infantry.

38 guns.

6,000 tribesmen.

Takht, 6 miles North-West of Spin Baldak.—

1 regiment of cavalry.

3 battalions of infantry.

General Wapshare asked permission to attack the enemy but this was refused "unless the military security of his force was threatened". On the 20th of July, a resumption of hostilities was anticipated, as the Afghan delegates had not yet arrived at Dakka. Plans were made out for an attack on Murgha Chaman. Brigadier General O'Grady, commanding the 10th Infantry Brigade, assembled the following force at Kila Abdulla to attack the enemy left through the Toba plateau:—

1 troop, 13th Lancers.

No. 9 Mountain Battery, R. G. A.

1st Battalion King's (Liverpool) Regiment.

2/129th Baluchis.

Leaving Kila Abdulla on the 20th of July, the column arrived at Bogra springs on the 22nd. The attack was, however, abandoned owing to the arrival of the peace delegates at Dakka on the 24th of July.

Meanwhile, the situation at New Chaman became more intolerable. Interference with our patrols was carried to such an extent that our cavalry reconnaissances were confined to within a few miles of our defensive positions. The Achakzais were encouraged by our inactivity to make two attacks on the troops guarding the Khojak tunnel, whilst bands of raiders threatened our communications. After the 8th of August, when peace was signed, all enemy activity on this front ceased, and the tribesmen dispersed. Spin Baldak was handed over to the Afghans on the 14th of August, our troops returned to Chaman, and this portion of Baluchistan soon reverted to its normal condition.

CHAPTER X.

ZHOB.

On the 6th of May the troops in the Zhob were:—

Distribution of Troops.

Loralai.—

3rd Skinner's Horse.

2/11th Rajputs less detachments at:—

Kila Saifulla.
Maratangi.
Zara.
Murgha Kibzai.
Sarghundai.
Musa Khel.
Ghurlama.
Zarozai.

Fort Sandeman.—

3/1st Gurkha Rifles less detachments at:—

Kapip.
Babar.
Gwal.
Lakaband.
Adozai.

Harnai.—

1/5th Light Infantry.

The Zhob Militia who were 1,200 strong had their headquarters at Fort Sandeman and detachments scattered throughout the area.

Although an Afghan invasion of the Zhob was unlikely, yet it was possible to move troops into this area from Ghazni. The two routes by which Afghan troops could move most easily were:—

(1) By Gul Kach on the Gomal.

(2) By Kamr-ud-Din Karez.

From Gul Kach they could threaten Fort Sandeman, whilst Kamr-ud-Din Karez, which was 64 miles west of Fort Sandeman and the same distance north of Kila Saifulla, formed a base equally well situated for an attack on the Upper or the Lower Zhob.

Column at Kila Saifulla.

On the 20th of May, it was reported that 4 Afghan battalions had arrived at Wazikhwa, 34 miles north of Kamr-ud-Din Karez. Arrangements were, therefore, made to protect the Upper Zhob which was thus menaced. The 1/5th Light Infantry, who were relieved at Harnai by the 2/15th Sikhs on the 20th of May, and 2 squadrons of the 3rd Skinner's Horse from Loralai were ordered to proceed to Kila Saifulla, where they concentrated on the 1st of June. The information however, proved to be false, and the column at Kila

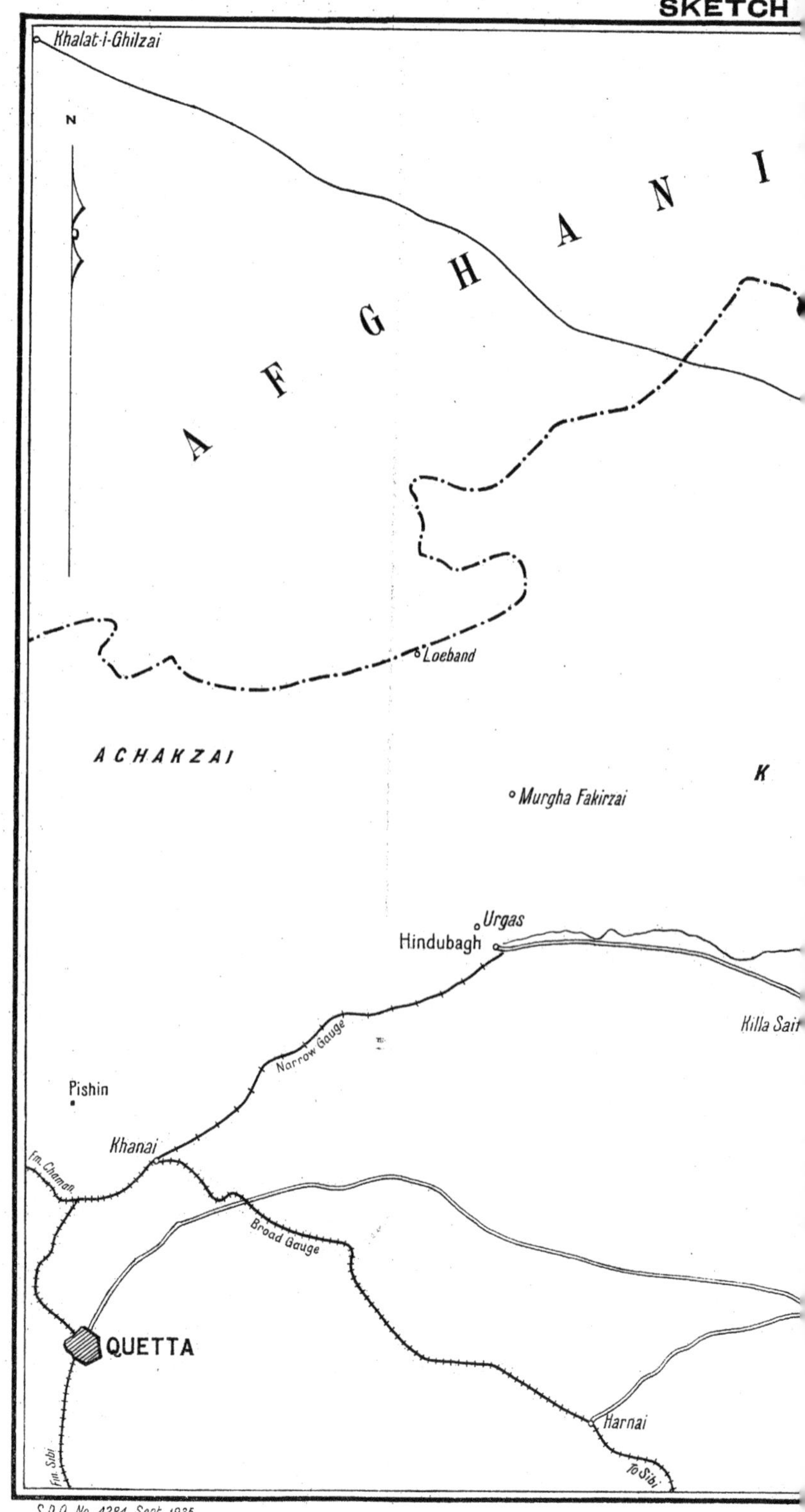

S.D.O. No. 4284 Sept. 1925.

Reg. No. 14 E. D. D. 1926 -1500.

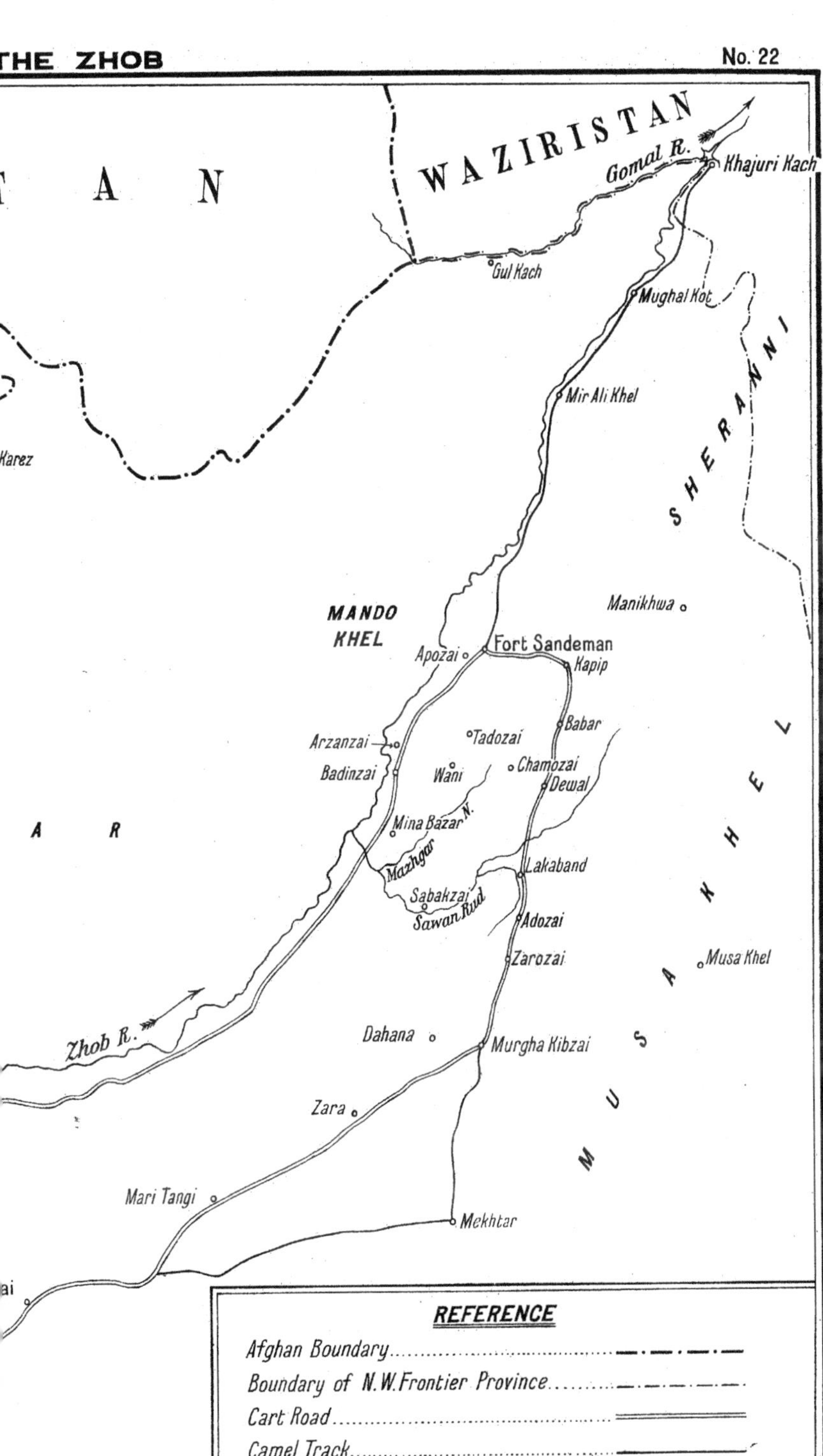

Heliozincographed at the Survey of India Offices, Dehra Dun

To face page 109

Saifulla was subsequently dispersed. No. 281 Company, Machine Gun Corps, were moved from Harnai to Loralai. A draft of 200 men of the 3/1st and 1/10th Gurkha Rifles was despatched to Fort Sandeman to bring the 3/1st Gurkha Rifles up to strength.

Major Russell at Moghal Kot.

It was not from Afghanistan that the peace of the Zhob was to be broken, but from Waziristan. As has been described in Chapter VI, Major Russell evacuated Wana and the Gomal posts, and arrived at Moghal Kot, 50 miles north of Fort Sandeman on the evening of the 27th of May. His party consisted of 7 British officers and about 300 men who had remained loyal. Moghal Kot was quickly surrounded by large bodies of Wazirs. Major Russell intended to march to Mir Ali Khel on the 28th of May, but his men were so tired and footsore after their running fight of 42 miles that he was compelled to postpone his departure for another day to rest them. More Wazirs continued to arrive during the day, and their numbers increased so rapidly that the South Waziristan Militia were unable to move on the 29th. There were only sufficient rations to last for the 30th and the water supply, which was outside the fort, was under heavy fire. There was no hope of relief. Fort Sandeman was garrisoned by 350 men of the 3/1st Gurkha Rifles and by the headquarters of the Zhob Militia, a force barely sufficient for the defence of the station. At Mir Ali Khel, 14 miles south of Moghal Kot, there were 150 infantry and 100 mounted infantry of Zhob Militia. Major Russell determined to cut his way out, and to retire on Mir Ali Khel with the help of the troops at the latter post. What afterwards occurred is described in "Operations in Waziristan, 1919-20", in the following words:—

Major Russell retires on Mir Ali Khel.

"One hundred and thirty rifles of the Zhob Militia, accompanied by one hundred mounted infantry of the same corps, were to leave Mir Ali Khel at 3 A.M. (on the 30th), and piquet half way to Moghal Kot. From this point the mounted troops were to push through towards Moghal Kot, where it was estimated that they should arrive at 6-30 A.M. On the following day (*i.e.*, 30th May), as there was no sign of the mounted infantry at 8-30 A.M., Major Russell ordered the evacuation to begin; heavy enemy fire was opened immediately by the tribesmen. Unfortunately the first piquet went too far and, failing to return when signalled to do so, moved in the direction of Mir Ali Khel. This movement became infectious and soon numbers of the Militia were to be seen fleeing in the direction of Mir Ali Khel, many abandoning their arms *en route*. The officers attempted to stem the route but in no case with success, for when an officer turned away from those he had collected, the men immediately disappeared. After four or five miles had been thus traversed the mounted infantry of the Zhob Militia appeared in sight holding piquets to cover the progress of the column. Efforts were again made to rally and reorganise the South Waziristan Militia in rear of the Zhob Cavalry. These were partly successful but the men were quite out of hand; the Pathan officers and N. C. Os. no longer had authority, and there were very few men who were at that time in possession of their rifles.

"The appearance and action of the Zhob Militia stopped the onrush of the Wazirs who had hitherto been carrying out a vigorous pursuit; and the survivors made their way to Mir Ali Khel.

"The officer casualties during the withdrawal from Mir Ali Khel were:—

Killed —

Captain G. T. Burn-Murdock, South Waziristan Militia.

Captain H. R. Traill, South Waziristan Militia.

Captain A. F. Reilly, Zhob Militia.

Lieutenant C. S. Leese, South Waziristan Militia.

Lieutenant E. J. MacCrostie, 1/25th London Regiment, Garrison Engineer, Wana.

Wounded —

Major G. H. Russell, South Waziristan Militia.

Lieutenant R. E. Hunt, South Waziristan Militia.

* * * * * * *

"The casualties among other ranks was not known accurately but are believed to have been about forty killed and wounded. Some of the column made their way *via* Manikhwa and the Sheranni country, and reached the Derajat some days later."

When the news of the arrival of Major Russell's party at Mir Ali Khel reached Fort Sandeman, it was realized that the local tribes would soon be in open rebellion. The evacuation of the Gomal posts and of the posts north of Fort Sandeman had left the way open for the Wazirs to overrun Northern Baluchistan, whilst the Sherannis and Mando Khels were now disaffected, as they thought that Fort Sandeman would also be evacuated.

Events at Fort Sandeman.

Lieutenant-Colonel Paul, the Commandant of the Zhob Militia, was the senior officer present, and he assumed command of the troops in Fort Sandeman. The 3/1st Gurkha Rifles were brought in from their barracks to the east of the fort to a perimeter camp covering the fort. Orders were also issued for the evacuation of all posts guarding the road between Fort Sandeman and Murgha Kibzai, and for the concentration of their garrisons at Fort Sandeman. Fortunately these orders were cancelled before they could be carried out, or the whole country would have been in a state of rebellion from the Afghan frontier to the borders of the Dera Ghazi Khan district. The garrison of Adozai actually retired on Lakaband, but returned the same evening.

Captain Yule moves to Lakaband.

The Zhob Militia and the survivors of the South Waziristan Militia arrived at Fort Sandeman from Mir Ali Khel on the 1st of June. The Sherannis now began to rise and desertions among the local Kakars and Mando Khels in the Zhob Militia became frequent. On the 2nd of June, the Sherannis gathered near Kapip and cut the telephone wires. On the 3rd of June, Captain Yule, the Assistant Political Agent, left Fort Sandeman with 45 mounted infantry of the Zhob Militia to escort the wounded officers of the South Waziristan Militia on their way to Loralai. As the main road through Kapip was blocked, he made use of the mule track through Tadozai and the Lwargai pass, 2 miles north-west of Chamozai, by which he reached Lakaband on the main road on the 4th of June without seeing signs of any enemy. Here motor ambulances were waiting, and the wounded officers were removed to Loralai on the same day.

At Lakaband Captain Yule was able to communicate with Quetta and to acquaint Baluchistan Force Headquarters with the actual state of affairs. He had another piece of unpleasant information to impart to them, as the Zhob Militia garrison at Manikhwa, 24 miles east north-east of Fort Sandeman, had tamely surrendered to a gang of 250 Sherannis on the 3rd of July. The men in this post were Ghilzais from Afghanistan, and the naïve explanation of their defection given by the three Indian officers who escaped to Fort Sandeman was that the enemy had placed a charm on their rifles, and that none of them would fire. He also explained to Force Headquarters that the Mando Khels and Kakars in the Militia had all deserted.

Surrender of Manikhwa post.

Captain Yule also obtained information by telephone from the posts north of Lakaband. The Gurkha Officer at Gwal reported that a body of the enemy had been seen moving from Kapip on Lakaband, whilst the inspector of police at Babar stated that Kapip had fallen into the hands of the tribesmen. Captain Yule rightly concluded that his own party, which had passed within a mile and a half of Gwal, had been mistaken for enemy. He had no means of ascertaining the truth of the fall of Kapip, which afterwards proved false. Mounted patrols were sent out to the north towards Gwal, and along the hills to the east of the plain which stretches from Gwal to Babar, but they failed to find any enemy. Gwal and Babar posts were, however, evacuated and their garrisons brought in to Lakaband.

The draft for 3/1st Gurkha Rifles.

On the 5th of June, the reinforcements for the 3/1st Gurkha Rifles arrived at Zarozai. They consisted of 2 British officers and 198 other ranks. Most of these were recruits of 6 to 8 months service, and there were no Gurkha Officers and few non-commissioned officers among them. As the evacuation of Babar and Gwal, and the capture of Kapip, if true, would have made their onward march to Fort Sandeman dangerous, Captain Yule left Lakaband for Adozai with his party of 45 mounted infantry at 2000 hours on the 5th to lead the draft to Fort Sandeman by another route.

March across country.

At 0900 hours on the 6th of June, the Gurkha draft arrived at Adozai, where they halted for the day. Here they exchanged their cart transport for donkeys. They marched at 2000 hours across country in a northwesterly direction, and reached the Sawan Rud, a tributary of the Zhob, at 0100 hours on the 7th. Here they camped till dawn, and then moved down the Sawan Rud. By 1000 hours the donkeys were exhausted, and their loads were transferred to the mules of the Zhob Militia. At 1200 hours, Sabakzai was reached, and a halt of 6 hours was made. At 1800 hours the march was resumed. The Gurkha rearguard began to straggle, so their place was taken by the Zhob Militia. At 2300 hours the column arrived just south of Mina Bazar, 22½ miles south of Fort Sandeman, where they camped for the night protected by piquets of the Zhob Militia.

At 0600 hours on the 8th of June, the force left camp, and, after a march of 2¼ miles, the Fort Sandeman-Kila Saifulla road was reached. They were now 22 miles from their destination. By

0900 hours, they reached Arzanzai, $2\frac{1}{2}$ miles north of Badinzai where a little water was procured. Many of the Gurkhas were thoroughly exhausted by this time and as many of them as possible were placed on horses, mules, camels and donkeys, whilst the rations previously carried on baggage animals were destroyed. The march was then resumed, and, at 1200 hours, the plain 12 miles from Fort Sandeman was reached. The troops were now all tired out and they were compelled to halt for half an hour. The Gurkhas had had no food since the previous evening and very little water all day. Attempts were made to get into communication with Fort Sandeman by visual signalling, but the sun was overcast and this was found to be impossible. A mounted orderly was, therefore, sent on to Fort Sandeman to ask for assistance, and for carts to be sent out to bring in the more exhausted men.

Attacked by tribesmen.

The march from here onwards was painfully slow, as the column moved at a pace of $1\frac{1}{2}$ miles an hour. At 1730 hours they had approached within 6 miles of Fort Sandeman, when the enemy suddenly appeared on the hills on the right front. Barring the advance to Fort Sandeman, were two small hillocks between which the road ran. Captain Yule promptly sent parties of mounted infantry to secure these features, whilst the Gurkhas deployed and advanced in open order across the plain. The hillock to the left of the road was taken, but the party sent to seize the one to the right was badly handled and failed to secure their objective. A party of Gurkhas was then moved to the right to form a right flank guard, whilst the remainder advanced by short rushes. The flank guard soon got into difficulties and lost heavily. The rest made for the hillock on the left of the road, where they joined hands with 50 mounted infantry of the Zhob Militia and 50 rifles of the 3/1st Gurkha Rifles, who had come out from Fort Sandeman to help them. This latter party were formed into a rearguard, which covered the onward march of the draft. No further opposition was encountered, and the wounded were got in safely.

Our losses in this action were:—

Killed—

Lieutenant Allison, 3/1st Gurkha Rifles.

Other ranks 26.

Wounded —

Other ranks 6.

Up to this time, the tribesmen in the vicinity of Fort Sandeman had indulged in a little sniping, but otherwise they had been comparatively quiet. On the nights of the 8/9th and 9/10th of June, however, they looted and burnt the bazar, fired on the bungalows and exchanged shots with the piquets. By day they took refuge in the hills south of the fort. On the morning of the 10th of June, Captain Spain with 70 rifles of the Zhob Militia attacked these hills under cover of long range machine gun fire, and drove the tribesmen out. His losses were 1 man killed and 2 wounded, whilst 10 dead bodies of the enemy were counted. After this, there was little sniping for a considerable time.

Kapip relieved.

The arrival of the above-mentioned reinforcements made it possible to send out a column to relieve Kapip. Accordingly, on the 11th of June, a force of 200 rifles marched out from Fort Sandeman. On the outward journey, no opposition was encountered. The garrison was changed and the column retired. On the return journey they were attacked by a body of 200 tribesmen. These were easily beaten off and 9 of their number were killed, whilst our troops suffered no casualties.

Gwal Mandi and Apozai burnt.

On the 14th of June, a column of 100 rifles visited the villages of Gwal Mandi and Apozai just south of Fort Sandeman to recover loot which had been taken from the latter place. At first the tribesmen offered some slight opposition, but, after losing 2 men killed, they dispersed. Two cart loads of booty were recovered and the villages were burnt.

Musa Khel attacked.

Meanwhile the Sherannis, who live to the north-east of Fort Sandeman, were collecting to attack the post at Musa Khel, 29½ miles east north-east of Murgha Kibzai, which was held by 15 sabres of the 3rd Skinner's Horse and 46 rifles of the 2/11th Rajputs. On the morning of the 10th of June, Major Bruce, the Political Agent at Loralai, left Murgha Kibzai with 25 sabres of the 3rd Skinner's Horse to reinforce this post. They were followed at 1500 hours by 54 rifles of the 2/11th Rajputs. The cavalry column reached Musa Khel the same night, but the infantry camped for the night at Sarghundai, 15½ miles from Murgha Kibzai.

On the following morning, the 11th of June, about 500 Sherannis advanced on Musa Khel, but they were driven off without difficulty. An aeroplane from Murgha Kibzai flew over the post just before the attack started, and on its return, reported that fighting was in progress. A squadron of the 3rd Skinner's Horse was sent out to Musa Khel immediately. They and the infantry detachment arrived there on the evening of the same day, only to find that the tribesmen had retired to their own country. The squadron and 16 sabres of the 3rd Skinner's Horse were withdrawn to Murgha Kibzai on the 12th, and a garrison of 25 sabres and 100 rifles were left in the post.

Mobile column formed.

As soon as the news of the disturbances in the Lower Zhob reached Quetta, arrangements were made to concentrate a force at Murgha Kibzai for the relief of Fort Sandeman, under Brigadier General H. de C. O'Grady, commanding the 10th Infantry Brigade. The movement of these troops is shown in the table below:—

Unit.	From	Date of Departure from station.
3/124th Baluchistan Infantry, less 2 companies	Quetta	6th June.
Patiala Lancers	Do.	7th June.
H. Q. 10th Infantry Brigade	Do.	8th June.
1/5th Light Infantry	Kila Saifulla	Do.
1 section, No 281 Co., M. G. C.	Loralai	

At 0100 hours on the 16th of June, this force had concentrated at Murgha Kibzai, and a forward move on Fort Sandeman was commenced on the same day. Zarozai was reached on the 17th, and Gwal on the 18th. The post at Babar, between Zarozai and Gwal, was found to have been burnt by the tribesmen. A party of 30 men fired on the advanced guard of the column 2½ miles north of Babar, but no other enemy were seen. Kapip was reached on the 19th of June, and here the column remained, as there was not sufficient drinking water at Fort Sandeman for such a large force. The telegraph wires had been thoroughly destroyed, and had to be replaced by the Signal Service. The neighbourhood was searched, but no trace was found of Wazirs and Sherannis, and it was believed that these marauders had returned to their own country.

Mobile column reaches Kapip

A fresh scheme was devised for the security of the road from Murgha Kibzai to Fort Sandeman which was to keep a force at Lakaband consisting of:—

1 squadron, Patiala Lancers.
1 section, No. 38 Mountain Battery.
3/124th Baluchistan Infantry less 2 companies.

This force was to provide strong escorts for the weekly convoy from Murgha Kibzai to a point 2 miles north of Babar, where they were to be met by a similar escort from Fort Sandeman. The posts at Kapip, Adozai, Zarozai and Gurlama were abandoned, and their garrisons were evacuated. The remainder of the troops who had marched with General O'Grady were to be withdrawn to Loralai after measures had been taken to punish the Abdullazai Kakars and the Mando Khels for their share in the late disturbances.

Punitive Measures against Mandokhel and Kakars.

The first of these punitive measures was carried out by a column consisting of one squadron of the Patiala Lancers and 250 rifles drawn from the 3/1st Gurkha Rifles and the Zhob Militia. This column left Fort Sandeman and proceeded to Badinzai, 17 miles down the Kila Saifulla road. Here they filled their transport with *bhoosa*, and burnt several of the villages in the neighbourhood. On their return journey on the 30th of June they encountered a body of 200 to 300 tribesmen near the 12th milestone. The drivers of the hired transport immediately took fright and left their carts. The enemy were turned out of their position without difficulty, but it was a long time before the transport was reorganized and the march resumed. The column reached Fort Sandeman without further incident, having lost 1 follower killed and 1 Gurkha Officer and 2 followers wounded.

On the 3rd of July, the troops which were to be withdrawn to Loralai were formed into a column, and left Kapip for Fort Sandeman. It consisted of:—

1 section, No. 38 Mountain Battery.
1 section, No. 281 Company, Machine Gun Corps.
1/5th Light Infantry less 1 company.

At Fort Sandeman it was joined by the following force under Captain A. W. Woodhead:—

200 rifles, 3/1st Gurkha Rifles.
100 rifles, Zhob Militia.
2 Lewis Guns.

The combined forces marched to Wani on the 4th with the surplus civil population of Fort Sandeman. The villages along this route were found to be deserted, and five of them were burnt. On the 5th of July, Captain Woodhead's party moved across country to Babar on the Loralai-Fort Sandeman road, whilst the main column moved to Mina Bazar. The latter burnt one village during the march.

At Mina Bazar, news was received that a body of Abdullazai Kakars about 140 strong was expected to arrive in the vicinity that night from the south west. This large gang had raided the large village of Mekhtar, 22 miles south of Murgha Kibzai, on the 1st of July. They had wrecked the telegraph office, and had carried off a large amount of loot. They had then made for Dahana, 6 miles west of Murgha Kibzai. The down convoy had reached the latter place on the afternoon of the 2nd of July, escorted by 2 troops of the Patiala Lancers and 100 rifles of the 3/124th Baluchistan Infantry. Hearing that the gang was in the vicinity, Captain Goolden, who commanded the escort, sent off Subedar Ghulam Unis Bahadur with two platoons totalling 50 men altogether (Khattaks) to Dahana at 0330 hours on the morning of the 3rd of July. Ghulam Unis arrived at Dahana at 0600 hours and found the village deserted. He pushed on towards the west, and came in contact with a piquet of the raiders. He opened fire on this party with his Lewis gun, and the enemy fled leaving 2 men dead and 2 wounded. He then advanced and found the place in which the raiders had camped for the night. This was deserted, but 2 rifles, 1 Webley revolver and 1 horse were captured. Ghulam Unis then marched north east and joined the up convoy at Zarozai after covering 24 miles during the day.

Raid on Mekhtar.

Gang ambushed near Mina Bazar.

To intercept this gang, an ambush was laid by 100 rifles and 2 Lewis guns of the 1/5th Light Infantry on the night of the 5/6th of July. They left camp at 2000 hours on the 5th, and took up a position in the bed of the Mazghar Nala, which joins the Sawan Rud near Mina Bazar. At 0200 hours, on the 6th, a party of the enemy were heard advancing up the nala. Very lights were sent up, and these disclosed a large number of men and animals in the stream bed. Fire was opened on them and they disappeared. In the morning, four camel loads of cloth were found, valued at Rs. 4,000.

On the 6th of July, the column marched to Mohammed Yar Karez on the Fort Sandeman-Kila Saifulla road. From here they turned south, and, after spending one night at Tangi Kats, reached Zara post on the 8th of July. Here General O'Grady left the force, and proceeded to Quetta. On his way through Loralai, he handed over command of the Zhob to Brigadier-General G. A. Gale.

To return to the party under Captain Woodhead, which reached Babar on the 5th of July. Here he took over the up convoy, a section of No. 38 Mountain Battery, which had transferred from Lakaband to Fort Sandeman and a wagon wireless section. With these he marched for Fort Sandeman at 0830 hours on the 6th of July. On reaching Kapip at 1130 hours, a few tribesmen were seen near the dak bungalow. One gun of No. 38 Mountain Battery and one Lewis gun were pushed forward, and, under their fire, the advanced guard, reinforced by 50 men of the Zhob Militia, passed through Kapip and occupied the hills to the north of the post. The transport was then parked in the Pareza Nala, and piquets were placed to the west to cover the onward march. Two miles west of Kapip, the road enters a defile (tangi), and this was found to be occupied by a body of 200 to 300 Sherannis. Attacks were made on both sides of the road on the hills commanding the defile, but our troops made little progress. Captain Woodhead then went forward to lead the attack on the left of the road, whilst 50 men of the Zhob Militia made a detour to the south and outflanked the enemy. At 1415 hours, the hill to the south of the road was captured. Meanwhile, Lieutenant Sinker, who had been slightly wounded earlier in the day, was endeavouring to take the hill which commanded the defile from the north. He reached a point close to the crest, but was held up by enemy fire. On perceiving this, 2nd Lieutenant Gilbert, commanding the section of No. 38 Mountain Battery, ran forward one gun and opened an accurate fire on the hill at a range of 1,000 yards, under cover of which Lieutenant Sinker captured the position. **Fight near Kapip, 6th July.**

The defile was now secured, and the convoy passed through. There were no further positions from which the enemy could oppose the march of the column, but it was getting late. Preparations were made to halt for the night, but it was finally decided to push on to Fort Sandeman, which was reached without further fighting at 2030 hours. Our casualties were:—

Killed—

3/1st Gurkha Rifles, 2.

Zhob Militia, 1.

Wounded—

Captain A. W. Woodhead, 3/1st Gurkha Rifles.

Lieutenant E. C. Sinker, 3/1st Gurkha Rifles.

Jemadar Mohammed Khan, No. 38 Mountain Battery.

Indian other ranks—

No. 38 Mountain Battery, 3.

3/1st Gurkha Rifles, 11.

Zhob Militia, 3.

The enemy left over 30 dead bodies on the ground, but their exact losses were never known.

In accordance with the scheme for the protection of the Fort Sandeman-Loralai road, one squadron of the Patiala Lancers and the 3/124th Baluchistan Infantry were located at Lakaband. Originally the section of the mountain battery was also there, but this had left for Fort Sandeman, as mentioned above. The accommodation in the fort was insufficient for this force, so a temporary camp was formed near the Sawan Rud, 2 miles north west of Lakaband. On the 2nd of July, work was commenced on a perimeter camp, into which it was proposed to move the force when completed. It was still unfinished on the 13th of July, when information was received that a body of 700 Abdullazai Kakars and Wazirs were assembling at Chamozai on the Sawan Rud, 13 miles to the north, with the intention of attacking **Tribesmen attack Lakaband.**

Lakaband that night. Lieutenant-Colonel B. F. R. Holbrooke, commanding at Lakaband, posted three piquets for the protection of the camp. No. 1 was on a low ridge 800 yards east of the camp, whilst No. 2 and No. 3 were on the banks of the Sawan Rud, which here takes a bend, so that No. 2 piquet was 100 yards to the north, and No. 3 was 400 yards to the west of the camp.

At 0240 hours on the 14th, a body of about 200 of the enemy crept down the Sawan Rud, and began to attack No. 2 piquet. They were beaten off without much difficulty. Desultory firing was kept up on the piquets and on the camp during the rest of the night, but no further attempt was made to attack. Lieutenant-Colonel Holbrooke was dangerously wounded early in the fight, and the command devolved on Captain F. L. R. Munn, M.C.

At 0530 hours, just before daylight, Captain Lord left camp with 150 rifles and 2 Lewis guns to counter-attack the enemy. He found them in position 600 yards north east of the camp. He attacked at once, and the tribesmen retreated towards the north east, where they escaped in the broken ground. Captain Lord then wheeled to the left and moved against Zhara hill, an isolated feature 1 mile north of the camp, whilst Subedar Ghulam Unis Bahadur attacked it from the south with 50 rifles. The hill was taken without difficulty, and the tribesmen dispersed. Our casualties were 1 man killed and Colonel Holbrooke and 3 men wounded. During the morning of the 14th, the whole force was transferred to the partially finished perimeter, 300 yards away from the temporary camp.

Tribesmen defeat our troops near Babar, 15th July.

The convoy should have left Lakaband for Fort Sandeman at 0630 hours that day (*i.e.*, 14th). At first it was decided to hold it up, but as there were no signs of the enemy, it finally started for Dewal at 1130 hours with an escort of 191 rifles of the 3/124th Baluchistan Infantry. At 0600 hours on the 15th, the convoy left Dewal for the point 2 miles north of Babar, where it was to be taken over by the escort from Fort Sandeman. The camp at Dewal was left standing with a guard of 40 rifles under Lieutenant Daws. On reaching Babar information was received that a body of 200 tribesmen had been seen in the vicinity. Captain A. W. Goolden, who was in command of the troops, decided to park the bullock carts of the convoy in the compound of the rest house at Babar. He then pushed on with the mule carts of the convoy with the intention of piquetting the remaining 2 miles of road, and of joining hands with the troops from Fort Sandeman.. He had not proceeded more than half a mile, when he was attacked by a body of 800 to 900 Wazirs.

A detailed account of what subsequently happened has never been obtained. From the accounts of the survivors it appears that Captain Goolden at first overcame the enemy resistance and pressed on in the hope of meeting the Fort Sandeman detachment. There were, however, no signs of the latter arriving, and the convoy was forced to halt by the ever increasing activity on the part of the tribesmen. As it was almost certain that no help would arrive, Captain Goolden ordered the convoy to retire. As soon as this order was issued, the 33 mule carts of the convoy stampeded, and the column reached Babar in a state of complete disorganization. Here an attempt was made to reform the convoy, preparatory to a further retirement on Dewal, but

No. 23

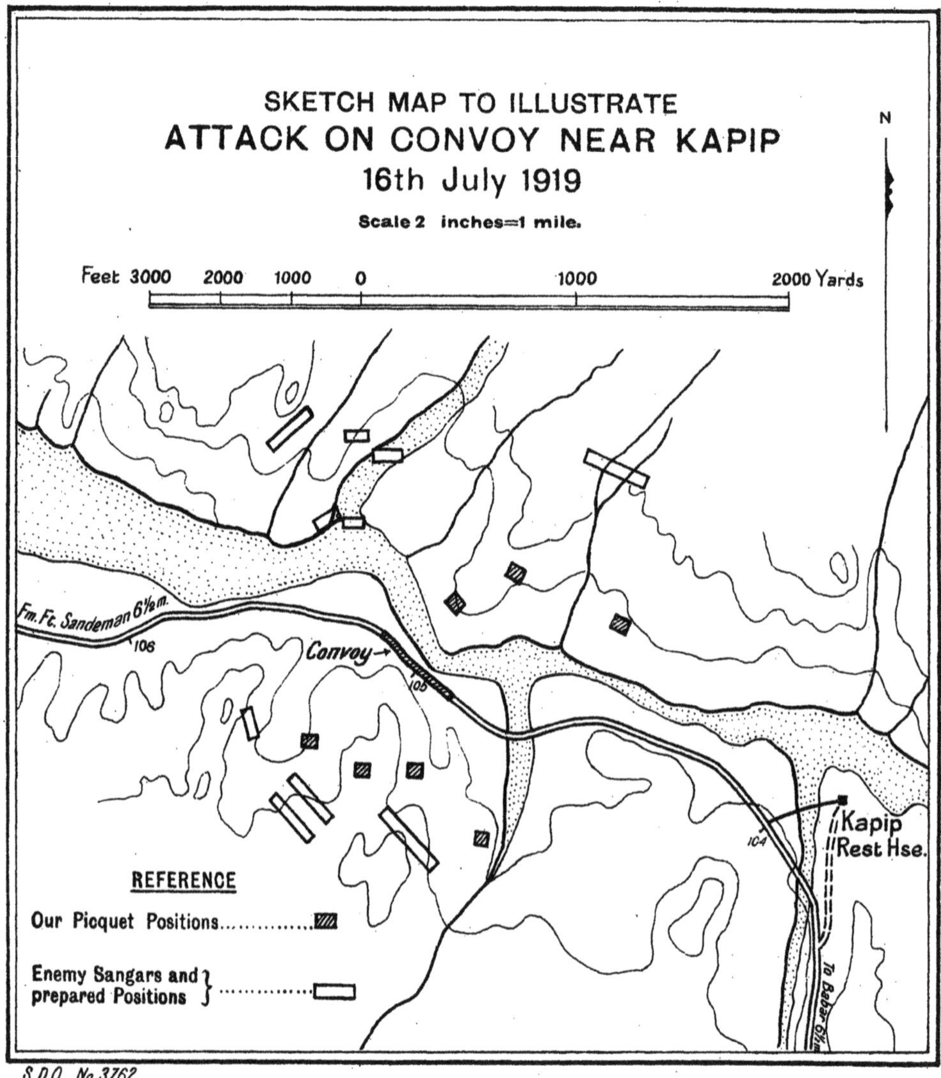

S.D.O. No. 3762

Reg. No. 14 E. D. D. 1926 -1500.

Heliozincographed at the Survey of India Offices, Dehra Dun.

To face page 119

it was found impossible to get the bullock carts out of the compound owing to the heavy fire brought to bear on it by the tribesmen.

The escort was now divided into two portions. A party of 2 Indian officers, 2 Lewis guns and 87 men under Subedar Saleh Mohammed installed themselves in the ruins of Babar post, and the remainder under Captain Goolden attempted to reach Dewal. The latter party was hotly pursued by the enemy and soon got out of hand. Captain Goolden was killed some 2½ miles north of Dewal, and after his death all organized resistance ceased.

Lieutenant Daws was first made aware of the state of affairs at 1230 hours, when the mule carts, which had again stampeded, passed his camp at a gallop. Behind them came large bodies of tribesmen. Lieutenant Daws judged that his small force of 40 rifles was not capable of affecting the situation materially, so he decided to retire on Lakaband. The tents were left standing, and the second line transport, whose animals were out grazing, was abandoned. The tribesmen immediately occupied the camp and looted it, whilst Lieut. Daws and his party made their escape unmolested to Lakaband where they arrived early in the afternoon.

As soon as he was made aware of the disaster, Captain Munn sent out a party to Gwal to assist Captain Goolden and his men, for the extent of the reverse was not then known. During the afternoon stragglers continued to arrive from the scene of action, many of them having been captured by the enemy and released after being deprived of their rifles, equipment and clothes. From their reports it was ascertained that Captain Goolden had been killed, and his force dispersed. An aeroplane from Fort Sandeman also dropped a message to say that there was no body of troops on the road retiring on Lakaband. The force which had proceeded to Gwal was, therefore, recalled, and it returned to Lakaband without having seen any sign of the enemy.

In view of the depleted garrison, the extent of the perimeter to be held, and the lowered morale of the garrison consequent on the results of the recent fighting, Captain Munn now decided to evacuate the camp, and to move to the unoccupied fort of Lakaband. This move was carried out on the 16th. The Police Station and the sarai were also placed in a state of defence and occupied.

In the meantime, the portion of the escort which had taken refuge in the post at Babar were surrounded by a body of 500 to 600 tribesmen, who made repeated and determined attempts to capture the post. These were all beaten off by the garrison, which maintained its position for 7 hours, until relieved by the escort from Fort Sandeman.

This escort consisted of 2 companies (225 rifles) of the 3/1st Gurkha Rifles, 75 rifles of the Zhob Militia and a section of No. 38 Mountain Battery. Owing to doubts as to the situation created by the attack on Lakaband, it had been delayed at Fort Sandeman for 3 hours, and had not left until 0900 hours on the 15th. On arrival at Kapip at 1330 hours, they were informed by a message dropped from an aeroplane of the situation at Babar. They immediately pushed forward to relieve the detachment of the 3/124th Baluchistan Infantry which was besieged in the post.

In the first 6 miles of their march from Kapip, no enemy were seen, but 1½ miles north of Babar fire was opened on them by a party of tribesmen who were in the hills east of the road. This body was attacked and dispersed and the column again moved forward. On approaching Babar, it was seen that the convoy was parked to the east of the post, which was being fired on from the high ground to the east and south. Guns and Lewis guns were then pushed forward and brought into action, and within half an hour they silenced the enemy fire. The column then advanced to the post. It was found that the garrison had suffered many casualties, whilst the dead bodies of 25 to 30 tribesmen lying round the post testified to the severity of the fighting.

Tribesmen defeat our troops near Kapip, 16th July.

The whole force then camped round the post for the night. A few shots were fired at them, but the majority of the enemy seemed to have disappeared. On the following morning, local inhabitants were sent out, and they reported that the road was clear as far as Kapip. It was decided to push on to the camp 6 miles east of Fort Sandeman, where they were to spend the night. Accordingly, at 1100 hours, the convoy and escort, together with the detachment of the 3/124th Baluchistan Infantry moved out of Babar. Piquets were pushed out, and spies from the village were sent out well ahead, but no signs of the enemy were seen until Kapip was reached. When approaching the defile which had been the scene of Captain Woodhead's fight on 6th of July, three men were seen dressed as Gurkhas. Lieutenant Dobbin went forward with three men to interrogate them, but they were fired on, and Lieutenant Dobbin was seriously wounded. It was then seen that the hills on either side of the defile were held by tribesmen. The column was, therefore, closed up, and Captain Copland, who commanded the troops, sent forward two parties, one under Lieutenant Dobbin (who although severely wounded refused to fall out) and one under Lieutenant ffrench to clear the hills overlooking the defile and to post piquets on them. These attacks were supported by artillery fire, but they only succeeded in establishing themselves on the lower spurs.

The enemy then began to press on the flanks and on the rear of the column. The convoy was advanced a few hundred yards close up behind the advanced guard. The enemy poured in a heavy fire from the hills and inflicted many casualties on men and animals. The advanced guard was unable to make further progress in spite of one gun being run up almost level with them. Captain Copland then went forward with all the men he could collect, which amounted to about 20, but he found it impossible to make any headway, and was forced to retire after his party had suffered many casualties.

The men were now utterly exhausted after the hard piquetting and fighting in which they had already been engaged. Captain Copland, however, managed to scrape together another small party with which he endeavoured to advance, but he was killed in the attempt. Soon after Lieutenant Dobbin and Lieutenant ffrench were also killed, and 2nd Lieutenant Gilbert, the only surviving British officer was left in command. His advance was barred in front by enemy *sangars*, the piquets on the hills to the north and south were in danger of being driven off, and the rearguard was threatened. Just as it was getting dark, the tribesmen opened a short burst of rapid fire and then charged the convoy. Fierce hand-to-hand fighting ensued, but the escort were outnumbered and were swept away. The two guns were captured after being put out of action by their gunners, and the convoy was seized. The carts were then plundered and their contents carried away by the enemy. Lieutenant Gilbert was with the rearguard at the time, and this party and a Lewis gun of the 3/124th Baluchistan Infantry were able to inflict casualties on the tribesmen as they made off to the north with their booty.

After this all was chaos, and the troops, with the exception of the rearguard of the Zhob Militia, split up into twos and threes and made their way to Fort Sandeman. 2nd Lieutenant Gilbert remained on the ground till 0115 hours on the 17th and then made a detour and reached the main road 4 miles from Fort Sandeman. He and his party reached the latter place at 0900 hours.

It was afterwards ascertained that the enemy consisted of a mixed force of 2,000 Wazirs, Sherannis and Suliman Khel Ghilzais from Afghanistan. Their losses in these engagements were never ascertained, but they must have been heavy. Our total casualties in the actions fought on these two days amounted to:—

Killed—

Captain A. W. Goolden, 3/124th Baluchistan Infantry.
Captain R. W. Copland, 3/1st Gurkha Rifles.
2nd Lieut. F. le F. Dobbin, 3/1st Gurkha Rifles.
2nd Lieut. E. D. ffrench, 3/1st Gurkha Rifles.

Other ranks—

No. 38 Mountain Battery, 1.
3/124th Baluchistan Infantry, 13.
3/1st Gurkha Rifles, 33.
Followers, 2.

Wounded—

2nd Lieut. V. J. Gilbert, R. A.
Jemadar Sher Zaman, 3/124th Baluchistan Infantry.

Other ranks—

No. 38 Mountain Battery, 7
3/124th Baluchistan Infantry, 29
3/1st Gurkha Rifles, 25
Zhob Militia, 5
Followers, 3

giving a total of 53 men killed and 71 wounded.

Mobile column formed.

As soon as the news of these reverses reached Loralai, arrangements were made to form another mobile column. The force in the Zhob was sufficient to deal with risings of the Kakars and Mando Khels, but the presence of large bodies of Wazirs, Sherannis and even Suliman Khel demanded additional troops to deal with these invaders. It was calculated that one regiment of cavalry, one battery of artillery, one machine gun company and three battalions of infantry were required in addition to the troops already in Baluchistan. Three battalions of infantry were already allotted to Baluchistan Force to strengthen the force at Kila Abdulla and Peshin, and these were to be diverted to the Zhob on their arrival. A mountain battery was placed at General Wapshare's disposal from army troops. As no machine gun company was available, it was decided to form one locally by training teams for 15 machine guns in Quetta. Thus arrangements were made for the whole force considered necessary with the exception of the regiment of cavalry. A table showing the concentration of troops at Murgha Kibzai is given below:—

Unit.	From	Quetta.	Harnai.	Murgha.
1-97th Infantry	Ambala	19th July	...	31st July.
1-153rd Infantry	Anandi	...	25th July	12th August.
2-153rd Infantry	Anandi	...	25th July	12th August.
No. 37 Mountain Battery.	Rawalpindi	...	24th July	12th August.

On the 17th of July, the 16th Rajputs arrived at Loralai, and on the 18th a small column consisting of:—

1 section, No. 38 Mountain Battery,

1 company, 2/11th Rajputs,

16th Rajputs, less 2 companies,

left for Murgha Kibzai where it arrived on the 21st of July.

Fort Sandeman was rationed up to the middle of September and Lakaband up to the 8th of August. It was decided that there was no need to send on the convoy, which should have left Murgha on the 18th and it was detained until conditions became more favourable. The tribesmen had collected at Kapip and were waiting for an opportunity to attack this convoy. As day after day passed, and no news of its arrival was received, they decided to lay siege to Fort Sandeman. A small party of 700 men appeared before the latter place on the 27th of July, and exchanged shots with the garrison. The noise of the firing caused a stampede among the animals, and 85 horses and ponies and 12 mules got away and were never seen again. On the following day the enemy numbers increased until about 4,000 men had collected. Their lack of cohesion, however, and their tribal jealousies prevented them from making any determined attack on the fort and perimeter. On the 3rd of August, an aeroplane from Quetta landed at Fort Sandeman after bombing the enemy encampments. It returned to Quetta on the same day. After this the tribesmen began to disperse, and they gradually disappeared. The mobile

Siege of Fort Sandeman.

column, which left Murgha Kibzai on the 12th of August, arrived at Fort Sandeman on 19th without encountering any opposition. The 3/1st Gurkha Rifles were relieved by the 1/97th Infantry, and the column withdrew.

Small parties of tribesmen had also penetrated as far as the Harnai-Loralai road, and on the 27th of July, a gang captured a tender belonging to the Royal Air Force near Raigora, 6 miles north west of Smallan. They got away with two Lewis guns, but one officer and 2 British other ranks escaped to Harnai, and 2 British other ranks escaped to Smallan.

Whilst these events were taking place, a force of 500 tribesmen, most of whom were deserters from the Zhob Militia, gathered in the hills north of Hindubagh and at Murgha Fakirzai, 25 miles north of the former place. On the 14th of July, a force consisting of 6 platoons of the Jind Imperial Service Infantry and 2 troops of the 3rd Skinner's Horse marched out from Hindubagh to engage a portion of this gathering in the vicinity of Mandak and Urgas, about 3 miles to the north and to the west of the post. A few enemy were met with, but the Jind Infantry showed a lack of training which would not have justified an attack being made on the breastworks held by the tribesmen. The fight was, therefore, broken off and the troops returned to Hindubagh.

Events at Hindubagh.

After this it was decided to replace the Jind Infantry by a detachment of the 2/15th Sikhs and to move the former unit to Harnai. Before this relief took place, the Extra Assistant Commissioner, with an escort of Jind Infantry, set out from Hindubagh on the 22nd of July with the intention of burning two towers in the village of Urgas. No opposition was expected, but suddenly 300 tribesmen attacked the right flank, and threatened the line of retirement. The men of the Jind Infantry got quite out of hand and expended their ammunition wildly. It was entirely due to the steadiness of a party of the 3rd Skinner's Horse under Captain Lyons, who opposed the enemy dismounted, that the survivors succeeded in reaching the post. The casualties among the Imperial Service Troops were:—

Killed—

Lieutenant A. Thomson.

Subedar Prem Singh.

Subedar Thaman Singh.

Other ranks, 12.

Wounded—

Major J. Masters.

Subedar Bishan Singh.

Other ranks, 20.

On receipt of this news at Quetta, an aeroplane was sent over to clear up the situation. A party of 80 tribesmen were seen about 1,000 yards from the post and these scattered on being bombed. In the evening, however, the enemy again approached, and kept up an intermittent fire on the post all night, killing one and wounding one of the garrison. The tribesmen also burnt the railway station and took away 16 hired camels and 2 ponies.

Two companies of the 1/102nd Grenadiers and 2 sections of No. 19 Motor Machine Gun Battery were ordered from Peshin to Hindubagh, where they arrived on the 26th of July without opposition. Prior to their arrival, the enemy had damaged the railway bridges and the rain had washed out the track, so that the line north east of Murgha Mekhtarzai was quite unserviceable.

On the 28th of July, Lieutenant-Colonel H. G. McRae, who was commanding the Railway Security Troops, moved up to Hindubagh with No. 11 Armoured Motor Battery. A party of tribesmen attempted to attack the armoured cars 7 miles from Hindubagh as they mistook them for transport lorries, but they were driven off and dispersed. A few shots were also fired from Karezgi fort, 1½ miles west of Hindubagh, which was in the hands of the enemy.

On arrival at Hindubagh it was found that the squadron of Skinner's Horse and a squadron of Alwar Lancers, who had arrived that afternoon from Kila Saifulla, were attacking Karezgi fort. The 2 sections of No. 19 Motor Machine Gun Battery were also in action in the hills to the north of the post. Colonel McRae considered that the arrangements for the attack were unsound, and he, therefore, ordered the fight to be broken off. On the following morning, the 29th, Karezgi was occupied without opposition, and a permanent garrison of 60 rifles was placed in the fort. The Jind Infantry left for Harnai on the 30th of July, and after this the district was less disturbed.

After the relief of Fort Sandeman there was no more fighting in the Zhob, but it was a long time before normal conditions were restored. Small gangs of raiders were active for a considerable period and it was found necessary to send a column to punish the Sherannis for their share in the attacks on our troops and for the raids they had carried out in the Dera Ismail Khan and Dera Ghazi Khan districts.

These and other measures taken to reduce the Zhob to order do not come within the scope of the present work although they were the aftermath of the Third Afghan War.

CHAPTER XI.

Administrative Measures. The Cholera Epidemic.

The foregoing chapters have dealt mainly with operations. It is now proposed to touch on a few of the salient points of the administration of the forces in the field. As has already been explained in Chapter III, India was unfortunately placed at the opening of the campaign. The absence of large numbers of units overseas, the shortage of transport animals, the lack of technical stores and the partial demobilization of the army, all combined to make a certain amount of improvisation necessary. The pages following deal with the difficulties encountered in maintaining the fighting forces in the field, and are not intended as an exhaustive study on the subject.

Railway and Concentration Arrangements.

During the early days of the war, the railway programme was well ahead of the scheduled time. This was due in no small measure to the restrictions placed on travelling in the Southern Punjab by Martial Law, which resulted in a quantity of rolling stock and a number of engines being available, which would otherwise have been absorbed in normal traffic.

Peshawar-Jamrud extension.

At the same time, the arrangements at railheads were far from satisfactory. The extension from Peshawar to Jamrud was a single line, which was roughly laid and poorly ballasted. Five miles west of Peshawar it crossed the dry bed of the Narai Khwar (stream) which was liable to floods when rain fell. There was no bridge, the lines being laid in the nala bed. A painted post showed the engine driver the depth of the water during spate, and he could then judge whether it was possible to cross without putting out his fires.

Jamrud railhead.

At the outbreak of hostilities, there were no sidings at Jamrud, and, although work was begun on these immediately, they were not ready for use until the beginning of June. Troops and stores had to be detrained at Peshawar, and much delay was occasioned by the congestion at the latter place. Mechanical transport, which should have been working ahead of Jamrud, was employed to convey stores between Peshawar and Jamrud, and its carrying capacity was thereby curtailed. The work of doubling the railway from Peshawar to Jamrud and of building a bridge over the Narai Khwar was put in hand, but was not completed until after peace was signed.

Khyber Ropeway.

In July the task of erecting an aerial ropeway from Jamrud to Landi Kotal was taken in hand, but this also was incomplete when hostilities ceased. A survey for a broad gauge railway through the Khyber was made during the operations, but the construction was not commenced till late in the year.

Kohat railhead.

At Kohat there were certain difficulties about the concentration camp. The ground itself belonged to small farmers, and was under cultivation in May 1919. The value of the crops had to be assessed, and the crops themselves cut before work could be started on the lay out of the camp.

Change of gauge at Kohat.

There was a break of gauge to contend with, as Kohat is the terminus of the broad gauge system, and a 2′ 6″ line ran from there to Thal. Broad fans were constructed in the concentration camp, with narrow gauge lines running between each pair of broad gauge lines. Even then, the distance between them necessitated the employment of a large amount of labour to handle the breaking of bulk and re-loading.

Mari Indus.

The railway communications to Bannu and Tank were more precarious. The broad gauge system ended at Mari Indus on the left, or east bank of the Indus river. Here bulk was broken, and stores were transferred to a narrow gauge line a mile long, which ran to the water's edge. The trucks were here transfe...ed to flats and towed across the river to Kalabagh, where they were dragged up into the sidings to be marshalled into rakes for despatch to Bannu and Tank. Troops had to march across the sandy bed of the river, and to cross by the steam ferry.

WATER SUPPLIES ON THE NORTHERN FRONT.

Water.

Water plays such an important part in campaigns on the North-West Frontier, that a brief description of the sources of supply in 1919, would not be out of place in a history of the campaign.

Peshawar.

Peshawar has a piped and filtered supply which is drawn from the Bara river, 8 miles to the south west. In normal times, the yield is ample for the requirements of the garrison. In 1919, with the large numbers of additional troops dependent on it, there was never any actual shortage, but at times arrangements had to be made to husband the supplies to provide for the needs of the garrison.

Kacha Garhi.

Kacha Garhi 5½ miles west of Peshawar, which should have been the concentration area, also drew its water from the Bara. There were, however, only 6 standpipes, which were insufficient for the number of troops which were actually located there.

Jamrud.

In 1919, a 2½″ pipe ran from Kacha Garhi to Jamrud. During the last week in May, a 4″ main was also laid. Even this did not give a supply sufficient for the needs of the large number of men and animals which passed through Jamrud during the course of the day. A brick conduit also brought water from the Bara River for irrigation purposes. This passed near several villages, and it was through drinking from this conduit that the troops contracted cholera in June.

Ali Masjid.

About 1½ miles above Ali Masjid was a perennial spring of pure wholesome water, with a yield of 500,000 gallons a day. Part of this water escaped underground, and the remainder formed the Khyber stream. The road crossed the water twice between its source and Ali Masjid, and the large number of men and animals which crossed the stream daily contaminated the water supply, which was derived from the Khyber stream. After the outbreak of cholera, the spring was railed off, and the water was piped down to Ali Masjid by gravitation. Later, a pumping plant was put up, and water from this source was forced up to Landi Kotal.

At Landi Kotal, water was obtained from the Tangi springs, and pumped up to the fort through a 4″ main. For several weeks only 12,000 gallons a day were obtained from this source, which was quite inadequate for the 8,000 men who were dependent on this supply. This gave about 1½ gallons a man on an average, whereas the actual requirements were found to be 3 gallons a man. The animals, which on occasions totalled 2,000 camels and 1,000 mules, had to be watered at the troughs at Tangi, 2 miles down the Landi Khana road. In July a 6″ pipe was laid from the Bagh springs, and 60,000 gallons a day were pumped up to a reservoir on the hill to the north of the fort, from whence it was piped by gravity to the fort and to the various camps. Landi Kotal.

At Landi Khana, water was obtained from the overflow of the Tangi and Bagh springs. Both of these streams go to earth before they reach the valley. By tapping the streams where they were still flowing, and by leading the water into cemented channels, an abundant supply of excellent water was obtained. Later, when the number of troops increased, a 4″ pipe was laid from the Tangi nala, and a 2½″ pipe from the Bagh nala, which gave an ample supply for all requirements. Landi Khana.

At Dakka, the Kabul river gave unlimited supplies of good water. Dakka.

At Kohat, water was obtained from the Bona spring, 3½ miles north west of the cantonment, whence it flowed by gravitation through a 5″ pipe. In normal times, this supply was sufficient for the needs of the garrison, but in the middle of June it was found necessary to lay an 8″ main to provide for the extra troops which had arrived in the area. In the mobilization camp, there was no piped supply previous to May, 1919. A 3″ main was completed on the 25th of May. Unfortunately the pipe was laid on the surface and not buried in the ground. Consequently, the water was so hot when it reached the camp that it was impossible to drink it. It was largely due to this that the troops and followers made use of the numerous irrigation channels which intersect Kohat, and this led to cholera. Kohat.

At Hangu, the water of a mountain spring was piped into iron tanks. These tanks proved insufficient for the number of troops eventually stationed there, but the provision of extra tanks remedied this defect. Hangu.

At Thal water was pumped up from a spring in the Sangroba Nala. After the siege, Roberts spring, a land spring ½ miles south west of the fort, was opened up, a reservoir was built on the highest point of the plateau, pipes were laid and water was pumped up to the reservoir. This proved sufficient for the force there. Thal.

It will thus be seen that in few cases was the water supply adequate for the number which had to be provided for. In most cases, arrangements had to be made after the outbreak of hostilities to provide sufficient for the troops concentrated in these various places. In the Khyber, political considerations had prevented the necessary work from being carried out; in the case of Jamrud and Kohat these measures could have been carried out in times of peace.

Cholera on the Northern Front.

During June and July there were violent outbreaks of cholera in the Khyber, and in the Peshawar and Kohat districts. What happened is best described in the following extract from a report by Major-General P. Hehir, C.B., C.M.G., C.I.E., M.D., I.M.S., Deputy Director of Medical Services to the North-West Frontier Force:—

" The outbreaks were the most extensive and sudden that have occurred in frontier warfare; at one time they threatened to immobilise the Forces; by the energy and devotion to duty of the medical services and the important and valuable help they obtained from other branches of the service this catastrophy was averted.

Cholera outbreaks.

" There were 7 explosive outbreaks in all, beginning at Hangu on the 1st of June, Kohat, Doaba, Thal and Jamrud on (or about) 5th June, Ali Masjid 6th and Landi Kotal on the 7th. By the 21st June cholera in an epidemic form had ceased but a few sporadic cases continued to occur.

Number of cases.

" There were up to the 8th July 1663 cases including 566 deaths, the vast majority of these occurred in followers, such as camel, bullock and labour corps, who were without sanitary establishments and medical officers. The comparatively small extent to which British troops were infected is most noteworthy and is attributed to the higher standard of work of their regimental sanitary detachments, but especially to the much better water discipline.

"The highest number of attacks in one day was 99 at Ali Masjid on the 15th of June, and 73 at Kohat on the 10th of June—these two garrisons bore the brunt of the epidemic, the former having had 404 and the latter 653 cases.

Difficulties in dealing with outbreaks.

"Many difficulties had to be combated in dealing with these outbreaks, the following, *inter alia*, being the more important:—

(*a*) Shortage of the authorised scale of water supply, especially at Kohat, Ali Masjid (during the epidemic), Landi Kotal and Thal, which caused Indian troops and followers to drink from water channels and other promiscuous collections of water, of many which were definitely proved by bacteriological examination to be infected with actual cholera germs.

(*b*) Shortage of medical officers and other medical personnel (and of sweepers) which rendered the supervision of sanitation and the actual treatment of cases a most laborious work for those engaged in it.

(*c*) Want of sanitary discipline in such units as labour, camel and bullock corps. It was difficult to prevent men of these corps drinking contaminated water to which practically all cases were due.

(*d*) The military situation which unavoidably hampered our work at Landi Kotal, Ali Masjid, Kohat and Thal, and prevented troops being moved from congested and infected areas to others more favourable.

(*e*) The Force, owing to the suddenness of the original advance, arrived in the area of operations in a poor state of protection from cholera, practically all units, including followers (about 100,000) had to be inoculated after arrival at areas of concentration.

(*f*) The lack of motor vehicles for the use of A. Ds. M. S. and sanitary officers, and of mechanical transport which made it difficult to get the equipment and medicines required to the infected posts at once.

(*g*) The high atmospheric temperature prevalent during the epidemic, almost all the cases having to be treated under canvas in which the temperature during the day varied from 114 degrees to 123 degrees fahr.

(*h*) The fact that cholera prevailed in the civil population; from this both troops and followers were in many cases infected.

"There has been no epidemic outbreak in Peshawar although several isolated cases have occurred....................

Lack of sanitary discipline among followers.

"The incidence of attacks and the degree of difficulty in controlling the disease was largely determined by the number of followers at the various stations and posts in which the disease appeared. These followers, consisting of labour, camel, bullock corps, *etc.*, are in the sanitary sense untrained and know nothing about water discipline and to control them in relation to the water they drink is an unsurmountable if not impossible task. They continued to drink specifically contaminated water though warned against it, and infected other harmless sources.

* * * * *

"It has to be confessed that although we were prepared for outbreaks of cholera we did not expect extensive outbreaks at several centres almost simultaneously.

* * * * *

Cause of the outbreaks.

"The direct cause of the disease was unequivocally the drinking of cholera-infected water from unauthorised sources."

Energetic measures were taken by the medical authorities. Cholera camps were established, inoculation was carried out, and arrangements were made to prevent the troops from drinking from water known or suspected to be infected. Early in July, the cholera died down and the outbreak was stamped out.

Rations.

The climatic conditions necessitated a more generous scale of rations being issued to the troops than had hitherto been the custom in frontier expeditions. On the 19th of May, the following scales were adopted:—

Scale of rations, British.

British troops.

Daily issues.

Bread	1 lb.
Meat	1 lb.
Bacon	3 ozs.
Potatoes	10 ozs.
Onions	6 ozs.
Other fresh vegetables	8 ozs.
Tea	$\frac{3}{4}$ oz.
Sugar	3 ozs.
Jam	3 ozs.
Condensed milk	2 ozs.
Tinned or dried fruit	2 ozs.
Salt	$\frac{1}{2}$ oz.
Vegetable oil for cooking	1 oz.
Fuel, wood	3 lbs.

Weekly issues.

Pepper	$\frac{1}{7}$ oz.
Mustard	$\frac{1}{7}$ oz.
Cigarettes or	20
Tobacco or	2 ozs.
Sweets	4 ozs.
Matches	2 boxes.

Thrice weekly.

Oatmeal with	3 ozs.
Condensed milk	1 oz.
Rice	$\frac{1}{3}$ oz.
Curry powder	$\frac{1}{8}$ oz.
Fresh lime juice	$\frac{1}{2}$ fluid ounce.

Scale of rations, Indian.

Indian Troops.

Daily issues.

Atta	$1\frac{1}{2}$ lbs.
Fresh meat	8 ozs.
Dhall	3 ozs.
Ghi	2 ozs.
Sugar	$2\frac{1}{2}$ ozs.
Potatoes	2 ozs.
Onions	2 ozs.
Other fresh vegetables	1 oz.
Tea	$\frac{1}{2}$ oz.
Fresh lime juice	$\frac{1}{2}$ fluid ounce.
Mixed condiments	$\frac{2}{7}$ oz.
Fuel, wood	2 lbs.

Weekly issues.

Tobacco or	2 oz.
Cigarettes or	40
Sweets	4 oz.
Matches	2 boxes.

Thrice weekly.

Ground nuts	2 oz.

The scale was a generous one, and ample for all requirements. Owing to the congestion at railheads, to the uncertainty of delivery by the railway, and to the shortage of transport, it was seldom that a full scale of rations was issued to the troops in the forward areas.

Ice and mineral waters. In addition to this ice and mineral waters were provided and proved very acceptable in the intense heat. Early in campaign, ice had to be brought up from Lahore and Rawalpindi; but the plant in the factories at Peshawar and Nowshera was enlarged and new factories were established at Landi Kotal, Kohat and Thal. In Quetta, the ice factory proved equal to all demands made on it.

Dairies. Dairies were opened at Dakka and Kohat in addition to the existing one at Peshawar, which was greatly enlarged. These provided pasteurised milk for the hospitals. **Canteens.** Field Canteens for British and Indian troops were established along the lines of communication, which supplemented the rations of the troops and followers, thereby helping to keep up their stamina, and adding to their comfort. At Quetta, vegetable gardens were planted, and the local fruit supply was tapped for the benefit of the troops.

Officers Messes. It was found necessary to arrange for officers messes at Peshawar, Kacha Garhi, Jamrud, Ali Masjid, Kohat and Thal, and these proved a boon to officers passing through these places.

Heatstrokes Stations. Heatstroke stations, well provided with ice, were put up to meet the needs of troops and followers along the lines of communication.

Mosquito nets, goggles and spine pads. To protect the troops from flies, sandflies and mosquitoes one mosquito net was issued to each combatant. A pair of goggles was also provided for each man to alleviate the strain caused by glare and dust. Spine pads were issued to all British troops, Gurkhas and Garhwalis, and proved very valuable during the heat waves of June and July.

Chaguls. To provide for the carriage of extra water, one canvas bag (chagul) was issued to each 2 combatants and one for each follower.

Red Cross and St. John's Ambulance. Before closing the chapter, mention should be made of the valuable aid given by voluntary societies. The Conjoint Red Cross and St. John's Ambulance Association largely supplemented the medical comforts and supplies which were provided for the hospitals. In addition to their scheduled articles, they supplied many other things such as Jost fans, fresh fruit and vegetables, clothing, bedding, furniture, toilet requisites and crockery.

Y. M. C. A. The Y. M. C. A. also did all within their power to keep up the reputation they had established during the Great War, and to bring home comforts and amusements within the reach of British and Indian troops.

CHAPTER XII.

Lessons of the War.

Political lessons.

Politically, there is much of interest in the events leading up to the Third Afghan War. Our previous campaigns had been deliberate offensives, carried out at times of our own choosing, to combat Russian influence in Afghanistan. In the Third Afghan War, the Afghans were the aggressors. At the time we were practically at war with the Bolshevik Government of Russia, which had taken the place of the Romanoff dynasty in 1917, and their influence was undoubtedly thrown into the scale against us. It was not this, however, which induced the Amir to commence hostilities against us. The primary cause of war was the desire of Amanulla to gain popularity in order to divert the attention of his subjects from the doubtful methods by which he had secured his throne. Such popularity could be gained by recovering the lost provinces of Afghanistan west of the Indus, and this territory, inhabited by a race alien from the people of the Peninsular, and allied in race, language and religion to the subjects of the Amir, must remain as a potential source of war till the tribes on our border are absorbed in the body politic of India. The opportunity occurred when the Southern Punjab practically rose in rebellion. Vain as the Afghans were, and are, it is inconceivable that they could have hoped for success in their enterprise against the disciplined and well equipped forces they were liable to meet, unless they found India in the throes of revolution. They undoubtedly hoped to find the military forces in India engaged in quelling civil disobedience and to a degree their hopes were not ill-founded. It should be borne in mind for the future that serious disturbances in India may be followed by an Afghan invasion, the avowed object of which would be the annexation of the Afghan " irredenta ".

Indian unrest.

Tribal menace.

The ease with which the Pathan tribes were raised against us shows how slight is our hold on them in times of religious and racial excitement. The subsequent cost to India in blood and treasure proves how dangerous these hordes of well-armed fighting men can be. Whilst these tribes remain independent and well armed, we must expect a portion, or all, of them to be hostile to us in the case of another war with Afghanistan. The inhospitable nature of their territory, and the absence of roads greatly increase our difficulties in dealing with these independent tribes. They lie across our main lines of advance from the North-West Frontier Province to Afghanistan, and large numbers of troops had to be employed to keep our lines of communication open through the Khyber. In the Kurram matters were somewhat better, but this was due in no small measure to the organisation of the Turi tribesmen by the Political Agent, whose efforts were rewarded by the efficient way in which the local inhabitants in the Kurram supported the troops and Militia.

Covering Force.

The plan of employing the Frontier Militias as a covering force behind which the Field Army could concentrate proved a failure in the Khyber and in Waziristan. That the scheme was not entirely unsound is shown by the steadfastness of the Chitral Scouts, the Mohmand Militia and the Kurram Militia. The lesson to be learnt is that irregular troops should not be left to meet the first onslaught of the invader, with regular troops in rear to support them as occasion requires. On the contrary, strong mobile Columns of regular troops should be located in the foremost line, from whence they can ensure, at all times, adequate and rapid support being afforded to the irregulars. These forward troops should not be part of the Field Army. They should form a protective screen behind which the Field Army can mobilize without hindrance or delay, and without being diverted from its function of delivering a crushing blow wherever we choose. The system in force in 1919 by which the 1st Division was replaced at Peshawar and Nowshera by the 2nd Division, which in its turn was pushed forward when relieved by the 16th Division, was unsatisfactory. The staff and transport became disorganised, and the Field Army disintegrated owing to the necessity of sending portions of the 16th Division to the Kurram and to Bannu. On the Southern Front, too, the 4th Division could not have taken the field complete, as the 10th Infantry Brigade was employed on purely protective duties.

Tactical lessons.

The tactical lessons of the campaign thoroughly vindicate the soundness of our text books. The susceptibility of the Afghans to a vigorous offensive was clearly demonstrated by the second action of Bagh on the 11th of May, by the fight at Dakka on the 17th of May, and by General Dyer's operations during the relief of Thal. The moral effect of these aggressive actions was to keep the Mohmands, Afridis and Orakzais quiet at a critical period. At the same time, moral effect is a thing which is purely local, and which quickly wears off. The inaction at Dakka, in the Khyber, in the Kurram, in Waziristan and at Chaman brought in all the tribesmen against us from the borders of Chitral to Baluchistan.

Moral effect of offensive.

Royal Air Force.

Although aeroplanes had been employed against the Mohmands in 1916 and against the Mahsuds in 1917, this was the first occasion on which they were used in any numbers within Indian limits. Little useful purpose can be served by drawing deductions from their performances during this campaign. The machines with which the R. A. F. were equipped when the Afghan War broke out were obsolete and worn out. Their climbing power was low, and this led to their being shot at from the hill tops as they passed along the valleys. Their moral effect was undoubtedly great, and the bombing of Dakka, Jalalabad and especially Kabul were factors which probably decided the Amir to sue for peace. The greatest credit is due to the officers of the Royal Air Force for the courage and skill which they displayed in performing their duties in these antiquated machines. They proved the value of the aeroplane in long-distance strategical reconnaissances, in bombing areas of concentration, supply depots and transport, but in short-distance tactical reconnaissances they were of no great value. The terrain was difficult and the tribesmen soon learnt how to break into small groups and to keep still when an aeroplane was overhead. The result of this was that bodies of the enemy were difficult to locate and negative information from the air had to be regarded with suspicion.

Cavalry.

The value of cavalry was fully demonstrated in the plains of Dakka and Peshawar, in the Upper Kurram and on the Chaman front. In spite of the heat, men and animals kept fit and put in valuable work. Their moral effect is still great on the frontier, and their mobility gives them a great advantage over the tribesmen. The only occasion when the " arm blanche " was used was at Dakka on the 16th of May. In the hills, they must be prepared to assume the role of mounted infantry, and to be capable of acting independently on all occasions. One famous cavalry regiment was described with pride by the infantry brigade commander as " the best infantry in my brigade."

Armoured Cars. Another mobile arm which showed its usefulness during the campaign was the armoured car. It possessed great fire power and mobility, whilst offering a small and almost invulnerable target to the enemy. Not only were they employed on the roads, but on occasion they moved across country with complete success as in the case of the attack of Karawal on the 23rd of July. They did invaluable work in patrolling roads and in escorting mechanical transport convoys. They are, however, liable to engine trouble, and the heat in the turrets when closed becomes intolerable.

Artillery. As regards artillery, the value of howitzer fire was very notable. The moral effect of the gun against both tribesmen and Afghan regulars was great. When firing on men in the open on the razor-backed hills which are such a common feature of the country, it was found that the howitzer with its high angle fire gave better results than the gun with its flatter trajectory. The 3·7″ howitzer, then used for the first time in India, proved to be a distinct advance in the armament of pack artillery.

Neither Afghan regulars nor tribesmen ever held a position in great depth, and it was found that the effect of frontal fire was slight. Whenever possible, oblique or enfilade fire should be employed.

The tribesmen sometimes attempted to rush piquets by night, and on these occasions a few shells usually dispersed the enemy. Night lines should be employed, and an artillery plan should be prepared for night as well as day.

Machine guns. Machine guns were largely employed for direct over-head covering fire, and for this they were eminently suitable in hilly country. The fire unit usually employed in the attack was the section of four guns, and this was found to produce better results than by splitting into sub-sections of two guns. For the defence of camps at night, they should be sited singly or in pairs to form belts of fire obliquely along each face of the camp, whilst the vulnerable points in front can usually be allotted to Lewis guns. Machine guns were rarely employed in piquet positions or in detached posts, and then only for specific purposes. An example of this was at Kafir Kot near Landi Khana, when a particular hill much used by snipers was out of range of rifle fire. A machine gun was placed in the Kafir Kot Piquet, and it successfully dealt with all enemy efforts to fire on the road or on the camp.

Lewis guns. Lewis guns were not a platoon weapon, as two were allotted to each company of infantry. They proved themselves to be eminently suitable for mountain warfare. Carefully used and firing short bursts, they provided a suitable and effective form of covering fire. It was found, however, that when the numbers in units dwindled owing to the wastage of war, that the number of Lewis guns had to be reduced so as to prevent the company becoming all covering fire without the bayonet strength necessary to take the offensive.

Grenades.

The Mills grenade proved useful on occasions, but large numbers of them failed to explode. Some had defective fuzes, and some split on the rocks when they fell. A far larger proportion were thrown without the pins being removed, which showed that the troops had not received training in their use sufficient to make the extraction of the pins a habit.

Permanent piquets.

The system of providing for the security of the lines of communication by establishing permanent piquets was first inaugurated by the 1st Division in the section between Dakka and Haft Chah. This proved safer and more economical in men than the old method of placing day piquets which were withdrawn when the convoy had passed through. The permanent piquet has the advantage, also, of keeping the ground under continuous observation. At the same time it must be borne in mind that troops shut up in permanent piquets lose all mobility, and this tends to have a lowering effect on the moral of troops, similar to that brought about by trench warfare in other theatres of war. The fewer the number of troops so employed, the less the offensive spirit of the force as a whole will suffer.

It was forcibly brought home to the garrison of Thal that, however suitable round piquet posts with dry stone walls are against tribesmen, they are dangerous when subjected to artillery fire.

Fire and movement.

With a mobile enemy who are adepts at laying ambushes, the movements of even the smallest body of troops should be covered by fire. This principle of "fire and movement" is now thoroughly understood by the tribesmen themselves, as is exemplified by their rushing the convoy at Kapip on the 16th of July, by the attack on Barley Hill piquet near Ali Masjid on the 17th of July, and by the counter-attack on Twin Peaks near Dakka on the 23rd of July. On each of these occasions the actual assault was covered by a heavy rifle fire.

Value of Training.

Above all, the infantry require to cultivate dash, and a desire to close with the enemy with the bayonet. This should be combined with a high standard of individual weapon training and a stringent fire discipline. Keen observation and an intelligent use of the peculiarities of the terrain are essential factors in the employment of infantry in mountainous country. Unless troops have attained a high degree of training, and have developed confidence in themselves and in their leaders, they cannot be employed to full advantage on the North-West Frontier or in Afghanistan.

Increase in Transport.

In comparison with previous campaigns on the Indian frontiers, the amount of transport employed was very large. Additional equipment, the provision of articles previously looked on as luxuries, the extra ammunition required by the more extensive use of artillery and machine guns, all tended to increase the transport necessary to maintain the troops in the field, and to make necessary the thorough consolidation of the lines of communication as the advance progressed. The effect of this was to reduce the mobility of the forces.

Probable result on future campaigns.

Formerly our object was to forestall the enemy, and to occupy his country before serious opposition could be organised. In previous campaigns, long advances were usual. Under modern conditions it is almost certain that advances into tribal country will be deliberate and by short stages, and every endeavour will have to be made to bring the enemy to action and to defeat him in the field as soon as possible after the opening of hostilities.

Railways.

The carrying capacity of the railways was found to be inadequate. This was mainly attributable to the shortage and bad condition of the rolling stock due to the great war. Perishable goods were received with the greatest irregularity, and rations were seldom in accordance with the authorised scale. The 2′6″ gauge line had a low carrying capacity, and proved unsuitable for the maintenance of large bodies of troops. In addition to this, the breaks of gauge at Nowshera, Kohat and Mari Indus not only occasioned delays, but were wasteful in labour. The events in the Zhob show the desirability for a railway line to Fort Sandeman, if operations are to be undertaken in this locality. From a military point of view, the construction of a bridge over the Indus at Kalabagh is also most desirable.

Organisation.

The proper organisation of both the administration and defence of the lines of communication is of primary importance. A certain amount of overlapping was caused by the failure to divide the functions of the Quartermaster General's Branch of the Corps Staff from those of the Inspector-General of Communications. This should be avoided in the future, and arrangements should be made to define the limitations of each.

Conclusion.

In conclusion, it will not be out of place or redundant to mention that in spite of the almost over-whelming difficulties that confronted the Army in India at the outbreak of this war our arms were victorious. Reference has been made elsewhere in this account of Nadir Khan's "feat of arms" at Thal, in the Kurram Valley, which was described in Afghanistan as an Afghan Victory and celebrated at Kabul by the erection of a column with a chained lion, representing Britain, at the base. Many instances can be quoted in which nations, defeated in war, have laid claims to a larger degree of success than later history records, but it is seldom that a nation has gone so far as to claim victory when it has been defeated. The Afghan regular troops were defeated every time they were encountered and gained no single success throughout the period of the war. A few minor reverses were sustained at the hands of the tribesmen due to the wide extent of the front of operations, bad communications, the shortage of experienced officers and the rawness of some of our troops.

APPENDIX I.

ORDER OF BATTLE—6TH MAY 1924.

Order of Battle :—Shewing peace stations of units, formations, etc., when hostilities commenced.

General Headquarters	A. H. Q. Simla.	

Royal Air Force.

Headquarters R. A. F. (India)		
No. 114 Squadron R. A. F. (less 1 flight) . .	Quetta.	
Aircraft Park (India)	Lahore.	

General Headquarters Troops.

35th (Reserve) Indian Mountain Battery . .	Rawalpindi.	
37th „ „ „ „	„	
Engineer Base Park	Lahore.	
No. 1 Field Signal Park	Poona.	For Rawalpindi.

CENTRAL RESERVE.

4th Cavalry Brigade.

Headquarters	Meerut.	
21st Lancers	„	
13th Lancers	„	
14th Lancers	„	
"X" Battery, R. H. A.	„	
4th Cavalry Brigade Ammunition Column . .	„	
No. 23 Squadron Machine Gun Corps . . .	„	
4th Cavalry Brigade Signal Troop	„	
No. 3 Field Troop, 2nd S. & Miners	„	
No. 44 Brigade Supply Troop	„	
Nos. 505—507 Bakery Sections	„	
Nos. 505—507 Butchery Sections	„	
62nd Draught Pony Corps	Pathankot.	
66th Pack Pony Corps 4½ Troops . . .	Secunderabad.	Under formation.
No. 9 Combined Cavalry Field Ambulance .	Meerut.	
No. 13 Indian Mobile Veterinary Section . .	„	

16TH DIVISION.

43rd Infantry Brigade.

Headquarters	Lahore.	
2-6th Royal Sussex Regiment	„	
2-10th Jats	„	
2-27th Punjabis	Agra.	
1-124th Baluchistan Infantry	Lahore.	

44th Infantry Brigade (Brig.-Gen. W. M. Southey, C.M.G.).

Headquarters	Ferozepore.
1-1st Kent Regiment	„
1-30th Punjabis	„
2-30th Punjabis	„
1-6th Jat Light Infantry	Jhansi.

45th Infantry Brigade (Brig.-Gen. R. E. Dyer, C.B.).

Headquarters	Jullundur.
1-25th London Regiment	„
2-41st Dogras	Sialkot.
2-72nd Punjabis	Multan.
2-150th Infantry	Ambala.

DIVISIONAL TROOPS.

Headquarters 16th Division	Lahore.
1 Squadron, 4th Cavalry	Mardan.
2-61st Pioneers	Dhond.
No. 260 Company Machine Gun Corps	Dalhousie.
No. 288 „ „ „	Lahore.

Divisional Artillery.

Headquarters	Lahore.
217th Brigade R. F. A.—	
Headquarters	Lahore.
79th (Howitzer) Battery, R. F. A.	„
1091st Battery, R. F. A.	„
1093rd „ „	Jullundur.
No. 12 Divisional Ammunition Column	Lahore, Amritsar.
No. 1 Indian Mountain Artillery Brigade:—	
Headquarters	Abbottabad.
24th Mountain Battery (F. F.)	„
30th „ „	„

Divisional Engineers:—

Headquarters	Lahore.
No. 53 Field Coy. 1st S. and M.	„
No. 76 „ „ 2nd „	Kirkee.
No. 40 Divisional Signal Company	Lahore.

Divisional Supply and Transport Units.

No. 3 Divisional Supply Company	Lahore.
Nos. 71 to 80 Bakery Sections	„
Nos. 71 to 80 Butchery Sections	„
59th Draught Pony Corps (4 troops) 200 carts	Jullundur Temporarily at Manzai.

Divisional Supply and Transport Units—contd.

60th Draught Pony Corps (4 troops) 200 carts	Ambala. Temporarily at Manzai.
66th Pack Pony Corps (3½ troops) 200 carts	Secunderabad. Under formation.
67th „ „ „ (3 „) „ „	Lucknow. Under formation.
68th „ „ „ (2 „) „ „	Poona. Under formation.
49th „ „ „	Overseas.
51st „ „ „	„
6th Government Camel Corps (2 troops)	Sirsa.
7th „ „ „ (3 „)	Multan.
6th Draught Bullock Corps (200 carts)	Bangalore. Under formation.
11th „ „ „ (400 „)	Poona.

Divisional Medical Units.

No. 25 Combined Field Ambulance	Lahore.
„ 26 „ „ „	„
„ 27 „ „ „	„
„ 7 Sanitary Section	„
„ 14 Indian Mobile Veterinary Section	„

MOBILE BRIGADES.

46th Mobile Brigade.

Headquarters	Ambala.
12th Cavalry (H. Q. and 2 Squadrons)	
1096th Battery, 218th Bde. R. F. A. (Less 1 Section)	„
No. 3 Motor Machine Gun Battery	„
1-5th Hampshire Regt.	„
2-151st Infantry	„
2-7th Gurkha Rifles	„
1 Section Trench Howitzers (Stokes)	„
No. 74 Field Company, 3rd S. and M. (2 Sections)	Jubbulpore.
„ 46 Mobile Brigade Signal Section	Ambala.
Section Ammunition Column	To be improvised.
No. 58 Brigade Supply Section	Ambala.
Nos. 411 to 415 Bakery Sections	„
„ „ Butchery „	„
64th Pack Pony Corps	„
No. 16 Combined Field Ambulance	„
„ 22 Indian Mobile Veterinary Section	„

47th Mobile Brigade.

Unit	Station	Remarks
Headquarters	Jubbulpore.	
35th Scind Horse (H. Q. and 2 Squadrons)	„	
1089th Battery, 216th Brigade, R. F. A. (Less Section)	„	
No. 14 Motor Machine Gun Battery	„	Temporarily at Bombay.
1-4th Border Regt.	„	
2-21st Punjabis	„	
2-76th „	„	
2-91st „	„	
1 Section Trench Howitzers (Stokes)	„	
No. 74 Field Company, 3rd S. and M. (Less 2 Sections)	„	
47th Mobile Brigade Signal Section	„	
Section Ammn. Column	„	To be improvised.
No. 76 Brigade Supply Section	„	
Nos. 154—158 Bakery Sections	„	
„ 154—158 Butchery „	„	
65th Pack Pony Corps	„	
No. 47 Bullock Half Troop (detachment)	Allahabad.	
„ 17 Combined Field Ambulance	Jubbulpore.	
„ 23 Indian Mobile Veterinary Section	„	

60th Mobile Brigade (Surplus to original Organization Scheme and formed to provide reinforcement for Kohat).

Unit	Station	Remarks
Headquarters	Ambala.	For employment with Kohat Force.
2-26th Punjabis	Ambala.	For employment with Kohat Force.
2-39th Garhwal Rifles	Ambala.	For employment with Kohat Force.
2 Battalions from Kohat Brigade	Kohat.	
No. 60 Improvised Field Ambulance	Meerut.	For Ambala.
No. 103 Brigade Supply Section	Delhi.	Being formed.

61st Mobile Brigade (Surplus to original Organization Scheme).

Unit	Station	Remarks
Headquarters	Jubbulpore.	
16th Rajputs	Arangaon.	For Jubbulpore.
1-43rd Erinpuras	Erinpura.	
1-102nd Grenadiers	Mhow.	For Jubbulpore
104th Wellesley's Rifles	„	
No. 104 Brigade Supply Section	Delhi.	Being formed.
„ 61 Improvised Field Ambulance	Mhow.	For Jubbulpore.

62nd Mobile Brigade (Surplus to original Organization Scheme).

Unit	Station	Remarks
Headquarters	Dhond.	
2-90th Punjabis	„	
2-103rd Mahrattas	Belgaum.	For Dhond.
2-125th Rifles	Poona.	„ „
1-105th Indian Infantry	Dhond.	Temporarily at Bombay.
No. 105 Brigade Supply Section	„	
„ 62 Improvised Field Ambulance	Poona.	For Dhond.

63rd Mobile Brigade (Surplus to original Organization Scheme).

Headquarters	Lucknow.	
2-4th Rajputs	Agra.	For Lucknow.
1-69th Punjabis	"	" "
82nd Punjabis	Jhansi.	" "
1-90th Punjabis	Kamptee.	" "
No. 63 Improvised Field Ambulance . . .	Lucknow.	
" 106 Brigade Supply Section	Delhi.	Being formed.

64th Infantry Brigade (Surplus to original Organization Scheme).

Headquarters	Chaklala.	
1-55th Coke's Rifles	Ambala.	For Chaklala.
2-69th Punjabis	"	" "
Patiala I. S. Infantry	Patiala.	" "
Gwalior I. S. Infantry	Gwalior.	" "

No. 1 Special Brigade (To be formed from Demobilisers).

Headquarters	Rawalpindi.	
No. 1 Special Service Battalion	"	
No. 2 " " " . . .	"	
No. 3 " " "	"	
No. 4 " " "	"	
No. 287 Company Machine Gun Corps . . .	"	
No. 38 Divisional Signal Company (Brigade Section and Draught Cable Wagon Section) . . .	Poona.	*En route* to Rawalpindi.
No. 14 Combined Field Ambulance	Quetta.	" "
No. 107 Brigade Supply Section	Rawalpindi.	
Nos. 651 to 658 Bakery Sections	"	
Nos. 651 to 658 Butchery Sections	"	

NORTH-WEST FRONTIER FORCE.

Headquarters	Peshawar.	

CORPS TROOPS.

Royal Air Force.

Headquarters 52nd Wing, R. A. F.		
No. 31 squadron R. A. F.	Risalpur.	

Artillery.

No. 60 Heavy Battery, R. G. A. 30 pr. B. L.	Rurki.	
,, 68 ,, ,, ,, ,,	Cawnpore.	

Machine Gun Corps.

No. 22 Motor Machine Gun Battery	Rawalpindi.	

Signal Units.

No. 1 Pack Wireless Troop No. 2 ,, ,, ,, No. 1 Wagon Wireless Section } No. 3 Wireless Squadron.	Rawalpindi. ,,	
Frontier Wireless Troop	Bannu, etc.	
Army Corps Signal Company	Secunderabad.	For Peshawar.

Sappers and Miners.

No. 58 Field Company, 1st S. and M.	Rurki.	For Peshawar.
No. 14 ,, ,, 2nd ,,	Bangalore.	,, ,,
Railway Battalion S. and M.		
No. 26 Railway Company	Sialkot.	
No. 27 ,, ,,	,,	
No. 28 ,, ,,	,,	
No. 6 Litho Section, 3rd S. and M.	Kirkee.	
No. 9 Printing Section, 1st S. and M.	Rurki.	
No. 7 ,, ,, 3rd ,,	Kirkee.	
No. 4 Pontoon Park, 1st S. and M.	Rurki.	
No. 6 ,, ,, 3rd ,,	Kirkee.	
No. 1 Engineer Field Park, 1st S. and M.	Peshawar.	
No. 3 ,, ,, ,, 1st ,,	Rawalpindi.	

Infantry.

1-55 Coke's Rifles	Ambala.	Absorbed in 64th Inf. Bde. Central Reserve.
2-69th Punjabis	,,	

Pioneers.

2-12th Pioneers	Lahore.	
2-34th ,,	Sialkot.	

Ordnance Services.

4 Ordnance Depot Units	Rawalpindi. Ferozepore.	To be formed mobilization.

Field Supply Units.

No. 61 Brigade Supply Section	Rawalpindi.	
Nos. 63—65 Bakery Sections	,,	
Nos. 63—65 Butchery ,,	,,	
No. 21 Divisional Supply Park	,,	

Transport Units.

61st Pack Pony Corps (3½ Troops, with 200 A. T. carts, latter provided locally).	Agra.	For Peshawar.
59th Grantee Camel Corps (4 troops) . . .	Rawalpindi.	
Nos. 1, 2, 4, 5, 6, 11 and 12 Bullock Half Troops (S. T.).	Peshawar, Rawalpindi and Ferozepore.	
No. 18 Bullock Half Troop A. T. (4 Tongas, 14 Bullocks).	Peshawar.	
Nos. 24, 25, 33, 34, and 39 Bullock Half Troops (S. T.).	Mount Abu, Jubbulpore, Delhi, Rurki and Agra.	

Mechanical Transport.

No. 789 M. T. Company, R.A.S.C. (for 68th Heavy Battery R. G. A.).	Cawnpore.
No. 1028 M. T. Company R.A.S.C. (for 60th Heavy Battery R.G.A.).	Rurki.

Medical Units.

No. 23 Motor Ambulance Convoy	*En route* from Mesopotamia.	
No. 28 " " "	Rawalpindi.	For Landi Kotal.
No. 28 Combined Field Ambulance . . .	Peshawar.	" " "
Nos. 7, 8 and 9 Combined Casualty Clearing Station .	"	" " "
Nos. 1 and 4 British Staging Sections . . .	Peshawar.	For Landi Kotal.
Nos. 53—56 Indian " " . . .	"	" " "
No. 38 Sanitary Section	"	" " "
No. 1 Advanced Depot Medical Stores . . .	"	

CAVALRY BRIGADES.

1st Cavalry Brigade.

Headquarters	Risalpur.
1st (King's) Dragoon Guards	"
1st Lancers, H. Q. and 3 squadrons	"
33rd Light Cavalry, H. Q. and 3 squadrons . .	"
"M" Battery, R. H. A.	"
1st Cavalry Brigade Ammunition Column . .	"
No. 15 Squadron Machine Gun Corps	"
No. 1 Field Troop, 1st S. and M.	"
1st Cavalry Brigade Signal Troop	"
No. 43 Brigade Supply Troop . . .	"
Nos. 502—504 Bakery Sections . . .	"
Nos. 502—504 Butchery Sections	"
29th Pack Mule Corps (5 troops) . . .	Nowshera.
45th Draught Mule Corps	Risalpur.
No. 8 Combined Cavalry Field Ambulance . .	Peshawar.
No. 9 Indian Mobile Veterinary Section . . .	Risalpur.

10th Cavalry Brigade.

Headquarters	Peshawar.	
4th Cavalry, H. Q. and 3 squadrons	Mardan.	(1 Sq. with 16th Division.)
30th Lancers (less 2 troops)	Peshawar.	Attached 1st Cav. Bde. from 25th May 1919.
21st Cavalry, F. F.	Rawalpindi.	
S. A. A. Section	To be formed on mobilization.	
No. 24 Squadron Machine Gun Corps	Risalpur.	
No. 4 Field Troop, 3rd S. and M.	,,	
10th Cavalry Brigade Signal Troops	,,	
No. 45 Brigade Supply Troop	Peshawar.	
No. 508 Bakery Section	,,	
No. 508 Butchery Section	,,	
29th Pack Mule Corps (3 Troops)	Nowshera.	
No. 56 Draught Pony Corps	Jhelum.	
No. 172 Indian Cavalry Field Ambulance	Peshawar.	
No. 16 Indian Mobile Veterinary Section	Ambala.	

DIVISIONS.

1st Division (Major-Gen. C. A. Fowler, C.B., D.S.O.).

1st Infantry Brigade (Br.-Genl. G. D. Crocker.).

Headquarters	Peshawar.
2nd Bn., Somerset Light Infantry	,,
1-35th Sikhs	,,
1-9th Gurkha Rifles	,,
1-15th Sikhs	,,

2nd Infantry Brigade (Maj.-Genl. S. H. Climo, C.B., D.S.O.).

Headquarters	Nowshera.
2nd Bn., North Staffordshire Regt.	,,
2-123rd Rifles	,,
1-11th Gurkha Rifles	,,
2-11th Gurkha Rifles	,,

3rd Infantry Brigade (Maj.-Genl. A. Skeen, C.M.G.).

Headquarters	Abbottabad.
1st Bn., Yorkshire Regt.	Peshawar.
2-1st Gurkha Rifles	Nowshera.
4-3rd Gurkha Rifles	Kakul.
3-11th Gurkha Rifles	Kakul.

Divisional Troops.

Headquarters 1st Division.

1 Squadron, 1st Lancers	Risalpur.
No. 263 Company Machine Gun Corps	Nowshera.
No. 285 ,, ,, ,,	,,
1-12th Pioneers	,,

Divisional Artillery.

Headquarters	Peshawar.
7th Brigade R. F. A.—	
Headquarters	Nowshera.
4th Battery, R. F. A.	"
38th Battery, R. F. A.	"
77th (Howitzer) Battery, R. F. A.	Peshawar.
No. 1 Divisional Ammunition Column	Nowshera, Peshawar. S. A. A. Sec to be formed on mobilization.
No. I.—British Mountain Artillery Brigade :—	
Headquarters	Peshawar.
No. 6 Mountain Battery R. G. A.	"
No. 8 " " "	"

Divisional Engineers.

Headquarters	Peshawar.
No. 7 Field Company, 1st S. & M.	"
No. 56 " " 1st "	Nowshera.
No. 36 Divisional Signal Company	Peshawar.

Divisional Supply and Transport Units.

No. 1 Divisional Supply Company	Peshawar.
Nos. 1 to 10 Bakery Sections	"
Nos. 1 to 10 Butchery Sections	"
"Local" Transport—(512 mules)	Peshawar Area.
40th Pack Mule Corps	Peshawar.
41st " " "	"
43rd " " "	"
47th Draught Pony Corps (with 400 A. T. Carts)	Nowshera.
50th Silladar Camel Corps	Campbellpore.
51st " " "	Rawalpindi.
52nd " " "	Jhelum.
Detachment of Half Troop of A. T. Bullocks (from Nowshera. No. 18 Bullock Half Troop) (12 Tongas 26 Bullocks).	

Divisional Medical Units.

No. 5 Combined Field Ambulance	Peshawar
No 6 " " "	"
No. 7 " " "	"
No. 5 Sanitary Section	"
No. 10 Indian Mobile Veterinary Section	Nowshera.

2ND DIVISION (MAJOR-GENERAL SIR C. M. DOBELL, K.C.B., C.M.G., D.S.O.).

Headquarters	Rawalpindi.

4th Infantry Brigade (Brig.-Gen. E. C. Peebles, C.B., C.M.G., D.S.O.).

Headquarters	Rawalpindi.
1st. Bn., Durham Light Infantry	"
1-33rd Punjabis	"
40th Pathans	Campbellpore.
2-54th Sikhs (F. F.)	Rawalpindi.

5th Infantry Brigade (Brig.-Gen. R. T. I. Ridgeway, C.B.).

Headquarters	Gharial.
1st Bn., South Lancashire Regt.	Rawalpindi, Sialkot in detachment all over Punjab.
2-35th Sikhs	Lahore.
3-39th Garhwal Rifles	Rewat.
3-5th Gurkha Rifles (F. F.)	Chamiari.

6th Infantry Brigade (Brig.-Gen. G. Christian, C.B., D.S.O.).

Headquarters	Chaklala.
1st Bn., Royal Sussex Regiment	Rawalpindi.
2-33rd Punjabis	Chaklala.
2-67th Punjabis	"
2-8th Gurkha Rifles	Rewat.

DIVISIONAL TROOPS.

Headquarters, 2nd Division.

1 squadron, 33rd Light Cavalry	Risalpur.
1-61st Pioneers	Ferozepore.
No. 222 Company Machine Gun Corps	Abbottabad.
No. 286 " " "	"

Divisional Artillery.

Headquarters	Rawalpindi.
16th Brigade, R. F. A.	
Headquarters	Rawalpindi.
89th Battery, R. F. A.	Campbellpore.
90th " "	Rawalpindi.
74th (Howitzer) Battery, R. F. A.	"
No. 2 Divisional Ammunition Column	"
(S. A. A. Section to be formed on mobilization)	"
No. II.—British Mountain Artillery Brigade :—	
Headquarters	Rawalpindi.
No. 3 Mountain Battery R. G. A.	"
No. 4 " " "	"

Divisional Engineers.

Headquarters	Rawalpindi.
No. 11 Field Company 2nd S. and M.	"
No. 64 " " 2nd "	"
No. 39 Divisional Signal Company	"

Divisional Supply and Transport Units.

No. 2 Divisional Supply Company	Rawalpindi.
Nos. 36—45 Bakery Sections	„
Nos. 36—45 Butchery Sections	„
'Local" Transport	Abbottabad.
19th Pack Mule Corps (1 troop) (*plus* 48 mules) .	Rawalpindi.
46th „ „ „	„
53rd „ „ „	Ferozepore.
54th „ „ „	Abbottabad.
58th Draught Pony Corps (4 troops) (200 carts) .	Kalka.
59th „ „ „ (4 troops) (200 carts) .	Jullundur.
1st Government Camel Corps	Campbellpore.
4th „ „ „	„
62nd Grantee Camel Corps	Rawalpindi.
Detachment of No. 3 Half Troop of A. T. Bullocks (9 Tongas 18 Bullocks). .	Nowshera.
Detachment of 18 half Troop of A. T. Bullocks (4 Tongas, 8 Bullocks). .	Peshawar.

Divisional Medical Units.

No. 12 Combined Field Ambulance	Rawalpindi.	
No. 13 „ „ „	„	
No. 41 „ „ „	„	
No. 2 Sanitary Section	„	
No. 11 Indian Mobile Veterinary Section . .	Lahore .	. Temporarily at Bombay.

PESHAWAR AREA AND L. OF C. DEFENCE.

Cavalry.

23rd Cavalry (F. F.)	Meerut .	. Temporarily at Ferozepore.

Artillery.

No. 1 Special Section, R. F. A.	Peshawar.
22nd (Derajat) Mountain Battery (F. F.) . .	Kakul.
Frontier Garrison Artillery	Peshawar and Jamrud.

Signal Units.

No. 4 L. of C. Signal Section	Poona.

Machine Gun Corps.

No. 1 Armoured Motor Brigade—	
Headquarters	Peshawar.
No. 1 Armoured Motor Battery "A" Class .	„
No. 2 „ „ „ „ „ .	„
No. 3 „ „ „ „ „ .	„
No. 15 Motor Machine Gun Battery . .	„

Infantry.

Unit	Station	Remarks
2-4th Border Regiment	Peshawar.	
1-4th R. W. Surrey Regiment	...	Temporarily at Jullundur.
37th Dogras	Jhelum.	
110th Mahratta Light Infantry	Belgaum.	
3-2nd Gurkha Rifles	Peshawar.	
1 Sub-Section Trench Howitzers (Stokes)	"	

Transport.

Transport to be improvised from Local resources.

Special for Malakand Posts.

Unit	Station	Remarks
Frontier Garrison Artillery	Malakand and Chakdara.	
2-2nd Rajput Light Infantry	Malakand and Posts.	
2-89th Punjabis	Dargai and Chakdara.	
1 Section Trench Howitzers (Stokes)	Malakand.	
Local Transport (including 144 Pack Mules 5 Tongas and 18 A. T. Bullocks).	Malakand.	

Special for Chitral.

Unit	Station	Remarks
1 Section 23rd (Peshawar) Mountain Battery (F. F.)	Chitral.	Additional section.
1-11th Rajputs	Chitral and Drosh.	
Chitral Section 2nd S. and M.	Chitral.	
Local Transport (266 Pack Mules)	"	
Chitral Scouts	"	
No. 1 Divisional Area Troops Supply Sections	Peshawar.	
No. 64 Brigade Supply Section	"	
Nos. 11 to 17 Bakery Section	"	

Special for Gilgit.

Unit	Station	Remarks
No. 1 Kashmir Mountain Battery	Gilgit.	
1st Kashmir Rifles	Satwari.	
2nd " "	"	
3rd " "	"	
Gilgit Scouts	Gilgit.	

Medical and M. T.

Unit	Station	Remarks
No. 2 Motor Ambulance Convoy (additional Section)	Lahore.	To be formed on mobilization.
No. 4 British Casualty Clearing Station (1 Section)	Peshawar.	
No. 4 " " " " (R. S. S. converted) Nos. 7 and 8.	"	

Medical and M. T.—contd.

No. 14 Indian Casualty Clearing Station	Peshawar.
Nos. 5 and 6 British Staging Sections	„
Nos. 91 to 94 Indian „ „	„
No. 18 Sanitary Section	„
No. 14 Advanced Depot, Medical Stores	„
A.-35 British General Hospital	„
A. B. C.-13 Indian General Hospital (for Peshawar)	„
D. & E.-13 „ „ „ (for Nowshera)	„
No. 3 Field Veterinary Section	„
No. 1 Advanced Repair Workshops M. T.	„
No. 4 M. T. Company (7 lorries)	Karachi.
No. 6 „ „ (M. T. detail No. 2 M. A. C.)	Lahore.

KOHAT AREA AND L. OF C. DEFENCE (MAJOR-GENERAL A. H. EUSTACE, C.B., D.S.O.).

Headquarters, Kohat Brigade	Kohat.

Cavalry.

37th Lancers, H. Q. and 4 Squadrons	Kohat.

Artillery.

23rd (Peshawar) Mountain Battery	Nowshera.
28th Mountain Battery	Kohat.
Frontier Garrison Artillery	Kohat, Fort Lockhart.

Machine Gun Corps.

No. 4 Armoured Motor Battery "A" No. 10 Brigade.	Kohat.
No. 22 Motor Machine Gun Battery	Rawalpindi.

Infantry.

3rd Guides Infantry (F. F.)	Mardan
1-57th Wilde's Rifles (F. F.)	Kohat.
1-109th Infantry	„
1-151st Sikh Infantry	Chaklala.
3-8th Gurkha Rifles	Hangu and Samana.
3-9th Gurkha Rifles	Kohat.
1 Section Trench Howitzers (Stokes)	„
No. 57 Field Company, 1st S. and M.	„
No. 44 Divisional Signal Company	Poona.
Section Ammunition Column	To be improvised.

60th Brigade.

Headquarters	Ambala	To be completed by absorbing 2 Battalions from Kohat Brigade.
2-26th Punjabis	Do.	
4-39th Garhwal Rifles	Dehra Dun	

Supply and Transport Units.

No. 11 Brigade Supply and Transport Headquarters .	Kohat.	
No. 31 „ „ Section	„	
No. 32 „ „ „	Rawalpindi .	Temporarily.
No. 11 Divisional Supply Park	„	„
No. 366 Bakery Section	„	„
No. 366 Butchery Section	„	„
19th Pack Mule Corps (4 troops)	„	„
38th „ „ „	Kohat.	
58th Draught Pony Corps (4 troops 200 carts) . .	Kalka.	
67th Pack Mule Corps (5 troops)	Lucknow.	Under formation.
5th Government Camel Corps	Kohat.	
53rd Silladar Camel Corps (5 troops) . . .	Sargodha.	
"Local" Transport (133 mules, 54 camels, 10 bullocks, 4 tongas).	Kohat.	
No. 3 Bullock Half Troops (6 tongas, 14 bullocks) .	Nowshera.	

Medical Units.

Nos. 45 and 60 Combined Field Ambulances . .	Kohat.	
No. 144 Indian Field Ambulance	Kohat and Rawalpindi.	
No. 8 Sanitary Section	Kohat.	
No. 3 Motor Ambulance Convoy (2 Sections) . .	Bombay.	Additional Section. To be formed on mobilization.
No. 27 Combined Casualty Clearing Station . .	Rawalpindi.	
A.-4 British „ „ „ . . .	„	
B. and C.-27 Indian „ „ „ . . .	„	
Nos. 11 and 44 British Staging Sections . .	„	
Nos. 81, 82, 96, Indian Staging Sections . .	„	
No. 16 Advanced Depot Medical Stores . .	„	
A.-36 British General Hospital	„	
A. B. and C. 29 Indian General Hospital . .	Meerut.	

Veterinary Units.

No. 19 Indian Mobile Veterinary Section. . .	Lucknow.	

Labour.

144th Labour Corps	Rawalpindi.	For Kohat.

WAZIRISTAN FORCE.

Headquarters Waziristan Force.

No. 3 Litho Section, 2nd S. and M.	...
No. 8 Engineer Field Park, 1st S. and M. . . .	...
1 Ordnance Depot Unit	...

Bannu Area.

Hadquarters Bannu Brigade	Bannu.

Cavalry.

31st Lancers (H. Q. and 4 squadrons)	Bannu.	

Artillery.

33rd (Reserve) Mountain Battery	Bannu.	
Frontier Garrison Artillery	„	

Machine Gun Corps.

No. 10 Armoured Motor Brigade—		
Headquarters	Bannu.	
No. 5 Armoured Motor Battery "A"	„	
No. 6 „ „ „ „	„	

Infantry.

1-41st Dogras	Bannu.	
1-103rd Mahratta Light Infantry	Miranshah.	
2-112th Infantry	Bannu.	
3-6th Gurkha Rifles	Miranshah.	
1 Section Trench Howitzers (Stokes)	Bannu.	
No. 55 Field Company, 1st S. and M.	„	
1 Brigade Section, No. 39 Divisional Sig. Co.	Rawalpindi.	
No. 1 L. of C. Signal Section	Poona.	
Section Ammunition Column	To be improvised.	

Supply and Transport Units.

No. 12 Brigade Supply and Transport Headquarters	Bannu.	
Nos. 34 and 35 Brigade Supply Sections	„	
No. 12 Divisional Supply Park	„	
No. 381 Bakery Section	„	
No. 381 Butchery	„	
"Local" Transport (554 Pack Mules, 282 camels, 12 A. T. carts, 7 tongas and 16 Bullocks).	„	
48th Pack Mule Corps (5 troops)	„	
3rd Jat Draught Bullock Corps	„	
8th Draught „ „	„	
12th „ „ „	„	
14th „ „ „ (½ Troops)	„	
3rd Govt. Camel Corps	„	
53rd Silladar Camel Corps (3 Troops)	Sargodha.	

Medical Units.

No. 4 Indian Field Ambulance	Bannu, Miranshah.	
No. 42 Combined Field Ambulance	Rawalpindi.	
½ No. 4 Sanitary Section	Bannu.	
1 Section No. 3 Motor Ambulance Convoy	Bombay.	Additional Section.
No. 13 Indian Casualty Clearing Station	Rawalpindi.	To be formed.
Nos. 12 to 16 British Staging Sections	„	„ „

Medical Units—contd.

No. 17 British Staging Section	Lahore.	
Nos. 66, 98, 99 and 100 Indian Staging Sections	Rawalpindi.	
No. 13 Advanced Depot Medical Stores	„	
No. 38 Indian General Hospital	Lahore.	
No. 20 Indian Mobile Veterinary Section	Rawalpindi.	

Derajat Area.

Headquarters Derajat Brigade	D. I. Khan.	

Cavalry.

27th Cavalry (H. Q. and 4 squadrons)	„	

Artillery.

No. 27 Mountain Battery	Tank.	

Machine Gun Corps.

No. 7 Armoured Motor Battery "A" (No. 10 Bde.)	D. I. Khan.	

Infantry.

66th Punjabis	Tank.	
1-76th „	D. I. Khan.	Tank.
2-2nd Gurkha Rifles	„	
1 Section Trench Howitzers (Stokes)	„	
No. 75 Field Coy. 3rd S. and M.	Tank.	
1 Brigade Section, No. 33 Divl. Signal Company	„	
No. 2 L. of C. Signal Section	Poona.	
Section Ammunition Column	To be improvised.	

Supply and Transport Units.

No. 13 Brigade S. and T. Headquarters	D. I. Khan.	
No. 13 Divisional Troops Supply Section	„	
No. 37 Brigade Supply Section	Tank.	
No. 396 Bakery Section	„	
No. 396 Butchery „	„	
No. 13 Divisional Supply Park	Lahore.	Temporarily.
"Local" Transport (756 pack mules, 346 camels, 12 A. T. carts, 7 tongas, 16 Bullocks)	D. I. Khan.	
48th Pack Mule Corps (2½ troops)	Bannu.	
6th Govt. Camel Corps (6 troops)	Sirsa.	
8th Patiala Camel Corps	Kalka.	
57th Silladar „ „	Multan.	
71st Govt. „ „	D. I. Khan.	

Medical Units.

No. 2 Indian Field Ambulance	D. I. Khan.	Tank.
43 Combined „ „	„	Rawalpindi.
½ No. 4 Sanitary Section	Tank.	
1 Section No. 4 Motor Ambulance Convoy	Quetta.	(Additional Section—to be formed.)

Medical Units—contd.

No. 118 Indian Casualty Clearing Station . .	D. I. Khan.
Nos. 18, 19, 20, 41, 42 and 43 Brit. Staging Sections	Lahore.
Nos. 59, 60 and 79 Indian Staging Sections . .	D. I. Khan.
No. 11 Advanced Depot Medical Stores . . .	Rawalpindi.
A. B. and C.-43 Indian General Hospital . . .	Lahore.
No. 21 Indian Mobile Veterinary Section . .	Meerut.

Lines of Communication.

Under D. I. G. C., Kalabagh—	
Nos. 162 to 164 Supply Depot Sections . .	Bannu.
¼ No. 22 Supply Workshop Section . .	„
No. 77 Supply Tally Section	„
No. 22 Supply Depot Headquarters . . .	D. I. Khan.
Nos. 165—168 Supply Depot Sections . .	„
¾ No. 22 Supply Workshop Section . . .	„
Nos. 74—81 Supply Tally „ . .	Rawalpindi.
No. 172 Supply Depot	„
Nos. 174 and 175 Depot.	„
½ No. 23 Supply Workshop Section . .	„
Nos. 84 and 85 Supply Tally „ . . .	„
48 Pack Mule Corps (detachment 9 mules) . .	Bannu.
No. 7 Bullock Half Troop (A. T.) . . .	„
No. 9 „ „ „ „ . . .	D. I. Khan.
No. 10 „ „ „ „ . . .	Sialkot.
No. 14 „ „ „ „ . . .	Jullundur.
No. 30 Bullock Half Troop (A. T.) . . .	Bombay.
No. 36 „ „ „ „ . . .	Bannu.
No. 38 „ „ „ „ . . .	Dehra Dun.
No. 40 „ „ „ „ . . .	„
No. 42 „ „ „ „ . . .	Kotdwara.
No. 49 „ „ „ „ . . .	Fyzabad, Lucknow.
No. 50 „ „ „ „ . . .	Bannu.
No. 54 „ „ „ „ . . .	Lucknow, Cawnpore
15th Labour Corps	Bannu ?
103rd „ „	„ ?
105th „ „ (detachment)	„ ?

Headquarters Inspector General of Communications, Northern, Supply Units.

Under D. I. G. C., Kohat—	
Nos. 159 to 161 Supply Depot Sections . .	Kohat.
½ No. 21 Supply Workshop Section . . .	„
Nos. 74 to 76 Supply Tally „ . . .	„
No. 21 Supply Depot Headquarters . . .	„
Under D. I. G. C., Jamrud—	
Nos. 276 to 280 Supply Depot Sections . .	Peshawar.
½ No. 37 Supply Workshop Section . . .	„
Nos. 133 and 134 Supply Tally Sections . .	„

Transport Units.

48th Pack Mule Corps (detachment) (½ troop)	Bannu.
No. 3 Bullock Half Troop (A. T.) (detachment)	Nowshera.
No. 15 " " " "	Rawalpindi.
No. 16 " " " "	Ferozepore.
No. 17 " " " "	Ambala.
No. 37 " " " "	Agra.
No. 41 " " " "	Rawalpindi.
No. 43 " " " "	Bareilly.
No. 44 " " " "	Rawalpindi.
No. 45 " " " "	Campbellpore.
No. 47 " " " "	Allahabad.
No. 48 " " " "	Dinapur.
No. 53 " " " "	Bareilly.
No. 55 " " " " (detachment)	Calcutta, Cawnpore.
No. 59 " " " " "	Calcutta.
No. 60 " " " " "	Dum Dum.
No. 61 " " " " "	Calcutta.
19th Pack Mule Corps (2¾ Troops)	Rawalpindi.
43rd " " " (1½ Troops)	"
61st " Pony " (4½ Troops)	Agra.
No. 3 Bullock Half Troop (A. T.)	Nowshera.

Mechanical Transport.

D. I. G. C., Kohat—	
No. 1 M. T. Company	Peshawar.
D. I. G. C., Jamrud—	
No. 2 M. T. Company	Rawalpindi.
D. I. G. C., Kalabagh—	
No. 3 M. T. Company (30 lorries)	"
No. 630 M. T. Company R. A. S. C. (M. T. details 28 M. A. C.)	Peshawar.
D. I. G. C., Jamrud—	
No. 692 M. T. Company R. A. S. C.	Rawalpindi.
D. I. G. C., Kalabagh—	
No. 693 M. T. Company R. A. S. C. (less 1 section), Peshawar	Peshawar.
D. I. G. C., Kohat—	
No. 694 M. T. Company R. A. S. C. 2 secs.	"
D. I. G. C., Kalabagh—	
Central M. T. Repair Workshop 2 secs.	"

Labour Units.

17th Labour Corps (detachment)	Jubbulpore.	For Peshawar.
100th " "	"	
101st " "	"	
102nd " "	"	
112th " "	"	

BALUCHISTAN FORCE.

Headquarters, Baluchistan Force . . . Quetta.

CORPS TROOPS.

Royal Air Force.

1 Flight, No. 114 squadron, R. A. F. . . . Quetta.

Signal Units.

No. 2 Wagon Wireless Section, No. 3 Wireless Squadron Rawalpindi. Under formation.

Sappers and Miners.

No. 71 Field Company, 3rd S. and M. . . . Nushki Extension.
No. 73 „ „ 3rd „ (2 sections) . „ „
No. 2 Engineer Field Park . . . . . Quetta.

Ordnance Services.

1 Ordnance Depot Unit . . . . . To be formed on Mobilization.

MOUNTED BRIGADE.

12th Mounted Brigade.

Headquarters . . . . Sheikh Mandah.
40th Indian Cavalry . . . . . . Baleli.
41st „ „ (less 2 squadrons) . . . „
42nd „ „ . . . . „
No. 22 Squadron, Machine Gun Corps . . . „
No. 7 Field Troop, 3rd S. and M. . . . Quetta.
No. 6 Cavalry Brigade Signal Troop . . . „
No. 49 Brigade Supply Troop . . . . Sibi.
Nos. 586 and 587 Bakery Sections . . . Quetta.
Nos. 586 and 587 Butchery Sections . . . . „
63rd Draught Mule Corps . . . . . „
Pack Mule Corps (2½ troops) . . . . To be allotted; transport not available.
No. 173 Indian Cavalry Field Ambulance . . Quetta.
No. 18 Indian Mobile Veterinary Section . . Baleli.

4TH DIVISION.

Headquarters, 4th Division . . . . . Quetta.

10th Infantry Brigade.

Headquarters . . . . . . Quetta.
2nd Bn. The King's (Liverpool) Regt. . . . „
1-5th Light Infantry . . . . . . Harnai.
2-56th Rifles (F. F.) . . . . . . Quetta.
2-129th Baluchis . . . . . . Karachi.

11th Infantry Brigade.

Headquarters	Quetta.	
1st Bn., West Riding Regt.	„	Temp. in Lahore.
1-4th Gurkha Rifles	„	
1-22nd Punjabis	„	
2-10th Gurkha Rifles	Chaman.	

57th Infantry Brigade.

Headquarters	Quetta.
1-4th R. W. Kent Regt.	„
2-119th Infantry	Pishin.
3-7th Gurkha Rifles	Quetta.
1-129th Baluchis	„

Divisional Troops.

Headquarters 4th Division.

25th Cavalry (F. F.)	Quetta.
2-23rd Pioneers	Ambala.
No. 270 Machine Gun Company	Quetta.
No. 281 „ „ „	Mhow.

Divisional Artillery.

Headquarters	Quetta.	
21st Brigade R. F. A.—		
Headquarters	Hyderabad (Sind).	
101st Battery, R. F. (18 prs.)	Hyderabad (Sind).	
102nd „ „ (18 prs.)	Quetta.	
1107th (Howitzer) Battery, R. F. A.	Hyderabad (Sind).	2 5" Hows. and 4 4·5" Hows.
No. 4 Divisional Ammunition Column	„ „	
No. IV.—British Mountain Artillery Brigade— Headquarters	Quetta.	
No. 1 Mountain Artillery, R. G. A.	Quetta.	
No. 9 „ „ „	„	

Divisional Engineers.

Headquarters	Quetta.
No. 17 Field Company, 3rd S and M. (2 sections)	Kirkee.
No. 24 „ „ 3rd „	„
No. 73 „ „ 3rd „ (less 2 sections)	Quetta.
No. 33 Divisional Signal Company	Quetta.

Divisional S. and T. Units.

No. 4 Divisional Supply Company	Quetta.	
Nos. 106 to 115 Bakery Sections	,,	
Nos. 105 to 115 Butchery ,,	,,	
"Local" Transport (173 mules)	,,	
14th Pack Mule Corps (with 200 carts)	,,	
52nd ,, Pony ,,	Jhansi.	
55th ,, ,, ,,	Quetta.	
60th Draught Mule Corps (4 troops) (with 200 A. T. carts).	Ambala.	
68th Pack Mule Corps (5½ troops)	Poona.	Under formation.
7th Government Camel Corps (5 troops)	Multan.	
Bahawalpur and Khairpur Camel Corps	Bahawalpur.	
Detachment of No. 20 Half Troop A. T. Bullocks (12 tongas, 26 Bullocks).	Quetta.	

Divisional Medical Units.

No. 15 Combined Field Ambulance	Quetta.
No. 52 ,, ,, ,,	,,
No. 51 ,, ,, ,,	,,
½ No. 35 Sanitary Section	,,
½ No. 24 ,,	,,
No. 15 Indian Mobile Veterinary Section	,,

FORCE IN EAST PERSIA AND L. OF C.

Meshed Force.

Force Headquarters	Meshed.
28th Light Cavalry	,,
12th Cavalry Brigade Signal Troop	E. Persia.
1-19th Punjabis	Meshed.
No. 48 Combined Cavalry Field Ambulance	,,
2 Secs. No. 178 Indian Cavalry Field Ambulance	,,
No. 20 Sanitary Section	,,
No. 53 Brigade S. and T. Directorate	,
No. 97 Brigade Supply Section	,,
Nos. 297, 307 and 308 Supply Depôt Sections	,,
Detachment 14th Mule Corps	Quetta.

LINE OF COMMUNICATION.

2 Squadrons, 41st Cavalry	Persia.
107th Pioneers	,,
1-98th Infantry (6 companies)	,,
120th Infantry	Saindak (Sistan).
½ No. 17 Field Coy., 1st S. and M.	Sistan.
No. 71 ,, ,, ,, ,,	,,
½ No. 73 ,, ,, ,, ,,	,,
Sistan Detachment, 3rd S. and M.	,,

LINE OF COMMUNICATION—*contd.*

No. 7 Litho Section	
104th Labour Corps	
Base Depôt	
2 Sections, No. 116 Indian Field Ambulance . .	
1 " " 118 " " " . .	
1 " " 175 " " " . .	
No. 6, and half No. 35 Sanitary Sections . .	
2 Secs., No. 17 Combined Casualty Clearing Section .	Returning to India.
1 Sec., No. 29 Indian Casualty Clearing Section .	
Nos. 4, 21 and 22 British Staging Sections . .	
Nos. 73, 74, 110 and 111 Indian Staging Sections .	
Nos. 58 and 59 Combined General Hospitals . .	
No. 12 Advanced Depôt Medical Stores . .	
2 Secs. Motor Ambulance Convoy	
No. 21 X-Ray Section	
1 Sec. No. 2 Base Depot of Medical Stores . .	
No. 63 Draught Pony Corps	Quetta.
2nd Govt. Camel Corps	
54th Silladar Camel Corps	
55th " " "	
1 Troop, 56th Silladar Camel Corps . .	
5 Troops, 60th Grantee " " . . .	
61st Grantee Camel Corps	
65th Govt. " "	
72nd Hired " "	
No. 5 M. T. Company (Ford Vans) and attached section.	
1 Light Lorry Section	
Locally purchased camels and donkeys . . .	
Locally hired mules	
No. 33 Divisional S. and T. Headquarters . .	
" " " Troops Supply Section . . .	
" " Brigade S. and T. Directorate . . .	
Nos. 98 and 99 Brigade Supply Section . . .	
No. 52 Brigade S. and T. Headquarters (L. of C.) .	
No. 54 S. and T. Headquarters (L. of C.) . .	
Nos. 41—43 Supply Workshop Sections . . .	
Nos. 601, 602, 603 and 604 Bakery Sections . .	
" " " " " " Butchery " . . .	
1 Advanced Ordnance Depot	
1 Stationery Depot	
1 Base Post Office	
15 Field Post Offices	

Baluchistan Area Troops.

Cavalry.

3rd Horse (Headquarters and 4 Squadrons)	Loralai.	
Alwar Lancers	Alwar.	
Gwalior Lancers	Gwalior.	Afterwards replaced by 13th Lancers.
Patiala Lancers	Patiala.	

Artillery.

38th Mountain Battery	Quetta.	

Signal Units.

No. 3 of L. of C. Signal Section	Poona.	

Machine Gun Corps.

No. 8 Armoured Motor Battery "A" (No. 6 Brigade)	Quetta.	Temp. Hyderabad.
No. 19 Motor Machine Gun Battery	„	

Infantry.

No. 17 Special Service Battalion	„	Under formation.
2-11th Rajputs	Loralai.	
2-15th Sikhs	Ferozepore.	
3-124th Baluchistan Infantry	Karachi.	
3-1st Gurkha Rifles	Fort Sandeman.	

Supply Units.

No. 4 Divisional Area Troops Supply Section	Quetta.	
No. 25 Divisional Troops Supply Section	„	
No. 73 Brigade Supply Section	„	
Nos. 116 to 118 Bakery Sections	„	
„ „ „ „ Butchery Sections	„	
Transport improvised locally.		
No. 13 Field Veterinary Section	Quetta.	

Lines of Communication.

No. 204 Supply Depot Section	Quetta, Harnai.	
No. 210 „ „ „	Sibi.	
No 98 „ Tally „	Quetta.	

Headquarters, Inspector General of Communications, Southern.

Transport Units.

68th Pack Pony Corps (detachment) (½ troop)	Poona.	Under formation.
No. 19 Bullock Half Troop (A. T.) (8 tongas, 22 bullocks).	Quetta.	
Nos. 20, 21 Bullock Half Troops (A. T.) (8 tongas, 22 bullocks).	„	

Transport Units—contd.

No. 22 Bullock Half Troops (A. T.) (8 tongas, 22 bullocks).	Karachi.	
Nos. 65, 66 Bullock Half Troops (A. T.) (8 tongas, 22 bullocks).	Bellary.	
Nos. 67, 68 Bullock Half Troops (A. T.) (8 tongas, 22 bullocks).	Secunderabad.	
No. 69 Bullock Half Troops (A. T.) (8 tongas, 22 bullocks).	Madras.	
No. 70 Bullock Half Troops (A. T.) (8 tongas, 22 bullocks).	Wellington.	
No. 71 Bullock Half Troops (A. T.) (8 tongas, 22 bullocks).	Mallapuram.	
No. 72 Bullock Half Troops (A. T.) (8 tongas, 22 bullocks).	Wellington.	

Medical Units.

2 Sections No. 4 Motor Ambulance Convoy . .	Quetta.	Additional Sections to be formed.
Nos. 18 and 36 Combined Casualty Clearing Station .	„	
Nos. 23 to 25 British Staging Sections . . .	„	
Nos. 46 and 47 British Staging Sections . .	„	
Nos. 119, 120, 157, 158, 161, 162, 163, 164, and 165 Indian Staging Sections.	„	
No. 41 Sanitary Section	„	
½ No. 24 „ „	„	
½ No. 42 „ „	„	
No. 17 Advanced Depot Medical Stores	„	
No. 43 British General Hospital	„	
No. 33 Indian „ „	„	

Labour.

107th Labour Corps (Wing.) . . . . . .

APPENDIX II.

*List of British Army units employed on the North-West Frontier in the operations against Afghanistan between the 6th **May** 1919 and the 8th August 1919.*

(Excluding Administrative units.)

Unit.	Force.	Date of joining Force.	From	REMARKS.
ROYAL AIR FORCE.				
Headquarters 52nd Wing R. A. F.	N.-W. F. F.	......	...	...
No. 20 Squadron R. A. F.	Ditto	......	...	...
No. 31 Squadron R. A. F.	Ditto	......	...	...
No. 48 Squadron R. A. F.	Baluchistan Force	......	...	...
No. 114 Squadron R. A. F.	N.-W. F. F.	......	...	...
	Baluchistan Force	......	...	...
CAVALRY.				
1st (King's) Dragoon Guards	N.-W. F. F.	In Force on 6th May 1919 (Risalpur).	...	To Dakka. Arrived 14th May 1919.
ARTILLERY.				
"M" Battery R. H. A.	N.-W. F. F.	In Force on 6th May 1919 (Risalpur).	...	To Dakka. Arrived 14th May 1919.
Hdqrs. 7th R. F. A.	Ditto	In Force on 6th May 1919 (Nowshera)	...	To Landi Kotal.
Hdqrs. 16th Bde. R. F. A.	Ditto	In Force on 6th May 1919 (Rawalpindi).	...	To Peshawar.
Hdqrs. 21st Bde. R. F. A.	Baluchistan Force	20th May 1919	Hyderabad (Sind)	To Chaman Area.
Hdqrs. 217th Bde. R. F. A.	N.-W. F. F.	9th June 1919	Lahore	To Nowshera.
4th Bty. R.F.A.	Ditto	In Force on 6th May 1919 (Nowshera).	...	To Landi Kotal.

List of British Army units employed ou the North-West Frontier, etc.—contd.

Unit.	Force.	Date of joining Force.	From	REMARKS.
ARTILLERY—*contd.*				
38th Bty. R.F.A.	N.-W.F. F.	In Force on 6th May 1919 (Nowshera).	...	To Jamrud.
74th Bty. R.F.A.	Ditto	In Force on 6th May 1919 (Rawalpindi).	...	To Peshawar.
77th Bty. R.F A.	Ditto	In Force on 6th May 1919 (Peshawar). 9th June 1919.	...	For Dakka.
79th Bty. R.F.A.	Ditto	9th June 1919	Jullundur	To Nowshera.
89th Bty. R.F.A.	Ditto	In Force on 6th May 1919 (Rawalpindi).	...	To Kohat.
90th Bty. R.F.A.	Ditto	In Force on 6th May 1919 (Rawalpindi).	...	To Budni Bridge.
101st Bty. R.F.A.	Baluchistan Force	14th May 1919	Hyderabad (Sind)	To Quetta.
102nd Bty. R.F.A.	Ditto	In Force on 6th May 1919 (Quetta).	...	To Chaman Area.
1091st Bty. R.F.A.	N.-W. F. F.	9th June 1919	Lahore	To Nowshera.
1093rd Bty. R.F.A.	Ditto	9th June 1919	Jullundur	Ditto.
1096th Bty. R.F.A.	Ditto	1st June 1919	Ambala	To Kohat.
1104th Bty. R.F.A.	Baluchistan Force	7th July 1919	Meerut	For Baluchistan Area.
1107th Bty. R.F.A.	Ditto	16th May 1919	Hyderabad (Sind)	To Chaman Area.
No. 1 Special Section. R.F.A.	N.-W. F. F.	In Force on 6th May 1919 (Peshawar).	...	...
1st Divisional Ammunition Column R.F.A.	Ditto	In Force on 6th May 1919 (Nowshera).	...	To Kacha Garhi.
2nd Divisional Ammunition Column R.F.A.	Ditto	In Force on 6th May 1919 (Rawalpindi).	...	...
4th Divisional Ammunition Column R.F.A.	Baluchistan Force	20th May 1919	Hyderabad (Sind)	To Chaman Area.
No. 12 Divisional Ammunition Column	N.-W. F. F.	9th June 1919	Lahore and Amritsar.	To Nowshera.
46th Bde. Ammunition Column R.F.A.	Ditto	1st June 1919	Ambala	To Kohat.

"A" Ammunition Column, R. H. A.	N.-W. F. F.	In Force on 6th May 1919. (Risalpur).	...	Absorbed in 1st Cavalry Brigade Ammunition Column.
1st Cavalry Brigade Ammunition Column.	Ditto	Formed on 25th June 1919. (At Dacca).	...	...
H. Q. Heavy Brigade R. G. A.	Ditto	4th July 1919	Rurki	For Peshawar.
No. 1 British Mountain Artillery Brigade.	Ditto	In Force 6th May 1919 (Peshawar).	...	To Landi Kotal 13th May 1919.
No. 2 British Mountain Artillery Brigade.	Ditto	17th May 1919	Rawalpindi	To Ali Masjid.
No. 4 British Mountain Artillery Brigade.	Baluchistan Force	In Force 6th May 1919 (Quetta).	...	...
No. 1 Mountain Battery R. G. A.	Ditto	In Force 6th May 1919 (Quetta).	...	...
No. 3 Mountain Battery, R. G. A.	N.-W. F. F.	In Force 6th May 1919 (Rawalpindi).	...	...
No. 4 Mountain Battery, R. G. A.	Ditto	Ditto	...	...
No. 6 Mountain Battery, R. G. A.	Ditto	In Force 6th May 1919 (Peshawar).	...	To Landi Kotal 11th May 1919.
No. 8 Mountain Battery, R. G. A.	Ditto	In Force 6th May 1919 (Landi Kotal.)	...	...
No. 9 Mountain Battery, R. G. A.	Baluchistan Force	In Force 6th May 1919 (Quetta).	...	...
60th (Heavy) Battery, R. G. A.	N.-W. F. F.	20th June 1919	Rurki	For Peshawar.
68th (Heavy) Battery, R. G. A. (Cadre only).	Ditto	10th July 1919	Do.	Absorbed in 60th Battery R. G. A.
Armoured Cars and M. G. Corps.				
No. 1 Armoured Motor Brigade	N.-W. F. F.	In Force 6th May 1919 (Peshawar)	...	...
No. 10 Armoured Motor Brigade	Waziristan Force	20th July 1919	...	For Dera Ismail Khan.
No. 1 Armoured Motor Battery	N.-W. F. F.	In Force 6th May 1919 (Peshawar)	...	...
No. 2 Armoured Motor Battery	Ditto	Ditto Ditto	...	...
No. 3 Armoured Motor Battery	Ditto	Ditto Ditto	...	...
No. 4 Armoured Motor Battery	Ditto	In Force 6th May 1919 (Kohat)	...	...

List of British Army units employed on the North-West Frontier, etc.—concld.

Unit.	Force.	Date of joining Force.	From	Remarks.
Armoured Cars and M. G. Corps—*contd.*				
No. 5 Armoured Motor Battery	Waziristan Force	In Force 6th May 1919 (Bannu)	...	...
No. 6 Armoured Motor Battery	Ditto	Ditto Ditto	...	Incomplete.
No. 7 Armoured Motor Battery	Ditto	In Force 6th May 1919 (Dera Ismail Khan).	...	...
No. 8 Armoured Motor Battery	Baluchistan Force	17th July 1919	Hyderabad (Sind)	For Baluchistan Area.
No. 11 Armoured Motor Battery	Ditto	20th June 1919	Ambala	To Quetta.
No. 15 Machine Gun Squadron	N.-W. F. F.	In Force 6th May 1919 (Peshawar)	...	To Dakka. Arrived 14th May 1919.
No. 22 Machine Gun Squadron	Baluchistan Force	In Force 6th May 1919 (Quetta)	...	...
No. 24 Machine Gun Squadron	N.-W. F. F.	In Force 6th May 1919 (Risalpur)	...	To Peshawar.
No. 3 Motor Machine Gun Battery	Ditto	1st June 1919	Ambala	For Kohat. To return to Ambala for 63rd Mobile Bde.
No. 15 Motor Machine Gun Battery	Ditto	In Force 6th May 1919 (Peshawar)	...	...
No. 19 Motor Machine Gun Battery	Baluchistan Force	In Force 6th May 1919 (Quetta)	...	...
No. 22 Motor Machine Gun Battery	N.-W. F. F.	15th May 1919	Rawalpindi	To Parachinar.
No. 222 Machine Gun Coy	N.-W. F. F.	In Force 6th May 1919 (Abbottabad).	...	To Peshawar Area.
No. 260 Machine Gun Coy.	Ditto	17th May 1919	Dalhousie	For Peshawar.
No. 263 Machine Gun Coy.	Ditto	In Force 6th May 1919. (Nowshera).	...	To Landi Kotal.
No. 270 Machine Gun Coy.	Baluchistan Force	In Force 6th May 1919 (Quetta)	...	To Chaman Area.
No. 281 Machine Gun Coy.	Ditto	21st May 1919	Mhow	To Quetta.
No. 285 Machine Gun Coy.	N.-W. F. F.	In Force 6th May 1919. (Nowshera).	...	To Dakka.
No. 286 Machine Gun Coy.	Ditto	1st June 1919	Rawalpindi	To Kohat.
No. 288 Machine Gun Coy.	Ditto	In Force 6th May 1919. (Lahore).	...	For Peshawar.

INFANTRY.				
2nd Bn. Somerset Light Infy.	Ditto	In Force 6th May 1919 (Peshawar).	...	To Dakka. Arrived 14th May 1919.
2nd Bn. North Staffords	Ditto	In Force 6th May 1919 (Nowshera).	...	To Landi Khana.
1st Bn. The Yorkshire Regt	Ditto	In Force 6th May 1919 (Kacha Garhi).	...	To Landi Kotal 11th May 1919. For Dakka Force.
1st Bn. Royal Sussex	Ditto	In Force 6th May 1919 (Rawalpindi).	...	To Ali Masjid. Arrived 22nd May 1919.
1st Durham Light Infy.	Ditto	In Force 6th May 1919 (Rawalpindi).	...	To Landi Kotal. Arrived 20th May 1919.
1st Bn. South Lancs.	Ditto	In Force 6th May 1919 (Rawalpindi).	...	To Nowshera.
2-4th Border Regt.	Ditto	In Force 6th May 1919 (Peshawar).	...	Detts. Nowshera and Kohat.
1-4th Royal West Surreys	Ditto	In Force 6th May 1919 (Jullundur).	...	To Nowshera.
2nd Bn. The King's (Liverpool)	Baluchistan Force	In Force 6th May 1919 (Quetta)	...	...
1-4th Royal West Kents.	Ditto	Ditto	...	To Peshin Area.
1st Bn. Duke of Wellington's Regiment.	Ditto	17th May 1919	Lahore	To Chaman Area.
1-1st Kent Regiment	N.-W. F. F.	20th May 1919	Ferozepore	To Nowshera.
1-25th London Regiment	Ditto	17th May 1919	Jullundur	To Amritsar. For Kohat.
2-6th Royal Sussex Regiment	Ditto	30th May 1919	Lahore	To Kohat.
1-5th Hants.	Ditto	Ditto	Do.	To Kohat. (To Simla Hills for 63rd Mobile Bde.)
No. 17 Special Service Bn.	Baluchistan Force	22nd May 1919	Deolali	For Quetta.

List of Indian Army units employed on the North-West Frontier between 6th May and 8th August 1919.
(Excluding Administrative units.)

Unit.	Force.	Date of joining Force.	From	Remarks.
CAVALRY.				
1st Lancers	N.-W. F. F.	In Force on 6th May 1919 (Risalpur).	...	To Dakka on 15th May.
3rd Horse	Baluchistan Force	In Force on 6th May 1919 (Loralai).	...	To Chaman on 28th July.
4th Cavalry	N.-W. F. F.	......	...	At Mardan.
12th Cavalry	Ditto	6th June 1919	Ambala	2 Sqdns. only. Remainder Ambala.
13th Lancers	Baluchistan Force	30th May 1919	Meerut	For Quetta.
17th Cavalry	N.-W. F. F.	6th June 1919	Lahore	1 sqdn. only. Remainder Lahore.
23rd Cavalry	Ditto	12th May 1919	Ferozepore	For Peshawar.
25th Cavalry, F. F.	Baluchistan Force	In Force on 6th May 1919 (Quetta)	...	To Chaman on 15th May 1919.
27th Cavalry	Waziristan Force	In Force on 6th May 1919 (D. I. K.)	...	......
28th Light Cavalry	East Persia	......	...	......
30th Lancers	N.-W. F. F.	In Force on 6th May 1919 (Peshawar).	...	To Dakka on 13th May.
31st Lancers	Waziristan Force	In Force on 6th May 1919 (Bannu).	...	......
33rd Light Cavalry	N.-W. F. F.	In Force on 6th May 1919 (Risalpur).	...	Ditto.
37th Lancers	Ditto	In Force on 6th May 1919 (Kohat).	...	......
40th Cavalry 41st Cavalry 42nd Cavalry	Baluchistan Force	In Force on 6th May 1919 (Quetta).	...	To Chaman, on 4th June 1919 (2 sqdns. 41st Cavalry to East Persia Force).
Patiala Lancers	Ditto	28th May 1919	Patiala	Zhob Mobile Column.
Alwar Lancers	Ditto	25th June 1919	Alwar	......
Navanagar Lancers	Ditto	4th July 1919	Karachi	For Loralai.
Bhopal Lancers	Waziristan Force	9th June 1919	Ambala	For D. I. K. and Tank.

ARTILLERY.				
Headquarters, No. 1 Mountain Artillery Brigade.	N.-W. F. F.	7th June 1919	Abbottabad	For Kohat.
Headquarters, No. 3 Mountain Artillery Brigade.	Ditto	24th June 1919	...	Ditto.
22nd Mountain Battery	N.-W. F. F.	Ditto	Abbottabad	For Nowshera.
23rd Mountain Battery	N.-W. F. F.	In Force on 6th May 1919 (Nowshera).	...	...
24th Mountain Battery	Waziristan Force	4th June 1919	Abbottabad	For Bannu.
	N.-W. F. F. (16th Div.)	12th July 1919	Bannu	For Mardan on relief by 35th Bty.
27th Mountain Battery	Waziristan Force	In Force on 6th May 1919 (Tank)	...	...
28th Mountain Battery	N.-W. F. F.	In Force on 6th May 1919 (Kohat)	...	...
30th Mountain Battery	N.-W. F. F.	13th June 1919	Abbottabad	For Nowshera.
33rd Mountain Battery	Waziristan Force	In Force on 6th May 1919 (Bannu).	...	...
35th Mountain Battery	Waziristan Force	11th July 1919	Rawalpindi	Relieved 24th M. Bty.
37th Mountain Battery	Baluchistan Force	24th July 1919	Ditto	For Quetta.
38th Mountain Battery	Baluchistan Force	In Force on 6th May 1919 (Quetta).	...	...
Frontier Garrison Artillery	N.-W. F. F. and Waziristan Force.	......	...	...
No. 1 Kashmir Mountain Battery	East Persia Force	......	...	...
No. 2 Kashmir Mountain Battery	N.-W. F. F.	In Force on 6th May 1919 (Gilgit).	...	...
SIGNALS.				
No. 33 Divisional Signal Company	Baluchistan Force	In Force on 6th May 1919	Quetta	...
	Waziristan Force	Ditto	Tank	...
No. 36 Divisional Signal Company	N.-W. F. F.	Ditto	Peshawar	To Dakka—Landi Kotal on 10th July 1919.
No. 38 Divisional Signal Company	Waziristan Force	15th June 1919	Rawalpindi	Less 2 sections.
	Baluchistan Force	Ditto	Ditto	2 sections.
No. 39 Divisional Signal Company	N.-W. F. F.	In Force on 6th May 1919	Peshawar	For Kohat (less 44th and 45th Sections).
No. 40 Divisional Signal Company	Ditto	30th June 1919	Lahore	
Army Corps Signal Company	Ditto	22nd May 1919	Secunderabad	For Peshawar.
No. 44 Divisional Signal Company	Ditto	12th May 1919	Poona	For Kurram (Kohat).

List of Indian Army Units employed on the North-West Frontier, etc.—contd.

Unit.	Force.	Date of joining Force.	From	REMARKS.
SIGNALS—*contd.*				
No. 1 L. of C. Signal Section	Waziristan Force	24th May 1919	Poona	For Bannu.
No. 2 L. of C. Signal Section	Waziristan Force	24th May 1919	Poona	For Tank.
No. 3 L. of C. Signal Section	Baluchistan Force	24th May 1919	Poona	For Quetta.
No. 4 L. of C. Signal Section	N.-W. F. F.	10th June 1919	Poona	For Kohat.
No. 5 L. of C. Signal Section	N.-W. F. F.	2nd July 1919	Poona	For Dakka.
1st Cavalry Brigade Signal Troop	N.-W. F. F.	In Force on 6th May 1919 (Peshawar).	...	To Dakka, 14th May 1919.
6th Cavalry Signal Troop	Baluchistan Force	22nd June 1919	Poona	For Quetta.
43rd Brigade Signal Section	Waziristan Force	2nd July 1919	Rawalpindi	For Khajuri.
44th Brigade Signal Section	N.-W. F. F.	20th May 1919	Lahore	For Peshawar.
45th Brigade Signal Section	N.-W. F. F.	24th July 1919	Lahore	For Peshawar.
46th Mobile Brigade Signal Section	N.-W. F. F.	1st June 1919	Ambala	For Kohat. (Left force on 30th June 1919 for 63rd Mobile Brigade.)
67th Brigade Signal Section	Waziristan Force	2nd July 1919	Rawalpindi	For Bannu.
68th Brigade Signal Section	Waziristan Force	In Force on 6th May 1919 (Tank)	...	......
No. 3 Wireless Signal Squadron (detachments).	N.-W. F. F. (Waziristan Force).	In Force on 6th May 1919	...	......
12th Cavalry Brigade Signal Troop	East Persia Force	......	...	......
Sappers and Miners.				
No. 1 Field Troop, 1st S. and M.	N.-W. F. F.	In Force on 6th May 1919 (Risalpur)	...	To Dakka, 11th May 1919
No. 7 Field Coy., 1st S. and M.	N.-W. F. F.	In Force on 6th May 1919 (Landi Kotal).	...	To Dakka, 21st May 1919.
No. 53 Field Coy., 1st S. and M.	N.-W. F. F.	22nd May 1919	Lahore	For Jamrud.
No. 55 Field Coy., 1st S. and M.	Waziristan Force	In Force on 6th May 1919 (Bannu).	...	......
No. 56 Field Coy., 1st S. and M.	N.-W. F. F.	In Force on 6th May 1919 (Jamrud).	...	......
No. 57 Field Coy., 1st S. and M.	N.-W. F. F.	In Force on 6th May 1919 (Kohat).	...	To Doaba, 19th May 1919.

No. 58 Field Coy., 1st S. & M.	N.-W. F. F.	23rd May 1919	Rurki	For Jamrud.
No. 8 Field Troop, 2nd S. & M.	Waziristan Force	23rd July 1919	Bangalore	For D. I. K.
No. 11 Field Coy., 2nd S. & M.	N.-W. F. F.	In Force on 6th May 1919 (Rawalpindi).	...	To Ali Masjid. Arr. 23rd May 1919.
No. 14 Field Coy., 2nd S. & M.	N.-W. F. F.	27th May 1919	Bangalore	For Jamrud.
No. 15 Field Coy., 2nd S. & M.	N.-W. F. F.	2nd August 1919	Rurki	For Peshawar.
No. 64 Field Coy., 2nd S. & M.	N.-W. F. F.	In Force on 6th May 1919 (Rawalpindi).	...	To Landi Kotal Arr. 15th May 1919.
No. 66 Field Coy., 2nd S. & M.	N.-W. F. F.	31st May 1919	Bangalore	For Kohat.
No. 67 Field Coy., 2nd S. & M.	N. W. F. F.	27th July 1919	Golra-Kushalgarh Road.	For Peshawar.
No. 68 (Burma) Field Coy. 2nd S. & M.	East Persia Force	...	...	...
No. 69 Field Coy., 2nd S. & M.				
No. 63 Field Coy., 2nd S. & M.	Working on the Golra-Kushalgarh Road.			
Sirmoor I. S. Sappers				
No. 76 Field Coy., 2nd S. & M.	N.-W. F. F.	25th May 1919	Kirkee	For Jamrud.
Chitral Section, 2nd S. & M.	N.-W. F. F.	In Force on 6th May 1919	...	Drosh.
No. 7 Field Troop, 3rd S. & M.	Baluchistan Force	In Force on 6th May 1919 (Quetta)	...	To Chaman arr. 29th June 1919.
No. 17 Field Coy., 3rd S. & M.	Baluchistan Force	20th June 1919	Kirkee	For Quetta 2 secs. only.
No. 24 Field Coy., 3rd S. & M.	Baluchistan Force	19th May 1919	Kirkee	For Quetta.
No. 71 Field Coy., 3rd S. & M.	Baluchistan Force	In Force on 6th May 1919 (Quetta)	...	To East Persia 1st July 1919.
No. 73 Field Coy., 3rd S. & M.	Baluchistan Force	In Force on 6th May 1919 (Quetta)	...	To Chaman. Arr. 24th May 1919.
No. 74 Field Coy., 3rd S. & M.	N.-W. F. F.	......	Jubbulpore	2 Sections only.
Sistan Dett., 3rd S. & M.	East Persia Force	......	...	...
No. 4 Pontoon Park, 1st S. & M.	N.-W. F. F.	28th July 1919	Rurki	For Peshawar.
No. 6 Pontoon Park, 3rd S. & M.	N.-W. F. F.	4th July 1919	Poona	For Peshawar.
No. 75 Field Coy., 3rd S. & M.	Waziristan Force	In Force on 6th May 1919 (Tank)	...	...
No. 26 Railway Coy., S. & M.				
No. 27 Railway Coy., S. & M.	N. W. F. F.	In Force on 6th May 1919	...	Railway Battalion.
No. 28 Railway Coy., S. & M.				
Nos. 1 & 3 Engineer Fd. Park, 1st S. & M.	N.-W. F. F.	......	...	...
No. 9 Printing Section, 1st S. & M.	N.-W. F. F.	......	Rurki.	...
No. 6 Litho Section, 3rd S. & M.	N.-W. F. F.	......	Kirkee.	..
No. 7 Printing Section, 3rd S. & M.	N.-W. F. F.	......	Do.	...

List of British Army units employed on the North-West Frontier, etc.—contd.

Unit.	Force.	Date of joining Force.	From	Remarks.
Sappers and Miners—*contd.*				
No. 10 Works Coy., S. & M.	N.-W. F. F.	......	...	...
Tehri I. S. Sappers	N.-W. F. F.	......	...	...
Maler Kotla I. S. Sappers	N.-W. F. F.	......	...	...
Faridkot I. S. Sappers	N. W. F. F.	......	...	...
Infantry and Pioneers.				
2-2nd Rajput Light Infantry	N.-W. F. F.	In Force on 6th May 1919	...	Malakand and Posts.
3rd Guides Infantry	Ditto	12th May 1910	Mardan	For Parachinar (Depot Mardan).
2-3rd Gaur Brahmins	Baluchistan Force	20th June 1919	Ahmedabad	For Quetta (Zhob Force).
1-5th Light Infantry	Ditto	In Force on 6th May 1919	...	Quetta.
1-6th Jat Light Infantry	N.-W. F. F.	20th May 1919	Jhansi	For Peshawar.
2-10th Jats	Waziristan Force	30th May 1919	Lahore	For Bannu.
1-11th Rajputs	N.-W. F. F.	In Force on 6th May 1919 (Chitral)	...	......
2-11th Rajputs	Baluchistan	Ditto ditto (Loralai)	...	......
14th Sikhs	Waziristan Force	3rd June 1919	Karachi	For Tank.
1-15th Sikhs	N.-W. F. F.	In Force on 6th May (Landi Kotal)	...	......
2-15th „	Baluchistan Force	19th May 1919	Ferozepore	For Quetta.
16th Rajputs	Ditto	30th June 1919	Arangaon	Ditto.
1-19th Punjabis	East Persia	......	...	......
1-32nd „	Baluchistan Force	In Force on 6th May 1919 (Quetta)	...	To Chaman Area early in May.
2-26th „	N.-W. F. F.	19th May 1919	Bareilly	For Kohat.
2-27th „	Waziristan Force	1st June 1919	Agra	For Bannu.
1-30th „	N.-W. F. F.	28th May 1919	Ferozepore	For Nowshera.
2-30th „	Ditto	Ditto	Multan	To Peshawar.
1-33rd „	Ditto	10th May 1919	Rawalpindi	To Landi Kotal.
2-33rd „	Ditto	In Force on 6th May 1919 (Chaklala).	...	To Ali Masjid, 10th May 1919.

1-35th Sikhs	Ditto	In Force on 6th May 1919 (Landi Kotal).	...	......
2-35th „	Ditto	12th May 1919	Lahore	For Kacha Garhi.
37th Dogras	Ditto	In Force on 6th May 1916 (Peshawar).	...	......
3-39th Garhwal Rifles	Ditto	18th May 1919	Rawalpindi	From Rewat to Kacha Garhi.
4-39th Garhwal Rifles	Ditto	Ditto	Ambala	For Kohat.
40th Pathans	Ditto	11th May 1919	Campbellpore	For Kacha Garhi.
1-41st Dogras	Waziristan Force	In Force on 6th May 1919 (Bannu).	...	......
2-41st „	N.-W. F. F.	24th May 1919	Sialkot	To Peshawar. For Kohat.
2-54th Sikhs F. F.	Ditto	13th May 1919	Rawalpindi	For Kacha Garhi.
1-55th Rifles F. F.	Waziristan Force	20th May 1919	Ambala	For Bannu.
2-53th Rifles	Baluchistan Force	In Force on 6th May 1919 (Quetta)	...	......
1-57th Rifles F. F.	N.-W. F. F.	Ditto ditto (Kohat)	...	To Parachinar.
1-66th Punjabis	Waziristan Force	Ditto ditto (Tank)	...	......
2-67th „	N.-W. F. F.	23rd May 1919	Chaklala	To Ali Masjid.
1-69th „	Ditto	25th May 1919	Lucknow	For Kohat.
2-69th „	Ditto	23rd May 1919	Ambala	Ditto.
2-72nd „	Ditto	24th May 1919	Multan	Ditto.
1-76th Punjabis	Waziristan Force	In Force on 6th May 1919 (D. I. K.).	...	......
1-82nd „	Ditto	4th June 1919	Jhansi	For Tank.
2-89th „	N.-W. F. F.	In Force on 6th May 1919	...	Dargai and Chakdara.
1-90th „	Ditto	7th July 1919	Chaklala	For Kohat.
2-90th „	Waziristan Force	26th June 1919	Dhond	For Bannu.
1-97th Infantry	Baluchistan Force	19th July 1919	Ambala	For Quetta.
1-98th „	East Persia	......	...	......
2-98th „	Ditto	......	...	......
1-102nd Grenadiers	Baluchistan Force	26th June 1919	Mhow	For Quetta.
2-102nd „	East Persia	......	...	......
1-103rd Mahratta Light Infantry	Waziristan Force	In Force on 6th May 1919 (Miranshah).	...	......
1-109th Infantry	N.-W. F. F.	In Force on 6th May 1919 (Kohat).	...	......
110th Mahratta Light Infantry	Ditto	14th June 1919	Belgaum	For Nowshera.

List of British Army units employed on the North-West Frontier, etc.—contd.

Unit.	Force.	Date of joining Force.	From	REMARKS.
INFANTRY AND PIONEERS—*contd.*				
2-112th Infantry	Waziristan Force	In Force on 6th May 1919 (Bannu)	...	......
2-113th "	Ditto	4th August 1919	Benares	......
2-119th "	Baluchistan Force	In Force on 6th May 1919 (Peshin).	...	......
120th "	East Persia	......	...	......
2-123rd Rifles	N.-W. F. F.	In Force on 6th May 1919 (Nowshera)	...	Landi Khana.
1-124th Baluchis	Ditto	30th May 1919	Lahore	For Kohat.
3-124th "	Baluchistan Force	7th June 1919	Karachi	For Quetta (½ Bn. Murgha).
2-125th Rifles	Waziristan Force	2nd July 1919	Dhond	For Bannu.
1-129th Baluchis	Baluchistan Force	In Force on 6th May 1919 (Quetta).	...	......
2-129th "	Ditto	20th May 1919	Karachi	For Quetta.
1-150th Infantry	Waziristan Force	30th June 1919	Dhond	For Tank.
3-150th "	N.-W. F. F.	25th May 1919	Ambala	For Kohat.
1-151st "	Ditto	In Force on 6th May 1919 (Kohat).	...	......
2-151st "	Ditto	1st June 1919	Ambala	For Kohat.
1-152nd "	Ditto	8th July 1919	Ahmednagar	Relieved 2-7th Gurkhas.
1-153rd "	Baluchistan Force	25th July 1919	Anandi	For Quetta.
2-153rd "	Ditto	Ditto	Do.	Ditto.
1-154th Infantry (200 rifles)	Waziristan Force	In Force on 6th May 1919 (D. I. K.).	...	......
Jind I. S. Infantry	Baluchistan Force	25th June 1919	Ambala	For Kohat.
Gwalior I. S. Infantry	Waziristan Force	23rd June 1919	Sangroor	......
Patiala I. S. Infantry	N.-W. F. F.	7th July 1919	Chaklala	For Kohat.
1st Kashmir Rifles (I. S.)	Ditto	5th July 1919	Abbottabad	Relieved 2-9th Gurkhas.
2nd Kashmir Rifles (I. S.)	Ditto	In Force on 6th May 1919	...	......
2nd Rifle Regiment (Nepalese)	Ditto	23rd July 1919	Abbottabad	For Gilgit and Mardan.
Kapurthala I. S. Infantry	East Persia Force	25th June 1919	Kapurthala	......
Nabha I. S. Infantry (½ Bn.)	Ditto	Ditto	Nabha	......

Pioneers.				
1-12th Pioneers	N.-W. F. F.	In Force on 6th May 1919 (Nowshera).	...	......
2-12th "	Ditto	In Force on 6th May 1919 (Jamrud).	...	......
2-23rd "	Baluchistan Force	14th May 1919	Ambala	For Quetta.
2-34th "	N.-W. F. F.	In Force on 6th May 1919 (Jamrud).	...	......
3-34th "	Ditto	2nd July 1919	Ambala	For Peshawar.
1-61st "	Ditto	15th May 1919	Ferozepore	For Kacha Garhi.
2-61st "	Ditto	26th May 1919	Dhond	For Jamrud.
1-81st "	Ditto	2nd July 1919	Delhi	For Kohat.
2-81st "	Ditto	12th June 1919	Bangalore	For Landi Kotal.
1-107th "	East Persia Force	...	...	Dett. Baln. Force.
Gurkhas.				
2-1st Gurkha Rifles	N.-W. F. F.	In Force on 6th May 1919 (Nowshera).	...	For Dakka.
3-1st " "	Baluchistan Force	In Force on 6th May 1919 (Fort Sandeman).	...	......
2-2nd " "	Waziristan Force	In Force on 6th May 1919 (Dera Ismail Khan).	...	......
3-2nd " "	N.-W. F. F.	In Force on 6th May 1919 (Peshawar).	...	......
4-3rd " "	Ditto	In Force on 6th May 1919 (Kakul)	...	For Dakka.
1-4th " "	Baluchistan Force	In Force on 6th May 1919 (Quetta)	...	To Chaman area.
3-5th " "	N.-W. F. F.	16th May 1919	Chamiari	For Kacha Garhi.
3-6th " "	Waziristan Force	In Force on 6th May 1919 (Miranshah).	...	......
2-7th " "	N.-W. F. F.	1st June 1919	Ambala	For Kohat (left Force on 6th July 1919).
3-7th " "	Baluchistan Force	In Force on 6th May 1919 (Peshin)	...	......
2-8th " "	N.-W. F. F.	11th May 1919	Rewat	For Kacha Garhi.
3-8th " "	Ditto	In Force on 6th May 1919 (Hangu)	...	......

List of Indian Army units employed on the North-West Frontier, etc.—concld.

Unit.	Force.	Date of joining Force.	From	Remarks.
Gurkhas—*contd.*				
1-9th Gurkha Rifles	N.-W. F. F.	In Force on 6th May 1919 (Landi Kotal).	...	......
2-9th ,, ,,	Ditto	1st June 1919	Ambala	For Kohat (left Force on 10th July 1919).
3-9th ,, ,,	Ditto	In Force on 6th May 1919 (Kohat)	...	......
2-10th ,, ,,	Baluchistan Force	In Force on 6th May 1919 (Chaman).	...	......
1-11th ,, ,,	N.-W. F. F.	In Force on 6th May 1919 (Nowshera).	...	Landi Khana.
2-11th ,, ,,	Ditto	In Force on 6th May 1919 (Nowshera).	...	Ditto.
3-11th ,, ,,	Ditto	In Force on 6th May 1919 (Kakul)	...	Dakka.

GIPD—L 79CGS—13-4-26—1,500.

www.ingramcontent.com/pod-product-compliance
Ingram Content Group UK Ltd.
Pitfield, Milton Keynes, MK11 3LW, UK
UKHW021834270726
14058UKWH00001B/139